Jean-François Champollion, Egypt, July 1829
by Salvador Cherubini © Rénéaume

EGYPTIAN DIARIES

HOW ONE MAN SOLVED THE MYSTERIES OF THE NILE

J.-F. Champollion

Decipherer of the Rosetta Stone

GIBSON SQUARE BOOKS

This edition first published in 2001
by
Gibson Square Books Ltd
15 Gibson Square
London UK-N1 0RD
tel: +44 (0)20 7689 4790 / fax: +44 (0)20 7689 7395
books@gibson-square.com
www.gibsonsquare.com

Distribution and UK Sales by Turnaround
Unit 3, Olympia Trading Estate
Coburg Road
London UK-N22 6TZ
tel: +44 (0)20 8829 3000 / fax: +44 (0)20 8881 5088
oders@turnaround-uk.com
www.turnaround-uk.com

Austria, Benelux, France, Germany, Switzerland: Michael Geoghegan
Tel: +44 (0)20 7436 1662 / Fax: +44 (0)20 7435 0180
mgsales@davidbowie.co.uk
14 Frognal Gardens
London, UK-NW8 6UX

Spain, Portugal: Peter Prout, Iberian Book Services
Tel: +34 91 803 4918 / Fax: +34 91 803 5936
Sector Islas, Bloque, 12, 1.* B,
28760 Tres Cantos, Madrid, Spain
E-mail: pprout@bcsnetwork.es

Sweden, Norway, Denmark, Finland, Iceland: Pernille Larsen:
p-larsen@mail.tele.dk
Thorshavnsgade 20, 3.th.
DK-2300 Copenhagen S Denmark

Middle & Far East: Julian Ashton
Tel: +44 1732 746 093 / Fax: +44 1732 746 096
sales@ashtoninternational.com
www.ashtoninternational.com
P.O. Box 298, Sevenoaks
Kent, UK-TN13 1WU

ISBN 1-903933-02-1

Typeset by Villiers Ltd, Ashford
Printed by WS Bookwell Ltd

Contents

Publisher's Note

Champollion wrote these diaries and letters from May 1828 to March 1830 during a time when the political situation France was in a turbulent state. The reign of the reactionary Bourbon king Charles X was slowly moving into the direction of the July Revolution of 1830 that would force him to abdicate on 2 August 1830. Moreover, Egyptology continued to be a highly sensitive subject for the clergy. The texts of ancient Egypt, which had been unintelligible for most of Christianity, could deal a severe blow to the orthodoxy and the authority of the (Catholic) church.

Champollion's frankness in these diaries and lively letters may, therefore, seem surprising. He and his older brother Champollion-Figeac, however, had worked together for most of their lives, exchanging views in crisp notes interspersed with blunt advice. In addition, Champollion had evidently decided to publish his early findings through the journalism of his brother rather than, as before, through letters to a distinguished person. Champollion-Figeac was to take from the letters what he could for his paper, the *Moniteur*, to keep Parisians informed about his brother's progress. After Champollion's death in 1832, he published the first edition of these popular letters. Later, in 1909, Professor Hermine Hartleben published the standard work of the writings, which has remained in print ever since; the present book is based on this volume. It is the first time that they are published in the English language.

In their original, Champollion's letters contain hieroglyphs, Arabic, Coptic and some Latin and Greek, as well as sketches of various cartouches as he interpreted them, or other small details spotted and remarked on in tombs. This book does not aim to reproduce these from the Hartleben edition (which itself leaves out parts of the letters) as only a number of specialists will be able to enjoy them. For the same reasons large sections of not totally related material have also been omitted as the aim here is to recreate the historical context of his frame of mind in 1828-1830: a virtually blank canvas - ancient Egypt itself. Hartleben's extensive notes have been incorporated here. Champollion's spelling of some names is strange to present usage - some of these have been changed (or notes added in square brackets) to help clarity, but others close to the modern name, and thus easily identifiable, have been left.

Jean-François Champollion, posthumously,
by Léon Cogniet, © RMN

'While Champollion's work is well known, how much is really known about the man himself? The answer is 'not a lot' in as much as there is no biography of him available in English, although in recent years two have been published in France. It is through his letters written on that momentous journey that he made to Egypt in 1828 to 1829 that we can begin to see the man. Here we share his enthusiasm, both scholarly and almost at times schoolboyish, as he writes to close friends and to elevated people such as the Grand-Duke of Tuscany... The publication in English of these enthusiastic letters of description and report not only reveal the man, his weak health that he strove to overcome in his headlong pursuit of his goal, but also the scholar who was prepared to chance all...'

Peter Clayton, FSA

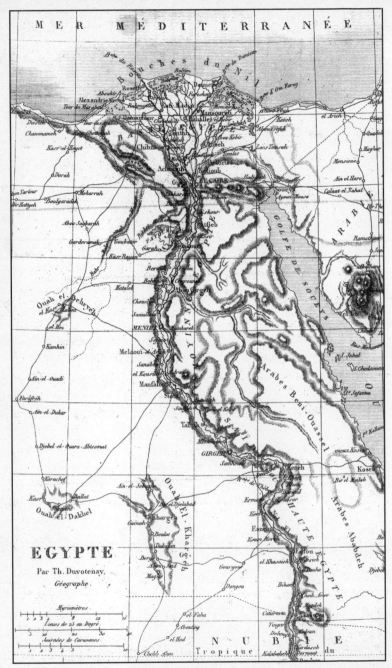

Egypt up to the Ist Cataract

Introduction

Jean-François Champollion was born in Figeac in north west France on 23 December 1790. Less than ten years later, the young Napoleon would try to realise his ambitious plans in the Valley of the Nile. His idea was to conquer Egypt in order to build the Suez Canal and open up the route to India for France and thus strike a devastating blow to the British economy. Like Julius Caesar before him, however, Napoleon was at the same time deeply interested in understanding the people he was conquering. He brought with him a delegation of scholars whose task it was to describe Egypt and its monuments, and the news of their early work and discoveries very quickly reached Europe where it whetted a popular appetite for ancient Egypt that had hitherto been limited to scholars and universities.[1]

Napoleon's expedition was a military disaster, yet its significance today lies in its scientific results. A 'Commission of Egypt' gathered 167 artistic and academic savants who had come over voluntarily in 1798, after an appeal to the Institut de France by Napoleon. With the aid of the chemist Berthollet he recruited cartographers, bridge engineers, zoologists, botanists, mineralogists, painters, draughtsmen, journalists and economists. The Commission held its first meeting in an ancient Cairo palace abandoned by the Mamelukes, and for three years it produced an impressive number of artistic and scientific studies on just about any aspect of Egypt.

Apart from the artist Vivant Denon, one of Champollion's heroes, it was mostly to the engineers of the Commission that the early nineteenth century owed its knowledge of pharaonic art. After scientific sorties into the Said (the south of Egypt) in 1799, it became possible to recreate on paper the architecture, sculpture and crafts of the New Kingdom (1600-1000 BC) and the Ptolemaic period (300-30 BC).[2] Returning to France, the French savants brought back portfolios stuffed with notes and drawings. These results, published in the twenty one volumes of the *Description de l'Égypte* (1809-1828) under the editorship of the geographer Edmé Jomard, at last provided a reliable image of ancient Egypt, and through them the members of the expedition laid down the procedures for objective description that became the exclusive method for publishing Egyptian antiquities until the use of photography. Thus, from 1809 Champollion had access to Egyptian texts which were reproduced with sufficient precision to allow his breakthrough — finding the code of the hieroglyphs.

DESCRIPTION
DE L'ÉGYPTE,
OU
RECUEIL
DES OBSERVATIONS ET DES RECHERCHES
QUI ONT ÉTÉ FAITES EN ÉGYPTE
PENDANT L'EXPÉDITION DE L'ARMÉE FRANÇAISE,
PUBLIÉ
PAR LES ORDRES DE SA MAJESTÉ L'EMPEREUR
NAPOLÉON LE GRAND.

1 - PLANCHES.

A PARIS,
DE L'IMPRIMERIE IMPÉRIALE
M. DCCC. IX.

The most important consequence of the Egyptian campaign was the discovery of the famous Rosetta Stone. In July 1799 a French officer, P.F.X. Bouchard, discovered in the foundations of Fort St Julien near Rosetta a fragment of basalt with some 'inscriptions which would appear to be of interest'. The Rosetta Stone was covered with text in two languages and two scripts: hieroglyphs, demotic (cursive, late-Egyptian) writing and Greek. The French realised instantly that this fragment of basalt would one day provide the key to deciphering ancient Egyptian. In 1801, after the French surrender to General Sir John Hutchinson, the savants refused to hand over the fruits of their work, their notes, threatening to burn them all. One of them put it thus: 'Without us this material is useless; neither you nor your people [the English] will understand it. Rather than be party to such evil and allow spoliation, if not vandalism, to take place, we will destroy everything that belongs to us, we will scatter it across the Libyan sands, we will hurl it into the sea, we will burn all these riches. Everyone is aware that you want to claim them as your own. Do so, but beware: history has a long memory; you too will be guilty of having burnt the library of Alexandria.' The savants could keep their notes, though the Rosetta Stone (which is today in the British Museum) was confiscated.

The French had however taken the precaution of making several copies. It was on one of these that Champollion would be working as the last one in a long line of scholars obsessed with breaking the hieroglyphic code. When in 535 AD the Byzantine Emperor Justinian forbade the cult of Isis and closed its temple on the island of Philae there was no longer anyone capable of reading the long pharaonic litanies that covered the Egyptian temples. Even though the Coptic spoken by the Egyptian peasants (*fellahs*) was a language that had developed from ancient Egyptian, they had become unintelligible because written Coptic used the Greek alphabet to which several characters were added to transcribe sounds which were unknown to the Greeks.

Well into the Renaissance, these mysterious signs excited the imagination of scholars, without leading to any significant efforts to penetrate their mysteries. During the sixteenth century, however, reading Roman and Greek writers became popular again and several new attempts were made. But scholars continued to take as the basis for their studies the *Hieroglyphica* of Horapollo, written around the fourth century AD and containing information that was of little use. At the same time, potions produced from mummy powder became a trusted medical treatment and some merchants sold papyri in the Coptic language alongside, supplementing their profits from the lucrative business of trafficking unprocessed mummies. These became sought after because they contained information relevant to biblical studies. A Jesuit, Athanasius Kircher (1628-1680), thus developed a lively interest in the study of Coptic. He was the first to grasp one of the strands of ancient Egyptian when he suggested that Coptic and hieroglyphic writing were one and the same language, written in two different forms. Basing himself on the *Hieroglyphica* of Horapollo, Kircher unfortunately also thought that hieroglyphic writing was exclusively based on the use of images. His lapidary scientific methods and lack of a critical

Athanasius Kircher

mind, moreover, gave free rein to his fertile imagination. Instead of translating a cartouche as the name of the Pharao Apries, for example, he put forward the following extravagant translation: 'the rewards of the divine Osiris must be procured by means of sacred ceremonies and a chain of geniuses so that the rewards of the Nile may be obtained.' After such flights of fantasy no serious scholar dared touch the subject again. Everyone agreed that there was a dramatic shortage of accurately copied ancient Egyptian texts.

This dearth of reliable material only disappeared upon the return of the French savants from Egypt, after the surrender to the English in 1801. At last, it was possible to set to work with some chance of success. However, there still remained an obstacle to decoding the hieroglyphs: Horapollo continued to be treated as a key to the language and scholars remained convinced that hieroglyphs related to ideas rather than sounds.

One of the aspects of Champollion's genius was to detach himself from this idea. When he set to work on penetrating the great enigma he was the only scholar for whom the conditions for breaking the code coincided. He had an excellent understanding of Coptic as well as a thorough understanding of, notably, Semitic, Syrian, Arab and Hebrew, and he even learned Chinese because he thought that perhaps the alphabet of this language was influenced by ancient Egyptian. But, most important of all, he had at his disposal the work of the Commission of Egypt and a copy of the Rosetta Stone.

Thomas Young

Champollion was not without competition however. The English physician Thomas Young (1773-1829) was also trying to decode the hieroglyphs. He had identified the proper names of the kings mentioned on the Rosetta Stone (it was known from the eighteenth century that these were surrounded by a 'cartouche'). He also tried to translate the name of Ptolemy. But instead of translating his Roman epithet 'autocrator' he misunderstood this word and translated it as the surname of several Ptolemies,

'Evergetes'. Likewise, where the hieroglyphs said 'Caesar', he thought they said 'Arsinoe'. Young failed because he did not know any Semitic languages and his knowledge of Coptic was cursory; besides, his research only extended to a few ancient Egyptian texts. Young, however, can claim the distinction of 'having discovered that hieroglyphic writing is not alphabetic and that hieratic and demotic writing – which derived from the hieroglyphs – is determined by the same principles'.[3] These results made him think that he could deny all importance of Champollion's work and accuse him of plagiarism. Nonetheless, the starting point of Champollion's success lies where he left off.

*

In order to understand the stages of Champollion's achievement, one has to understand the principles of hieroglyphic writing. 'Everything starts with a drawing.' In order to write 'goose' they used the image of the animal. But 'adhering strictly to this system would not allow you to write very ordinary words such as father, son, etc…, and one would be unable to indicate any grammatical inflection. You therefore have to resort to a very simple procedure: you replace the thing that needs to be characterised with a sign that has the same sound. "Goose", which has the same consonants as the word "son", serves [also] to write the word "son". Or else you add a sign to images which can be read in several ways which is only for reading.'[4] Thus the word which is transcribed in our alphabet as 'RM', meaning fish, consists of three elements in Egyptian: two phonetic signs, the 'R' and the 'M', and a figurative sign without a phonetic value (the image of a fish) which 'determines' to which category the word belongs.

The hieroglyphic system contains thus three types of signs: the first are figurative (or ideographic), directly representing the object, the second are phonetic, and the third are determinatives. Champollion already wrote in 1810, when he was barely twenty, that hieroglyphs 'possess the characteristic of producing sounds' because they transcribe proper names; he combined the brilliant intuition of a genius with rigorous methodology. This is how he himself described the method underlying his analysis: 'The care I took not to invent anything myself but to have everything present itself through a multitude of facts, observed with attention and compared with strictness, this care, I would say, gives some weight to my conclusions and to the ideas which continue to be put forward by me.'

Between 1810 and 1820 Champollion assembled an impressive documentation which allowed him to decipher the name of one of the Ptolemies in the text of the obelisk on the island of Philae near Aswan. He proved that the name of the pharaoh was followed by the epithets: 'living-forever' and 'loved-by-Ptah'. Moreover he succeeded in identifying in the same text the words 'son of Osiris'. Here we see the first great step towards the unveiling of the mystery of these writings.

A little later, after having located the name 'Cleopatra' in the same text, he had the idea of comparing the Egyptian and Greek forms of this name. Thus, step by step, he increased the number of known letters of ancient Egyptian. More importantly, he started to understand the principles of the hieroglyphic system: Champollion had, in effect, discovered the use of the determinative. He was now close to translating the names of all the Roman emperors.

But there was one question that continued to vex him: could it not be that this phonetic writing was introduced in Egypt under the influence of the Greeks so as to transcribe names which were foreign to the Egyptian language? In that case the hieroglyphs used before the arrival of the Greeks could have been purely based on images, as had been generally assumed by scholars in the centuries before him.

It was on 14 September 1822 that he made his conclusive discovery. On that day Champollion received a number of documents sent by the architect Jean-Nicolas Huyot from the great temple at Abu Simbel. In them he found a crucial cartouche of four characters. Its last two characters were already known to him; they were two s's. The first character stood for the sun, which in Coptic reads as 'Ra'. As for the central character, this one was also engraved on the Rosetta Stone in an expression which translated the Greek word 'anniversary'. There it read: day of birth. Champollion immediately saw that the final missing character should be equated with 'm', which, followed by the 'ss', transcribed the word mise: 'put on the world'. Through this he rediscovered the name in Egyptian of its most celebrated Pharao, Ra-m-s(e)s. 'Ra put him on the world'.[5] After having announced his great discovery to his older brother, Champollion-Figeac, Champollion fainted, shattered by tiredness and emotion. His famous Lettre à M. Dacier wasn't written until five days after his becoming unconscious. In it Champollion set out the principle of hieroglyphic writing, showing that it was 'at the same time figurative, symbolic and phonetic, a character could represent either a simple sound, or two consonants, or an idea.'

With the official announcement of his discovery the dispute about hieroglyphs broadened sharply. One might understand the attitude of

Edmé-François Jomard

Thomas Young, which was driven by jealousy and bitterness, but the one by Edmé Jomard (1777-1862), one of the original members of Napoleon's Egyptian campaign, is much more difficult to understand. Jomard reckoned that the contents of this work could not be surpassed. Through him Egypt had spoken its final word; Egypt did not belong to this young upstart from the provinces. Any means would do to disparage the 'decipherer' Champollion: political denunciations, support to Thomas Young and even the writing of anonymous letters.

Hence, from 1822, Champollion's career would consist of a careful negotiation of the traps laid by the powers that be in Egyptology.

However, the road now lay open for the understanding of ancient Egypt. Champollion was in a hurry to check his discovery on the ground, in Egypt itself. But he preferred to first serve an apprenticeship in Italy. This country possessed the richest collection of pharaonic antiquities after Egypt due to their relevance to Biblical studies. On 7 June 1824, he arrived in Turin where he thought he would spend only a few days, though the abundance of papyri and statues was such that he stayed in this city until the 1st of March 1825. He got through a stupendous amount of work: perfecting his reading of hieratic and demotic writings, redrafting the list of pharaohs and their chronology, accumulating information concerning geography, religion, institutions, etc. Here Champollion had to convince himself of yet another a new idea (which he vindicates in these letters);

the autonomy of Egyptian art in relation to Greek art. These results were set out in two 'Letters to the Duke de Blacas d'Aulps about the Museum of Turin', published in 1824 and 1826.

On his return to Paris, Champollion found a very different atmosphere from the one before he left. The reign of Charles X had become much less severe towards former Bonapartists like himself and his resounding Italian successes obliged opponents such as Jomard to behave with more decency and subtlety. In the end Champollion found himself entrusted with an important mission by the government as he had succeeded to wrest from the government their consent to an important acquisition of Egyptian antiquities. This concerned the acquisition of the magnificent Egyptian

Bernardino Drovetti

collection of the English consul in Egypt, Sir Henry Salt (1780-1827), for the Louvre. Champollion was charged with its transport to Paris. During this second voyage to Italy he heard of his appointment, on 14 May 1827, as Director of the Egyptian section of the Louvre. He founded the Egyptian museum with the Salt collection and next added a second one, procured by the French consul in Egypt, Bernardino Drovetti (1776-1852), the man who would turn out to be his next great foe.

Champollion was now ready to leave for Egypt, the crowning glory of his work. He had minutely prepared his itinerary, as is clear from the memo he addressed to the king petitioning for this expedition:

The members of the Commission of Egypt and the majority of travellers who have followed in its footsteps, convinced perhaps that one would never be able to understand hieroglyphic characters, have attached less importance to copying exactly the long inscriptions in sacred signs which accompanied the figures represented in the historical bas-reliefs: they are almost all neglected, and often, while copying a few scenes of these bas-reliefs, one was satisfied with merely indicating the place these cartouches occupied... In our time... exact copies of the hiero-glyphic inscriptions, which were inserted in such huge numbers, have acquired an immeasurable value and will realise, if not completely at least to a very large degree, the high expectations which the historical sciences attach to them.' Among his most important goals was gathering the history 'of the delivery of Egypt from the yoke of the Hyksos herdsmen, the event to which the arrival and captivity of the Jews is related...

He also wanted to acquire 'exceptional works of art, which 'are most suitable to enrich our royal collections and to enlighten the historical work of our scholars.'

On 18 August 1828, when Champollion set foot on Egyptian soil at last, he did not ignore modern Egypt. His letters often contain obser-vations on life in Cairo. He 'loved to admire the city "of a thousand minarets", embraced by the setting sun behind the Mokattam mountain whose picturesqueness had thrilled him from the moment he first set eyes on it, and whose richness and curious nummulite shapes promised a great store of pleasures.'6 'A lot of bad things are said about Cairo; for me, I feel quite at home, and these roads of a width of eight to ten feet which have been so maligned appear to me to have been perfectly well designed to avoid the summer heat, which is too hot. It is a city which is utterly monumental... still a city of a Thousand and One Nights,' though the Turkish dictator, Pasha Muhammad-Ali, had destroyed or allowed a large part to be destroyed of the delicious products of Arab art and civilisation.

Henry Salt

'The Egyptian' – Champollion's nickname – relished in the sights of the sacred places of the Islam.7 'I paid my first respects to one in the mosque of Ibn Thulun, a building from the ninth century, a model of stylish elegance which I couldn't admire more, even though it is half-destroyed. While I was looking at the gate an old sheik suggested that I enter; I eagerly accepted and proceeding slowly through the first gate, I was abruptly stopped at the second one; you have to enter this holy place without shoes. I was wearing boots but no socks; this was a genuine problem. I took off my boots, borrowed a handkerchief from my Janissary to bundle around my right foot and another one from my Nubian servant Muhammad for my left foot, and shuffled over the marble parquet of the holy courtyard; without any doubt it is the most stunning Arab monument in the whole of Egypt. The delicacy of its sculpture is unbelievable and its suite of porticoes and arcades bewitching.'

Cairo, whose Arab name means 'the Victorious', was a jumble of pharaonic, Christian or Muslim monuments. Yet the Cairenes were sympathetic to Champollion, as were the religious feasts which they organised. He gave for example a lively description of the Anniversary of the Prophet: 'the large and important Ezbekieh Square, flooded in the middle, was thronged with people surrounding troubadours, dancers, singers, and extremely beautiful tents under which acts of devotion were practised. Here seated Muselmen read chapters of the Koran rhythmically: elsewhere, three hundred devotees arranged in parallel lines, seated, ceaselessly moving the top of their bodies backwards and forwards like mechanical puppets, sang in choir "Ia Allah, all'Allah", further on five hundred possessed, standing upright, arranged in circles and touching their necks, jumped in cadence, and reached from the depths of their exhausted chests for the name of Allah, repeated a thousand times, but in such a dull, cavernous tone that I never heard a more infernal choir; this terrifying murmur seemed to come from the depths of the Tartarus. Alongside these religious demonstrations circled musicians and prostitutes; merry-go-rounds, swings of all kinds were in constant operation; this blend of profane pleasures and religious practices, joined with the alienness of their figures and the extreme variety of costumes, formed an infinitely curious spectacle and one which I will never forget'.

If the Islamic monuments of Cairo enchanted him, the atmosphere in the Alexandrian salons were far from being pleasant and hospitable towards him. From the moment of his arrival, Champollion was considered a hindrance to the trafficking of antiquities by the antiquarians and diplomats *en poste* in Alexandria. 'The dealers in antiquities all squirmed when they heard about my arrival in Egypt for the purpose of doing excavations. Their cabal hatched the moment my request for official permits for the excavations was presented. minister Boghoz and the Pasha were deceived, and his highness said that he would only give permission to his friends Drovetti and Anastazy. The attitude of the diplomatic personnel in Egypt and the Republican ideals of his youth made him particularly sensitive to the plight of the *fellahs* (farmers), as well as the oppression of the regime. Regarding a gift which had been presented to him by the Pasha, he said: 'Knowing that the ancient Egyptians represented this land as a cow, he milks and exhausts it day and night, waiting for it to collapse, which won't be long. That is in truth what good and beauty the noble advice of Drovetti, the great Jomard and other pastors of their ilk bring about.' His archaeological mission was an expedition whose conditions couldn't be less touristic.

Thanks to Champollion's journey, ancient Egypt ceased to be mute, as he made its aged stones speak. In one stroke the pharaonic civilisation had become loquacious, prolix even, because the discoveries of 'the Egyptian' were validated on each monument, on each papyrus. His scientific contributions to the nascent discipline of Egyptology consisted of innumerable dates from the texts, copies of scenes, plans of monuments. But these important results caused anxiety about the future of his discoveries: 'I am startled by what I am reading fluently, rather than by what my imagination has been able to come up with. I have results (and this should remain between the two of us) which are extremely embarrassing for a regiment of theories, which we shall have to keep under wraps.'

What then were these 'extremely embarrassing results'? Essentially, they concerned chronology. 'Despite the ban by Rome and the opposition of the Protestant clergy, the [issue of the] fifteen dynasties preceding the sixteenth resurfaced, attested by monuments or by vestiges of monuments, and they returned to claim their place in the annals of world history no matter what the consequences would be for the biblical chronology; the discoveries he made concerning the astronomic knowledge of the ancients smashed the Egyptian chronology calculated from 1000 BC and which had held sway until then; Egypt, idolatrous only in appearances, possessed in the subtle structure of its dogmas, deliberately masked from the eyes of the mob to the point of being unrecognisable, a "notion of divinity which was at least as pure as Christianity itself, especially, equally rooted in the Trinity".'

Here lay a real danger for the young science of Egyptology.'[8] Champollion was the first person to fathom Egyptian religion for two thousand years. No matter what sites were visited, he gathered all images of the various divinities of the temples, religious inscriptions, mythological scenes, instruments of worship, etc. in order to 'know from the start the ensemble of Egyptian worship, the source of all western pagan religions' and of Christianity.

Champollion's method of gathering information shows that he was operating like a true scientist and not as an enlightened amateur — a completely new phenomenon at the time. His discoveries were much more than travel souvenirs. In order to establish a rigorous order in his collection of numerous treasures, and in order to avoid repetition, Champollion analysed and classified each night in alphabetical order the copies, impressions and drawings made during the day, thus creating a transparent collection which was assuming an imposing shape. His portfolios weren't published until after his death, but the contents of these publications are still of use today because a number of monuments have since disappeared and his are the only records of them.

Champollion left Egypt a happy man. When he arrived in Paris, the authorities could no longer obstruct his career for political reasons as they had done before in 1816. His inexorable rise seemed to be about to take off. He was appointed as an Academician and professor at the Sorbonne in 1831 but he was only able to teach but a few lectures because he died on 4 March, 1823, at the age of 42. He was exhausted, physically and mentally, by the resurrection of the lost civilisation of Egypt, one of the great ancient histories, in the ten years following his great discovery. Not only did he create Egyptology, he had also created Egyptian archaeology, 'basing it on scientific foundations, and this twenty years before that of Mesopotamia and fifty years before Greece.'[9]

R.L.

1.

Lucky Escape

After Champollion's momentous discovery in 1822, an expedition to Egypt became increasingly urgent. Not only was Champollion quickly reaching the limits of what he could achieve with the hieroglyphic texts available to him in Europe, but under the fierce Muslim rule of the Turkish viceroy in Egypt, Pasha Muhammad-Ali, the ancient monuments of Egypt were being pillaged and razed at an alarming rate. The thick fog that lay over ancient Egypt seemed to be on the verge of becoming impenetrable. With his pupil Ippolito Rosellini, the twenty-seven-year-old professor of Oriental Languages at Pisa, Champollion planned an expedition to Egypt that was half French, half Tuscan. As he wanted to preserve inscriptions and monuments for posterity, eight of the twelve other members of the expedition were artists and draughtsmen (Duchesne, Bertin, L'Hôte, Lehoux, Cherubini and Angelelli) and architects (Bibent and Gaetano Rosellini, the famous uncle of Ippolito). The other four members were the physician Ricci, the only one who had been in Egypt before, the Egyptologist Lenormant and the famous botanist Professor Raddi and his assistant Galastri.

Preparations for the expedition were troubled, however, by the scheming of Champollion's enemy at the court of Charles X, Edmé Jomard, and by the unrest in the Mediterranean due to the Greek war of independence against the Turks. Egypt had decided to support the Turkish Port (Sultan), which had resulted in their disastrous defeat in the Battle of Navarino of 20 October 1827 against the allied fleets of France, Britain and Russia. When Champollion heard a few months later that Egypt blamed the Turks rather than the Europeans, he and Ippolito Rosellini wrote long letters to their respective consuls in Egypt, MM. Drovetti and Rosetti, for permission from the Pasha for their expedition, while Champollion arranged for passes to go to Egypt on a French navy vessel. The letter below was Drovetti's response to Champollion.

Bernardino Drovetti to Jean-François Champollion — 3 May 1828, Gémialé, Egypt

The second of the letters you have honoured me with reached me on 18 February; please trust that after you no one other than me could take a more passionate interest in the important expedition you are proposing to undertake. I regret, more than anyone, that under the current circumstances I am not able to encourage you to embark on the project for the duration of this year, unless from August the sanctions imposed against the Turks by the signatories of the Treaty of London yield their intended results. In Egypt, as in all other parts of the Ottoman empire, a spirit of animosity against Europeans reigns which could conceivably produce unrest and harm to the personal safety of those who live here or find themselves travelling here. If only Pasha Muhammad-Ali's guarantee to prevail over this unrest were required, little would be easier to secure from him than what you are asking me, but he himself is the object of this animosity because of his beliefs and European leanings, and he does not wish to give me the assurances that I have asked him for on behalf of you and your associates.

If, in the meantime, a change occurs in the stance of the signatory powers towards Turkey you may embark on your journey without having to wait for new advice; your expedition shall not cause unrest and will be well-protected by the local government. Rosellini has asked for the same permission and received the same response.

Please trust that I deeply regret not to be able to be of greater help to these plans which are without doubt underscored by colleagues of the sciences which you have advanced with such success.

At the time of writing to say the Pasha declined his permission, Drovetti, who was an important dealer in antiquities as well as the French consul general in Egypt, no longer had any intention of letting Champollion succeed with his request. The balance of power at the Pasha's court had changed dramatically in his favour after the death of the British consul, the eminent collector Sir Henry Sal. Drovetti was now the most influential foreigner in Egypt. His long-standing opponent out of the way, Drovetti had no need at all for the presence of France's most celebrated Egyptologist to make an impression on the Pasha.

Because Champollion was unaware of Drovetti's reasons he interpreted this surprising reversal of support as a move brought about by Edmé Jomard. The appointment in January of two crucial ministers who were on his side seemed to make all this irrelevant. Royal support was swiftly obtained on 26 April at an impromptu confidential meeting between Charles X and Champollion, arranged by Viscount de La Rochefoucauld, minister of the Royal Household. From that day, oblivious of the letter which Drovetti would send him a few days latter from Egypt, Champollion started selecting his fellow expedition members. He was very keen to enlist his close friend from his Turin days, the abbot Costanzo Gazzera, librarian of the University of Turin and a gifted Egyptologist.

To Costanzo Gazzera — 26 May 1828, Paris

Dearest friend,

I am counting on your indulgence and friendship and I hope that you will forgive the long silence that I have maintained towards you. The endless vicissitudes that are part and parcel of an organisation such as my museum, where everything had to be set up, forced me to abandon my correspondence and hobbies. But now I am almost relieved of it all, and I see with satisfaction that a whole year of pleasure and study lies ahead of me, and for you too, should you wish so.

My expedition to Egypt has been fixed definitely for this year, 1828. The funds that are needed have been deposited by the bureaucrats, and as of now I can have my papers well and duly stamped. I reckon I will embark in Toulon in the first days of August and arrive in Egypt towards the first of September. The expedition will last no more than a year.

I have always assumed you would join our ranks and, though cuts that have been imposed do not allow me to offer you money for your return trip, I have arranged matters in such a way that you will be able to come with me and go back to Europe without your having to incur any expenses. It would cost no more than coming from Turin to Toulon, which is not very far, and I will take care of the rest. We will be taken to Alexandria on a navy vessel, and we shall go up the Nile in a large and comfortable river boat. We shall live there like brothers and in the best way we can, under the protection of God and his Prophet [Muhammad].

Think of the moment when we shall say our prayers in the cathedral of Thebes. Hold that secret thought, should it amuse you, and start making sure that you will be able to get a year off counting from July, while keeping your job so that you can return to it. I shall write to you in a few days to give you the firm date for meeting in Toulon. Get there and I will take care of the rest.

I like to believe that they will not be such barbarians as to refuse you less than a year off, as that will be all that you will be asking for. Should it be necessary that I write myself, do let me know; I shall write to whomever whatever you would like me to say.

You won't have to organise any provisions. I shall be thinking of everything and that is my job. Limit yourself to bringing no more than the clothes and habits you strictly need, and that's all. The least possible luggage. What is our friend Costa up to? He could every now and then let me know what he is doing – such laziness! Or stoicism!

My love to Plana, Boucheron, Pa[uli]. Tell Peyron that if he needs copies of our papyri to turn to Letronne,[1] who I have authorised to send them to him. – If the Royal Academy would require you to make a few acquisitions for the Egyptian Museum [in Turin] that would be marvellous, particularly if they gave you a purse of 1,200 francs for purchases; that might be reason for certain people to give you more happily a year off till the end of 1829. – See whether you might be able to take advantage of this idea which could serve as a flyleaf for your journey. – I await your answer to all this.

Yours ever, J.-F. C.

Leopold II, the Grand-Duke of Tuscany, had immediately agreed to the expedition, which in turn no doubt influenced Charles X's decision to give his support to Champollion.

To the Grand-Duke of Tuscany – 11 June 1828, Paris
Your Imperial and Royal Highness,
It is a real pleasure for me to see at last that fate favours a project to which science evidently attaches great hopes, and that I am able today to announce the forthcoming expedition of this scientific voyage to a Prince

whose generous protection and enlightened concerns are well inclined to assure its success.

The King has commanded that the funds necessary for a complete exploration of Egypt with regard to its historical monuments shall be placed at my disposal, and I have been authorised to enlist the help of a number of artists, draughtsmen or architects to copy accurately the numerous bas-reliefs and all inscriptions on monuments which so urgently need to be studied, and which in this way shall be seized from certain destruction at the menacing hands of ever more active savages.

The departure for Egypt shall take place towards the end of next July, or during the first days of August, and it is absolutely necessary that the Tuscan Commission, which Your Imperial and Royal Highness has deigned to instruct with the same goal as the French Commission, shall embark at the same time and on the same ship. The Minister of the French Navy is charged with providing safe passage on a Royal vessel to people who are part of this scientific and non-military expedition while the Mediterranean and Orient are subjected to the movements of a theatre of war; relying on the fact that Pasha Muhammad-Ali must understand where his real interests lie, we have grounds for hoping that our research in Egypt and Nubia shall take place under the most complete security.

I hope you will allow me to renew here the deep sentiment with which I remain yours

Costanzo Gazzera decided in the end not to join the expedition but had tentatively agreed to see Champollion off in Toulon (a plan he would cancel for the same reason, lack of good health).

To Costanzo Gazzera – 9 July 1828, Paris

I cannot tell you with how much pleasure I will greet you in Toulon should your work permit you to come. It will be a tremendous pleasure for me. – Do come if it doesn't cause too much inconvenience for you. – Send my love to Costa; say goodbye to him from me; and to Plana, Peyron, Boucheron, Pauli and the entire Sclopis family. Goodbye. I am glad to be able to think that I will once more be embracing you before embarking. Goodbye, with my entire heart and soul.

P.S. – If Peyron has a few notes to give to me for his research in Egypt, I am entirely at his disposal. Send him my love. – *Addio carissimo, addio*

Champollion to his schoolfriend Augustin Thevenet,
a shopkeeper in Grenoble – 10 July, Paris

I would not want to leave Europe, my little friend, without saying goodbye to you, my oldest comrade, and the one who has always remained foremost in my affection. I dare say I am not dealing with a Judas and that I still have in your heart the place that I used to occupy, because neither of us is of an age where one makes new friends at the expense of those who have developed and grown up with one. If you thought after my silence towards you that my love for you has diminished over time and distance, you would be mistaken, because I am always taking a lively interest in everything good that might happen to you or anything sad and disagreeable that might overcome you. I want to pass through Grenoble to give you a hug, but I am so pressed for time that I won't be able to give in to this wish. I absolutely have to be in Toulon on the 25th of this month because the corvette the *Églé*, which will take me and the fourteen people who accompany me to Alexandria, will sail on the 30th without tolerating delays.

I shall be in Lyons on Friday the 18th; I will stay there until the evening of Sunday 20th, when I will leave for Aix, where I will have to stay for a day. If your business were to allow you to come and meet me in Lyon and stay with me for two days, that would be delightful. I am leaving for such a hazardous journey that I am anxious to embrace everyone who is dear to me, and you can imagine how thrilled I would be to see you again before I thrust myself among the tanned faces that await me on the shores of Africa.

Do try and arrange this pleasure trip because it would be so sweet, and the distance is so small! You will find me in the Hôtel du Nord, near the Place des Terreaux, or, better still, you can get my address from M. Artaud, the curator of the Museum of Lyons at the Palace of Saint-Pierre. I almost count on the pleasure of seeing you; I will not say goodbye, then, as I know that you will do your very best [to see me]. I embrace you, like I love you, with all my heart.

Champollion to Champollion-Figeac – 18 July 1828, Lyons

I am now in Lyons in very good health. I found my friend Artaud prepared to be my host, and I settled in at his place with Rosellini. Last night, spent in a comfortable bed, completely revived me. My gout has not flared up… and I am beginning to hope that I will be able to keep ahead of it until Toulon. There it may do as it pleases; I will be able to treat it while at sea and the first heat of Africa will properly deal with it. At the Museum of Lyons they showed me, among other curiosities, a bronze statue of a height of seven inches, representing the God of the Nile, an excellent piece of workmanship. I am having it drawn for my *Pantheon* [of Egyptian deities]; it is, up till now, a unique object, and I am thrilled to have seen it.

My friend Artaud wrote today to M. Sallier in Aix to announce the fact that we will be passing through his town. I anticipate a great harvest from his ample collection and I will devote two days to it if necessary… When you write your article announcing the Egyptian expedition don't forget to include Salvador Cherubini as one of the members of the French expedition: Rosellini pays for his travel expenses but Salvador wants, for a reason, be reported as belonging to my French draughtsmen… Goodbye, then. I will write to you from Aix without fail.

Salvador Cherubini, the son of the composer and brother-in-law of Rosellini, became Champollion's most trusted member of the expedition. He concerned himself with the many practical concerns and dealt with concerns that arose among the French expedition members along the way. Writing to Champollion-Figeac from Aix-en-Provence, where they stopped to study the collection of Mr Sallier (now in the British Museum),[3] His letter confers the thrill about this serendipitous discovery of a papyrus that would a few months later turn out to contain the intact text of an important but fragmented temple inscription.

Salvador Cherubini to Champollion-Figeac – 23 July 1828, Aix
After a long family dinner, your brother has been kind enough to choose me as his secretary…

The Cabinet of M. Sallier includes, apart from beautiful drawings, a large number of rather valuable antiquities… But what is exciting everyone more than anything is a beautifully preserved papyrus dating back to the eighth year of the reign of Sesostris. It is a very important object; M. Champollion, too, is keen to come back after his return in order to stay here for a longer time. M. Sallier forgot to show it to him yesterday and only now, rather late in the day, did he remember to do so, as he hadn't attached to it quite the importance it deserves.

As a result, now that he has been made aware of the treasure he possesses, I think he has rather lost his head, which nonetheless will not prevent him from giving his attention to your text of Diocletian...

Your devoted Salvador Cherubini

Champollion to Champollion-Figeac — 25 July 1828, Toulon
I arrived here at night yesterday in excellent health, my dear friend, and after a journey which was less tiresome than one might expect from the summer season and the Provençal sky. Leaving Aix at three in the morning we were in Toulon at six o'clock in the evening; I barely noticed the heat during the trip thanks to the furs and wool which covered me; which made me think that the commonplace 'What keeps out the cold keeps out the heat' must be one of the perennial truths of human experience.

It was impossible to write to you from Aix as I had planned; M. Sallier's cabinet kept me busy for the two days I stayed in that old city. I found a number of important pieces which I copied or had drawn. Only on the second day did Sallier put in my hands a packet of non-funerary papyri, among which I found... a roll of which the first pages are missing but which contains eulogies and the exploits of Ramesses-Sesostris in a biblical style, that is to say in the form of an ode dialogue between the gods and the king.

This one is of the greatest importance, and the little time that I have given to its examination convinced me that it is a real historical treasure. I lifted from it the names of about fifteen conquered nations among which are particularly mentioned the Ionians, Iouni, Iavani and the Lyceans, and then Ethiopians, Arabs, etc. It talks about their chiefs who were taken hostage and the payments which those nations had to bear. The manuscript amply justifies my idea that the group [see drawing] identifies the names of foreign countries and those of individuals in a foreign language. I have carefully taken down all the names of conquered people which, being perfectly readable and in hieratic writing, will help to recognise the same names in hieroglyphs on the monuments of Thebes and to reconstruct them if they are partly worn off.

This is an enormous discovery. The most curious thing is that the hieratic manuscript is dated on the last page: 'It is written [says the text] in the ninth year, in the month of Paoni of the reign of Ramesses the Great.' I want to study this papyrus in depth when I come back from Egypt. Don't speak to anyone about it unless they are trustworthy and then only with circumspection. We must let sleeping dogs lie. Sallier promised me not to show it to anyone until I come back to Aix. I haven't yet told you anything about our friend Artaud. He has helped us. Do return the favour at his request.

M. Sallier promised to give me a paper impression of three stones which carry fragments of a Roman decree regarding the prices of food and merchandise; I would have done it myself but he has been silly enough to cover the letters of the text in hardened plaster. He will have them washed and cleaned. Write to him soon to remind him of his promise. He is a very good man... Warn the minister of the navy that, among the fourteen passes which he granted me, there are those of the Tuscan commission and that he can and ought to take credit for that with the Tuscan minister, who may talk to him about it. This is important...

Champollion to Champollion-Figeac – 29 July 1828, Toulon
Dear friend,
I received your [letter] 'no. 1', which I was already impatiently waiting for. My numbering won't start until after embarking, and my first will be dated from Neptune's pastures because I hope that on the way we will come across a few ships returning to Europe and that it will be possible to send via them a letter to France. But if we happen to be alone on the world's grand cross road you will not have my news for two months at the earliest, as departures for France from Alexandria are extremely rare. Our corvette, intended to act as convoy to merchant vessels, will not be escorting anyone. No one ventures out to sea, not because there is physical danger, but because trade with Egypt suffers from a complete state of paralysis; Egypt itself no longer exports cotton. Nonetheless, the Admiral assures me that our relationship with the Pasha is most cordial. I shall obtain more positive news on our position vis-à-vis Egypt because I just received an invitation from M. Léon de Laborde, who arrived from Alexandria in thirty days, to meet at the Toulon Lazaret. He will doubtless tell me what I may expect or should be wary of; the tone of his letter is really very reassuring and I foresee nothing but good news. I shall not close his letter until after seeing him. I met the commander of the *Églé*

and his aide-de-camp. I cannot but thank fate for having placed us in their hands. M. Cosmao is a man of forty, very agreeable – good conversation and excellent manners. He is very keen to let me have his room and I am obliged to accept as he is our commander. We treated him and his second-in-command yesterday; an alliance that is both offensive and defensive was forged amidst an explosion of champagne. I brought him over to our side.

Our Parisians arrived this morning, and our Tuscans this evening after a journey lasting fifteen days. They had all sorts of trouble getting through a blockade at the Piedmontese frontier raised by the King of Sardinia. That good man, deluded by the lies and exaggerations of one merchant captain who disembarked in Genoa, imagines that the Provence is infested with the plague; his regiments have marched up to close all passes through the Alps and letters coming from France are opened and dipped in vinegar. Newspapers are treated as if they are gherkins, which might benefit the *Gazette* and the *Quotidienne* immensely. In Italy they think that here and in Marseilles we are dying by the bushel, while we are having superb weather owing to a westerly breeze which refreshes the air and which will fling us into the open sea in less than an hour.

I think His Majesty the King of Sardinia confuses in his mind the physical plague and the moral plague that according to some minds is wasting our dear France. It is a good thing that brains and common sense cannot be strained through vinegar.

The sea is promising to be excellent. I have tested my stomach and I think it is well seasoned after having crossed by boat a bay with a violent sea… Cherubini, Duchesne and Bertin have ventured on a similar outing and have withstood it with honour… I bathed three times in the bay and this exercise has done me infinite good. I take advantage of this remedy whenever I am near salted water.

(Léon de Laborde wanted to inform Champollion about the discoveries of his recent archaeological research in Egypt.)[4]

Champollion to Champollion-Figeac – 30 July 1828, Toulon

I was unable to see M. de Laborde: the breeze was too strong for any exchange without danger with the Lazaret in a tiny keelless boat. He suggests a new meeting for tomorrow, but by that time I will already be far away from Toulon as our embarkation will take place between nine and ten o'clock in the morning. Our bulk luggage is on board and our suitcases will go tomorrow, and then we are ready to say our goodbyes to the mainland. They are making me hope that we will stop-over in Sicily. I have asked the Admiral to allow the captain to let us disembark for a few hours in Agrigento; which is agreed. It is up to the sea now to let us do so. If she behaves, I will write to you from underneath the shade of one of the Doric columns of the temple of Jupiter.

Goodbye, my dear friend, don't worry, the gods of Egypt are watching over us…

Drovetti's letter had still not reached Champollion, for a good reason. He had put his letter in a parcel to Champollion's older brother, Champollion-Figeac, who received it a few days before his brother's departure from Paris on 16 July. Champollion-Figeac decided not to mention the letter to anyone and by the time he forwarded it from Paris to Toulon his brother had left, as planned, for Alexandria with the corvette the *Églé*. Attempts were nonetheless made to intercept the *Églé*.[2] Furthermore, on 10 August Doctor É. Pariset, a specialist on the plague and a friend, was about to join Champollion on his own medical expedition to Egypt and Syria but was ordered by telegraph not to leave from Marseilles.

Champollion to Champollion-Figeac – 3 August 1828,
at sea between Sardinia and Sicily

I will try and write to you, dear friend, despite the movements of the ship. It is being propelled forward by the wind we were hoping for, and it is making steady progress towards the European coast of Sicily which, it appears, we shall see this evening. Up till now the crossing has been most fortuitous, and the most difficult part is over: my stomach has survived all these tribulations and I feel perfectly fine at the moment… The enforced rest from which one benefits on board, and the hopelessness of doing anything of consequence, are proving a boon to my health. My young people have suffered little and I am about to let them go up to the bridge after having taught them Arabic, which they are studying with great enthusiasm; I am teaching them how to draw linear hieroglyphs and they are doing quite well already. – Here in a few words is all the news on board. I won't talk about the past two days, when all I saw were the sea and the sky. This canvas, though interrupted by a few spinning porpoises and the massive appearance of two sperm whales, would be too boring. The desolate dryness of the Sardinian coast, a rather impressive country through the sight of its ancient Nuraghes [stone fortification towers], doesn't offer much of interest either.

I will therefore talk to you about the more interesting prospect that we will go ashore in the middle of the temples of the old Agrigento. Our commander promises that this will happen tomorrow evening if Aeolus and Neptune will kindly grant us that favour. I shall no longer depend on M. Cosmao; he has had to accept the return of his room and bed. At my feet and on mattresses, spread out on the wooden floor, sleep Rosellini, Raddi and father Bibent: his comical apathy and lethargic 'resurrection' enthrals the second-in-command. He sleeps on the bridge or deck for half of the day and perched on the rigging for the remainder...

4 August

We cleared during the night the western tip of Sardinia, and are pointing towards the shoreline of the south, Africa proper. This morning we saw nothing but the sky and sea. Towards the evening we saw the island of Maritimo, the farthest European tip of Sardinia, but a hapless calm prevented us from moving forward.

5 August

After a night of tacking we saw Maritimo again in the early morning at a distance of two or three miles. When at last the wind picked up the ship went by the islands of Favignana and Levanzo: we saw Trapani (Drepanum), the ancient arsenal of Sicily, and Mount Eryx, so much praised in the *Aeneid*. In the afternoon we passed Marsalla and enthusiastically hailed its vineyards: and a respectful salute when we passed that city which was once Lilibee, the main Carthaginian settlement in Sicily. This Mediterranean coast has a perfect beauty.

6 August

I wasn't able to hail the ruins of Selinunte, as we passed them at night. The coast is a bit drier here, though still picturesque and with a pleasant hint of Africa. We dropped anchor in the Bay of Agrigento (Grigenti): there is a bevy of Greek monuments which we wanted to visit and study. But it is now probably a certainty that we will have to live with the disappointment of coming within four hundred *tois* of these temples without even being able to see them. We are paying heavily for the stupidity of the Marseillais

Champollion-Figeac (1778 - 1867), curator at the Royal Library and journalist for the *Moniteur in* which chronicled Champollion's progress

captain who spread the rumour in Genoa of that famous plague of Marseilles. Going with the commander to the Lazaret of Agrigento as his interpreters, they told Rosellini and me that orders from Palermo, which had arrived the evening before, expressly forbade clearing any ship coming from the southern ports of France. I replied that Toulon is a northern port; the Sicilian answered that 'he knew this very well' but that, having received no orders on the northern ports, he couldn't let us go ashore without authorisation from the governor of the province of Agrigento. They promised us an answer by eight tomorrow morning; and we returned to the corvette with heavy hearts and with no hope that we would be able to admire the temple of Concordia. Fate plays its hand very well; at last I understand the exasperation of Tantalus.

7 January, six o'clock

We haven't yet received any news from the mainland. I have given up all hope. I am going to end this letter in order to be able to send it in an hour and a half from now by land, in order to let them put it in the post through all the usual fumigations. We are all looking very healthy, good appetite, sparkling eyes, superb tans, and they insist on treating us as plague infested! I will reopen my letter if I am able to let you know that they have allowed us to go to Agrigento, which is no more than two thousand steps away; I would be so delighted to go ashore among those venerable ruins! But I dare not count on it... My respects to M. Dacier [the permanent Secretary of the Academy of Inscriptions in Paris], who is often talked about during our conversations, which take place at night on the poop deck and under the most gorgeous sky in the entire world. Tell my *ancien* [Champollion's former tutor] that the time has come to take our share of bad luck; we will have the time to brace ourselves.

If we don't have our passes by eight o'clock we will sail immediately in the direction of Malta.

Goodbye, my dear friend. My love with all my heart to you and to all who are on our side.

2.

Treacherous Alexandria

From Champollion's diary

18 August – We saw early in the morning on the bleached coasts of Africa, at a location which is today deprived of all vegetation, as it may as well have been since the beginning of time, the site of ancient Toposiris or Taphosiris, today Abousir. We noticed, at first through a telescope and then with our bare eyes, the vestiges of this little city, whose position is marked by a mound with a square building. This appears to be an Egyptian edifice from the Ptolemaic times or the [Roman] emperors', as the stones seemed to me to be proportionally small. Not far away from these ruins and a little nearer the sea rises up a modern tower known to navigators as the Arab Tower.

Towards the afternoon, we could, through a telescope, see the Column of Pompey and the harbour of Alexandria. The sight of this town became more imposing the nearer we came. A forest of masts extended across the whole surface of the Old Port and one could see across masts the whitened low buildings that make up the modern city. To the left lay the house of Ibrahim-Pacha [the son of the Pasha], built on the seashore; the small cottage is occupied by Minister Boghoz. A much larger house, painted white like the other two, was once the residence of the Pasha. But, having built a vast wooden house of much larger proportions a little further inland, his old home has become the place where the Divan assembles and the location where His Highness gives his audiences and governs the affairs of state. The harem was moved to the new wooden building which, infinitely pierced by windows, has not yet been painted. Some twenty women who arrived from Cairo two days after the Pasha now reside in the new harem.

The Old Port is a magnificent ensemble and offers great safety to boats of all sizes, but its various approaches are highly treacherous, as the wrecks that encircle the harbour on almost all sides show. As we arrived from a distance, our curiosity was sharply aroused and increased from the moment that we noticed that there was not one French or British navy vessel patrolling the port of Alexandria, which, according to European newspapers, was supposed to be under boycott. Only after our entry into the Old Port, piloted by an Arab *reis* [captain] who had been beckoned from the shore by the commander with a cannon shot, did we see the French and English ships charged with the blockade of the harbour moored peacefully in the middle, blending in with Turkish boats and almost touching two Algerian vessels, which they are under orders to attack should they make a move to leave the harbour, or take by force if they dare to escape. – Not far removed from the European frigates and bricks sway Egyptian and Turkish vessels of all descriptions which escaped from the Navarino disaster, and which people are trying to repair. This mixture of ships of all nations, friends and enemies at the same time, is a rather bizarre spectacle and amply sums up our time. Having barely dropped anchor, senior officers of the French blockade came on board and told us of the peace treaty of the Peloponnese. Eight days earlier Admiral Codrington had arrived at the head of a small squadron in order to gauge the Pasha's intentions. Consenting to all its articles, he signed the convention and immediately sent out a large number of Egyptian and Moorish ships in order to transport the ammunition and provisions from the fortresses which the treaty leaves in Egyptian hands. European ships have likewise set sail for the Peloponnese; they are charged with bringing back Ibrahim-Pacha and the largest possible part of his army to Egypt. The Egyptian government intends to keep them in quarantine, to which purpose they have already dedicated a number of Syrian and Levantine buildings, and which together with the cordon sanitaire on the Syrian frontier has saved Egypt from the plague, which hasn't struck in Alexandria in five years.

The secretary of the French consulate, M. Cardin, came on board to congratulate me on my fortunate arrival with the *Églé* on behalf of M. Drovetti, who I knew to be in Alexandria like the Pasha and M. d'Anastazy. We arranged that on the very same night I would visit M. Drovetti;

Commander Cosmao wanted to join me and had his launch lowered and put to sea. At the agreed hour, towards six at night, the consul of Italy, Rosetti, sent us his janissary, Mustafa, and, weaving through the boats and vessels of all nations for half an hour (because the Old Port is immensely large), the pinnace let us out near the customs house. Thus preceded by two janissaries from the French and Tuscan consulates, who conjured up the Doryphores of the Persian kings with their white turbans, flowing red robes and tall staves with a silver knob, we took a few steps towards the city gates. But we had barely cleared the customs buildings when we were surrounded by a crowd of shouting young boys dressed in rags and guiding rather pretty donkeys, who urged us to use their modest mounts covered with a cleanish saddle braided with all colours. In a caravan, headed by our janissaries, who had also grabbed two donkeys, we made our entrance in the ancient seat of the Ptolomies. I have to say that the donkeys of Egypt, Alexandria's and Cairo's cabs, deserve all the praise lavished on them by travellers, and that it would be difficult to imagine a mount that is more gentle and agreeable in all respects. You must hold their bridle in order to make them trot and gallop. A little larger than those of Europe, and certainly more spirited, Egyptian donkeys carry their ears almost perfectly, practically straight up and pitched with a certain pride. This is mainly because when the donkeys are young their ears are pierced and, having been joined by a cord of horsehair, they are anchored with a second tie in such a way that they assume an upright position. Other than that these animals have very smooth coats; some of them are brown or black, but they are mostly reddish grey.

After having responded to the 'Who goes there?' of the watch, a soldier of the Nizam-Gedid [the élite corps of the Ottoman army] who was guarding the gates, we entered the streets of Alexandria, if one can give the name of street to a jumble of rather low houses mostly made of mud, irregularly pierced by occasional openings, and in no alignment to each other whatsoever. The appearance of its inhabitants, who despite nightfall cluttered up the streets, is so strange for the newly arrived from Europe that it is impossible to describe the surprise and virtual stupor that overcame us. This mélange of Egyptians of copper-brown tans, Barbars of a darker colour, Bedouins whose black colour contrasts with their white garb, blacks and Abyssinians, who touch and press against each other in order to avoid in the narrow streets the people on donkeys or horseback, and the long lines of sad and slow camels attached to each other — all this is so strangely new that they rather seemed to take part in an operatic scene. I could barely believe the picture I had before my eyes, which the lights of the shops that were still open lit up in an odd way. Our ears too were treated to a surprise and were stunned by the guttural sounds and wild cries which boomed from all sides.

Traversing this new world which changed at each pace, we arrived at the house of M. Rosetti, the consul of Tuscany. A few steps before the door our cavalcade was blocked by a European who, stopping the donkeys, flung his arms around me; it was Pietrino Santino, who had arrived from Livorno eight days earlier. The pleasure of embracing this dear and lovely friend immediately tore me from the peculiar spell which the journey across Alexandria had cast on me and brought me back to my senses.

I went up to M. Rosetti [the Italian consul] for a few moments, to compose myself, and then to M. Drovetti with the commander and M. Lenormand. The consul received me affectionately and said that he was not expecting me at all because he had written to me in May from the encampment in the Delta, where the Pasha was staying, to the effect that His Highness thought it might be better for me to adjourn the trip to Egypt because relations between France and the Sultan were most uncertain, and because the Pasha had been threatened with reprisals. Muhammad-Ali feared that all this would not dispose the Egyptian people well towards the French. His Highness had added that a voyage to Egypt undertaken by a large number of people under orders of a government practically at war with the Sultan would compromise him with the Sultanate; that he would like nothing more than that I came to Egypt, but that my arrival would be interpreted badly as there were a number of Turks among his ministers and generals. M. Drovetti told me that since his letter matters had changed somewhat and that the treaty signed to evacuate the Peloponnese lifted many of the obstacles; and that, moreover, 'as I was here', there was little he could do but welcome me, and that he was certain that the Pasha would not check the continuation of my journey and would give me all desirable official permits and necessary facilities. — It was agreed that I would stay with M. Drovetti and that a house would be rented in the neighbourhood for my travel companions as all *okels* [large houses] in Alexandria were already occupied by Europeans. — I left the consul and, accompanied by a janissary and a *sais* holding a lantern, we crossed the city once more in order to sleep on board the *Églé*.

19 August 1828 — A day passed on board in order to prepare for the final disembarkation tonight. M. Rosetti came to have lunch with us. At six o'clock in the evening, left the *Églé* in the commander's launch with the janissary seated on its poop. I settled myself in a pretty apartment with two rooms decorated with painted Parisian wallpaper. The one, the bedroom, depicted a rich fabric, the other a Swiss landscape. The whole wall of my room facing the alcove under the window is occupied by a large divan, elegant washstand, psyche [swing mirror], pendulum clock, expensive flower vases, exquisite chairs, settee — the apartment has everything. Upon entering this apartment it is impossible to imagine yourself in Africa, but what I notice most of all among all this European luxury are two ugly bluish clay carafes of ancient Egyptian design and filled with Nile water which remains fresh through perpetual transudation. When one asks a man who comes on shore after a crossing of a few months what he wants he will answer: really fresh water! I am one of these men and I gulped down Nile water! My two *gulah* (which is the name for these refrigerating carafes that, much more than the so-called god Canopus, are the saviours of the Egyptian people) were empty before nine at night when we went down for supper! One still has supper in Egypt.

Among our dinner guests were M. Méchain, son of the astronomer, an old member of the Commission, and French consul in Larnaca, who was staying with his friend M. Drovetti until the Cypriots had calmed down enough for him to return to his duties without being shot at during the disorders that are tearing that island apart.

20 August 1828 — After an excellent night in the alcove, where thirty years previously slept the victor of Heliopolis [a battle during Napoleon's campaign], General Kléber, whose administrative weakness precipitated the loss of Egypt but whose military courage regained it in a day, I woke up for breakfast at nine o'clock, as one does at the French consulate, with a cup of *café au lait* and bread rolls which resemble our hard buns. The milk, drunk pure, is not very agreeable and leaves an animal aftertaste, a smell of goat that is too pungent.

At half past ten, I went out to visit M. d'Anastazy, the Swedish consul in Egypt. He is a man with a pleasant figure, with open manners and enjoying an excellent reputation for uprightness. He does business on a vast scale, and of twelve ships freighted from Alexandria at least six will sail on his account. M. d'Anastazy, an Armenian, has rather a lot of credit with the Pasha, and most of all with his compatriot, Minister Boghoz. The Swedish consul received us while sitting on his divan and offered us a water pipe and coffee, after oriental custom, adopted by the French, who will gladly imitate everything the Muslim do when it concerns pleasure and comfort without worrying too much about practising their own habits and essential qualities. – At noon, dinner with M. Drovetti, whose usual guests are M. Méchain, his nephew, Bernardino Drovetti, and M. Lavison. The latter, originally from Marseilles, was chancellor of the Russian consulate and was about to be appointed as counsellor by Tsar Nicholas. He lives with M. Drovetti and has assisted M. Cardin after the Russian consul, under orders issued by the Pasha, was obliged to take down his flag, which he had continued to fly despite the declaration of war by Russia on the Sultan. – M. Lavison, an original mind and a nice man, is a very agreeable dinner companion. After dinner, water pipe and coffee, siesta – but I couldn't sleep. At five o'clock, left the *okel* to see Cleopatra's needles, called the needles of the Pharaoh by the Arabs, who are thus nearer the truth than the Europeans. These two monuments are located outside Alexandria proper in the Arab enclosure near Cape Lochias. After passing the gate of the enclosure one goes east across a multitude of mounds or sand dunes without any vegetation, formed from debris of pottery of all ages, glass, marble and materials of all types, which, discarded and mixed with sand, cover to a depth of many feet the remnants of Greek and Roman buildings in ancient Alexandria. At some places you come across exposed ruins in the middle of the sands, but they are insignificant remnants and for the most part brick buildings. A number of arches of these ancient edifices, filled with desert sand, are still visible above ground and are like cavernous mouths. Here, in these dens, which one can only enter by crouching, live miserable *fellah* [peasant] families amid venomous insects, lizards and millipedes. Many of these lairs, which are at very close proximity and near a cistern supplying foul water for two-thirds of the year, are called villages by the Alexandrines. I saw other hide-outs made of a roof of palm leaves placed on the edges of antique walls

View of the standing obelisk now in Central Park, New York

from which a man, women and completely naked children exited. They call this their home, and a few cats perching towards nightfall on the roofs join in this human misery.

Dogs live in complete freedom in Egypt, and while we were going to the obelisks we were accompanied by the barking of a drove of these creatures, each of which occupied the top of a dune while following us at a considerable distance with their throaty, muffled voices. These dogs of different sizes are of one and the same species: they are indistinguishable from jackals except for their fur, which is yellow-red. I am no longer surprised that in hieroglyphic texts it is so difficult to differentiate the jackal from a dog: their visual characteristics are the same. A dog is defined only by a tail curled up like a trumpet. This distinction is taken from nature: all Egyptian dogs carry  their tail pointing upward in this way. Continuing my route towards the sands and, after having had the chance to verify *de visu* the exactness of Herodotus when he described their way of urinating, I was accosted by an old Arab guided by a young half-naked child. The poor man was blind but approached me with confidence: 'Hello, citizen,' he said. 'I haven't yet had lunch, please give me something.' Caught unawares by this Republican greeting, I grabbed all the French *sous* I could find in my pockets and handed them to the Arab. He rolled them between his fingers and cried: 'These are no longer any good, my friend!' I then searched for a Turkish piaster and gave it to my blind compatriot.'This one is fine!' he said.'Thank you, citizen!' – In Alexandria you will find such souvenirs of our Egyptian campaign everywhere. At last I arrived at the obelisks, which are situated in front of a new enclosure which separates them from the sea, which is only a few *yards*² removed from them. Of the two monuments, one is still standing upright and the other toppled a long time ago.³ Both, made of pink granite like the ones in Rome and practically with an identical hue, measure about sixty feet in height, including their pyramidion. A quick scan of the three columns of hieroglyphs which are chiselled on each side told me that these beautiful monoliths were cut, consecrated and erected in front of the Sun Temple at Heliopolis by Pharaoh Tuthmosis III, which means that their age goes back to [blank] BC, i.e. [blank] before our present era. The lateral cartouches were afterwards added during the reign of Ramesses the Great; and the royal cartouche of Ramesses VII (Pheron), his immediate successor, was sculpted on the north and east façades, in between the lateral cartouches and the tip of the obelisk, but in tiny hieroglyphic characters. – So the obelisks of Alexandria go back to the pharaonic time – which the beauty of their incisions in any case amply shows – and were carved during three different eras, but mainly during the eighteenth dynasty. The first voyagers from Europe or the first Frenchmen who established themselves in Alexandria gave these monuments the name Needles of Cleopatra, which is as incorrect as the name Column of Pompey, given to a monument of early Roman times.

Champollion to Champollion-Figeac – 22 August 1828

I am risking these lines via a Tuscan ship which leaves tomorrow for Livorno. As it is rather doubtful that this letter will get to you before the one which the commander of the *Églé*, which will return to Europe, setting sail next Tuesday, has agreed to send, I am adding a provisional no. 1 to this, leaving all details for the second, which will be the real no. 1.

I arrived on the 18th of August on the Egyptian soil I have so long yearned for. Up till now she has been treating me like a caring mother, and all signs suggest I have maintained the good health with which I arrived. I have been able to drink as much fresh water as I want, and it is water from the Nile which is brought in by the Mahmoudieh canal, named in honour of the Pasha who had it built.

I saw M. Drovetti on the evening of my arrival and found out that he had written advising me not to come at all this year. My lucky star shone brightly on this important occasion as that letter didn't arrive in time. Since then things have rather changed. You have probably already heard about the evacuation treaty of the Peloponnese, agreed by Ibrahim-Pacha on 6 July and signed a dozen days ago by the viceroy, [Pasha] Muhammad-Ali. My crossing suffered no delays. The Pasha is aware of my arrival, and he has let me know that I am very welcome; I will be presented to him tomorrow or the day after, or maybe later. Everything is turning out in the best possible way for my future work, and the Alexandrinians are so pleasant that I have thrown out all prejudices which the Egyptian Commissioners [Edmé Jomard and a few other members of Napoleon's Commission of Egypt] instilled against them.

On the 19th I moved in with M. Drovetti, whose hospitality I neither wanted nor could refuse. In the palace of the French consulate I occupy an exquisite apartment with a view of the sea and which enjoys a pleasant coolness. The schedule of our projects in Alexandria and its environment is already set; it consists of the so-called obelisks of Cleopatra of which at last we have a copy, and next the column of Pompey. I have to find out at last what its exact dedication is and whether it contains the name Diocletian: we shall make a very good impression of it.

Our young people are stunned by what they have seen so far... The next one will have all the details: the series of letters with my observations will really start with that one.

Champollion to Champollion-Figeac – 23 August 1828, Alexandria
I suppose, my dear friend, that you will already have received the letter which our stop-over before Agrigento in Sicily gave me the chance to send to you by land and consign to the entire diligence of the Sicilian's authorities. I fear, though, that the same, endemic as it is in that delightful climate, may have let me down as far as Palermo... On the 18th, at five o'clock, senior officers from the French navy came on board to inform us of excellent news. We heard that, on 6 July, the admirals in command of the allied fleet in the Peloponnese had met Ibrahim-Pacha and suggested the outline of a treaty resulting in the withdrawal of Egyptian troops from

the Peloponnese; that seven days before our arrival Admiral Codrington had landed to have the Pasha sign the treaty which M. Drovetti had exhaustively prepared, and which the English admiral, who for the past month has snaked peacefully about the Mediterranean in order not to come across Admiral Malcolm, who has been appointed in his place and to whom he has to render his command, wants to use as a means to prepare a favourable reception in London by taking credit for these important negotiations.

But the fact of the matter is that the whole affair has been arranged by M. de Rigny and M. Drovetti. Many French and English vessels and a large number of Egyptian warships — as the Pasha still has a vast navy — have left Alexandria in order to look for Ibrahim-Pacha and the first division of his army in order to transport them back here, where they are expected in around fifteen days...

All descriptions that one may read about the city can at most give you an inkling of what it is like. It is a true antipodal apparition, and one is all of a sudden in a new world, where nothing resembles what one has seen so far: violent colours and strings of shops thronged with men of all races, sleeping dogs and camels tied by knotted cords, riotous shouts blending in with high-pitched female voices, and half-naked children, a suffocating dust, and here and there a gentleman in dazzling clothes on a magnificent horse — that is what a street in Alexandria is like!

After half an hour's trek and an infinite number of detours we arrived at M. Drovetti's, who received us in the best possible way. He admitted that he was rather surprised by my arrival, but was pleased that a letter which he had written me in May to delay my journey hadn't arrived, as since then things had changed, and I would not find any obstacles in my way; I should treat his house as my own, and he had had prepared an apartment for me...

Everything in this city breathes memories of our old power and shows how effortlessly French influence extends to the entire Egyptian population. Upon arrival I heard the drummers of the Pasha's troops sound the French retreat and their fifes play the same air as ours. All the marches of the Republic have been adopted by the Nizam-Gedid...

I couldn't be bearing up better to the heat; it seems as if I was born in this country, and the French have already remarked that I have the build of a Copt. My moustache, black in order to please and quite respectable, contributes considerably to the orientalisation of my face. In other respects I have adopted the customs of the country, strong coffee and three sessions of pipe a day. The tobacco is delicious while fusing each puff with a sip of coffee, and otherwise quite mild, and it is presented both when drinking or eating. Then the obligatory siesta after dinner, lasting two to four hours.

All my young men joined me at the sumptuous table of M. Drovetti, but all of them follow my example and are models of sobriety and know how to curb their appetites...

As you may imagine, I have already made a visit to Pompey's column, which is nothing exceptional, though I did all the same discover something that has been overlooked. I spotted, amid the antique disorderly debris that makes up its base, a section of crys-tallised sandstone, or

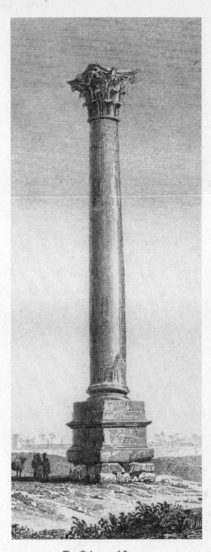

The Column of Pompey

perhaps more likely a sandy marble, which carried in hieroglyphs the royal legend of Psammetichus II.

Several times, always by donkey, a means of transport called 'Bon Cabal' by the young Arabs who guide them, I went to Cleopatra's obelisks, of which the one standing belongs to the king, who really ought to bring it back. Its neighbour, lying in the sand, belongs to the English. I already drew and had most of their inscriptions drawn. I will have, for the first time, a complete record: the theory of the Commission does not hold up. These obelisks of three columns of characters were erected by Moeris (Tuthmosis III) in front of the great sun temple at Heliopolis. The lateral inscriptions are from Ramesses VI (Sesostris), and I discovered, between the lateral columns of the front and back, two small hieroglyphic inscriptions which show the legend of Ramesses VII or Sesostris II; so three eras are represented on these monuments. Square and in pink granite, the antique daises on which the obelisks were fixed and which served as their footing still exist, and while the area around the dais of the English obelisk was being searched by Arabs, father Bibent, who is in charge of the search, noticed that the monuments were positioned on a plinth of three marches, in bad Roman taste. It is the most ancient example of an Egyptian monument corrupted by ill-considered embellishments. Bibent is very proud of this first discovery.

To Champollion-Figeac — 24 August
At eight o'clock this morning I had an audience with the Pasha. His Highness lives in a number of beautiful houses made out of wood with much care, and in the style of the palaces in Constantinople. These buildings, which look quite attractive, are situated on the ancient island of Pharos. M. Drovetti, who had to present us, took us, the commander, Lenormand and me, in his *calèche* harnessed with two spry horses which gracefully negotiated the tortuous and narrow streets of Alexandria thanks to the ceaseless attention of the driver.

Behind us, mounted on impetuous donkeys, galloped the young people in their best costumes.

Descending the grand staircase of the 'Salle du Divan', we entered a colossal room filled with public dignitaries, and we were immediately ushered into a second room that opened up, in the corner of which Muhammad-Ali was seated between two windows, dressed in very simple clothes and holding in his hand a pipe inlaid with diamonds. He is of an average size, and the whole of his physique exudes an air of esprit, which is surprising in a man who is absorbed by so many great things and weighed down by many concerns. What strikes you about his face are his

Pasha Muhammad-Ali (1769?-1849)

extremely vivacious eyes, which form an odd contrast with his white flowing beard, which extends to his stomach.

After having asked about us, His Highness told us we were very welcome and asked me about the schedule of my journey. I told him that I intended to descend [the Nile] till the Second Cataract, and that I was hoping to receive the necessary permissions from His Highness. He granted them on the spot, together with two of the Pasha's kavass [guards] to accompany us and make sure that we would everywhere be treated with due respect.

Next we spoke about the Greek situation, and His Highness told us the news of the day, the death of Ahmed-Pasha, the Patras, who was assassinated by Greeks who were let into his room by bought Albanian soldiers. This brave Turk, though already quite old, killed seven by hand but had to succumb to their large number. The story seemed to affect the Pasha of Egypt deeply.

He offered us a cup of coffee without sugar, after which we took our leave from His Highness, who saw us off with greetings by hand that couldn't possibly be more gracious. – The moment those permissions are in my hands, I will be on my way to Cairo, and from there to Lower Egypt. But I want to avoid the August heat and I shall stay in Alexandria until 12 September, using all my time for preparations, so that I will have to remain for as little time as possible in Cairo.

I am in my element here, deluged by everyone's attentions, particularly M. Drovetti's, although his health is in a parlous state. He absolutely has to get back to Europe as Dengue fever is killing him. M. Méchin, the consul of Larnaca in Cyprus, is thoroughly pleasant and a veteran of the Egyptian expedition who does not hide his views of poor Jomard. – M. d'Anastazy, the consul of Sweden, swaddles me with politeness; he is a highly respectable man according to all reports. I am also very grateful to M. Rosetti, the Tuscan consul, and to the Austrian consul, M. Acerbi. M. Drovetti's son-in-law, the Sardinian consul, Pedemonte, is one of my best friends from Turin, and he gave in to his father-in-law [to let me stay in his house] with great difficulty. – On the night of my arrival in Alexandria, the cavalcade of donkeys was stopped by Pietrino Santoni, who flung himself around my neck when I least expected him. – As you can see, my dear friend, I am very well and you may, must, not worry on my behalf...

Champollion to Champollion-Figeac – 25 August 1828

I am writing this letter, my very dear friend, for a very specific reason that is of deep interest to me. It concerns a favour to M. Poupel, lieutenant and second-in-command of the excellent *Églé* on which we had, thanks to the extreme kindness of its commanding officers, a crossing that couldn't have been more agreeable. I would be very grateful if, to repay my debt, you could apply to the University for a scholarship to a royal college for the benefit of the son of our lieutenant, Louis-Théodore Poupel, age eleven, pupil at the Collège de Cherbourg... His father, a Knight of Saint-Louis, has served for twenty-five years... and the grandfather of the young pupil, M. Augustin Poupel, Chevalier de la Légion d'Honneur and principal commissary of the navy, has served for forty-four years. I urge you to look after this instantly and I will take great pleasure in its success, which seems to me very likely as M. Poupel can genuinely lay claim to such aid.

Goodbye, my dear friend. Everything bodes well.

Ippolito Rosellini to Champollion-Figeac − 26 August, Alexandria
... the day after the presentation of the Saghir[4] to the Pasha, that is the
25th [of August], the Tuscan Commission was presented by our consul,
who has long been on intimate terms with the Pasha, and I gave him the
letter from the Grand-Duke. The distinguished Turk was charming. He particularly asked me to thank the Grand-Duke for the confidence he demon-
strated by sending us to his nation; assured us that Egypt should be
treated as our own country; that he had made available all means to ensure
our complete safety. He continued our conversation by asking political
questions on topical subjects.

One can see how pleased he is by this evacuation of the Peloponnese.
He also gave us coffee without sugar, but it would appear that this time
the coffee pot did not draw as it had the day before because Saghir got
very nasty coffee whereas ours was rather good.

Next we went to the Bey, the governor of Alexandria, who showered
us with courtesy and, in addition, offered us a pipe. He spoke about the
plague and told us that he thought Dr Pariset's voyage would prove
unproductive because there hasn't been any incidence of the plague in
Egypt for the past three years, and that they believe it is not endemic,
which means that only quarantine will protect them − may it be so! [5]

All the foreign consuls take every possible care of us, particularly
d'Anastazy. It would be funny for you to see Saghir's appearance with his
moustache and pipe, to which he has taken like an old Turk. In Cairo we
will dress in Arab clothes. Could I ask you, if you write another newspaper
article, to also highlight our presentation to the Pasha, and anything else
that you think is appropriate. − The toing and froing in the Mediterranean
ought to give you frequent opportunities to let us have news from you
and other things which might interest us.

I don't know whether you recall a certain Caviglia, who published
eight or nine months ago a mad letter on the magic and cabbala of
hieroglyphs. We met him here, and he is going to give me a colossus of
Sesostris in composite stone of thirty-three-foot height to present to the
Grand-Duke as a gift, which he found in Memphis, where it still is. To tell
you the truth, I think he is donating it because he cannot afford to bring
it back. If saws are able to successfully master it and cut it in pieces I will

certainly take it back.

... The great heat is a source of health; we melt like candles, yet curiously enough we grow fatter rather than slim.

I hope you are doing well, and my infinite friendship from your devoted friend

Champollion to Champollion-Figeac – 29 August 1828, Alexandria
I am taking advantage, my dear friend, of the delayed departure on the 30th of our brilliant captain in order to write to you a few more lines. This delay is a consequence of growing complex political developments which may be in favour of, or against, Egypt. I mentioned to you the evacuation treaty of the Peloponnese, agreed to by Ibrahim[-Pacha] and ratified by the Pasha. Towards the end of July they must have heard in Paris about the preliminaries for this treaty through the *Trident* and the *Hussard*, which we saw lying in quarantine when we arrived in Toulon. Here [in Alexandria] it is not quite understood why a military convoy left Toulon on 15 August, of which we were informed by the commander of the *Nisus*, arriving fifteen days ago with M. Gros, an envoy from Foreign Affairs. Accompanied by M. de Saint-Léger, a nephew of the Minister of the Navy, he arrived to stipulate the terms for the [evacuation] treaty which is already signed and in the process being executed; we have received news about the arrival in Navarino of the Turkish and allied fleet – joined and organised to bring back Ibrahim-Pacha and the first convoys of his troops to Egypt. The news of the departure of our army for the Peloponnese has excited a furious response here from the Pasha, who has ended up seeing no more in it than a reason to justify the treaty towards the Sultan by pretending that, hearing about the arrival of a French force superior to his, he had to seize the moment to save the twelve to fourteen thousand men stationed in the Peloponnese without being hindered.

Meanwhile, the Pasha is deeply angry about the French expedition, which compromises our government with the Sultan and places him, the Pasha, in an awkward position in respect of us. It is feared here, and I echo the thoughts secreted under well-informed hats and turbans, that our government has been duped by English policies which have driven us to this expedition through the promise of help and transport, none of which is available, aiming to pitch us against the Sultan while they themselves are signing an alliance treaty with Mahmoud, who is defending himself like a lion. They say that the Russians are already at Philippopoli, which is eight or ten miles from Andrinopoli, and that a horrendous fire has already devoured half of Constantinople. These words should be kept under wraps until they are more amply confirmed. In any case, in Paris they may congratulate themselves on having launched ten thousand men to sea, sending them to a god-forsaken country and into a season rife with illnesses. May the great Amon be our guide! Via the *Nisus* I received your letter of 28 July with the copy of

minister Boghoz

the letter of 3 May which M. Drovetti sent me from the Viceroy's camp in the Delta [Gemiale]. This letter must have worried you, and I must say that had I received it while I was in Paris I would not have left: thankfully it didn't arrive in time and it is the hand of Amon which delayed it. The Pasha thinks that it would have been better to wait, but he accepts with good grace that matters must proceed as the bottle has been uncorked. Moreover, the Egyptian population is more than ever on the side of the Europeans and particularly the French, whom they love. This is even more the case than the day before yesterday, when the news of the departure of our fleet from Toulon spread among the Alexandrian population. Ordinary people asked several representatives from the consulate whether 'the French would disembark tomorrow' and were thrilled by the thought of their arrival. This is because Muhammad-Ali isn't done any favours by the Turkish officers who surround him. They trample and suppress the people and the people detest them. The poor Egyptians involuntarily compare the regime of the Pasha to that of the French army, and all of it in favour of us. To say that they long for us would be exaggerating; religion stands in the way. Nonetheless, it is certain that they would welcome us without hostility; but the age of heroes is over. – I will therefore be well received by the population of Upper and Lower Egypt. M. Drovetti is at the moment pleased with my voyage, and it is he who is painting a most attractive picture of my impending journey. I count on staying here until 12 September in order to avoid the heat of Cairo, where a type of mild typhoid rages at the moment because the heat is lessening and the Nile is rising. The sacred river has caused a few worries over the last few days: it is short of a few *coudées* [approximately half a yard] that are needed for the next harvest.'Where is the Nile at?' was the question that resounded every quarter of an hour, from the palace of the Pasha to the remnants of the cistern where the poor *fellah* families live in the middle of the deserted enclosure of Greek Alexandria. The Nile made up its shortcoming and the rise in water level is assured for Lower Egypt; two more *coudées* would take care of Upper Egypt, and this is expected to happen. My health is still excellent, as is that of all my pilgrims.

Bibent has finished with the three marches of the obelisk which are known to the Commission, and I am about to verify them; they had expertly disfigured its hieroglyphic inscriptions. My drawings are making progress. I will next occupy myself with Pompey's column, on which there is no agreement regarding a few words. A good print on paper will decide the matter.

M. Drovetti is ill: worse even, he is delirious. It would be best if the Minister called him back as quickly as possible; if he stays here for another year he is a dead man. He has seen everyone who arrived at the same time as him twenty-six years ago succumb one by one, and this upsets him.

A thousand greetings to our wonderful M. de Férussac and ten thousand Arab pleasantries to Madame. My respects to the Colbert arcade [M. Dacier]. Embrace Dubois for me and tell him that I will write as soon as I have something that will interest him.

Goodbye with my entire heart.

Champollion to Champollion-Figeac – 10 September
I should hope, my friend, that you will have received by now my no. 1, dated 24 August, which came to France via the return of the corvette the *Églé*. M. Cosmao Dumanoir, our brilliant commander (of whom I hope

Ibrahim-Pacha

you will speak well in any way you can think of to the minister of the navy, via our friend M. de Férussac), will from the moment of his arrival in Toulon not have lost time opening and perfuming my letters and rather posted them straight away. They will all reassure you regarding our present and future mission, as I am sure you must have felt some concern about how we were received in Egypt after you received the letter from M. Drovetti, and when the government chose his side which it appears to have done by revoking the commission for my departure via a telegraphic dispatch, if I am to believe a Parisian newspaper which we received. Happily, very happily, neither the letter nor the dispatch arrived in time. It was clearly arranged up there that I would see 'my' Egypt this year, despite the political clouds which are cruising the skies of the Orient propelled by northern winds, and most of all by the eastern winds whose bearing we don't understand at all well. My voyage will be accomplished with all possible assistance and without the least danger. If I were to judge the future by the past, it isn't the Muslim population who will hinder me but rather the European one, that is to say 'Christians', who, as in the rest of the Levant, are the worst of their kind.

The news of the departure of the military expedition from Toulon and its arrival in the Peloponnese have produced no impression whatsoever on the people here. Only the Pasha's feathers were ruffled at first because, after having agreed to the evacuation of Egyptian troops from the Peloponnese and leaving a very weak garrison in five fortified locations, he could do little but be an uneasy spectator to the sudden arrival of the French to occupy the country, fearful that the Sultan would brand him a traitor. But he has taken this reversal well, and it will serve to show satis-factorily to the Sultan that his was a wise decision to withdraw his son and troops, which in any case are plagued by disease and might be considered lost if they had wanted to engage with the French troops. Muhammad-Ali's only fear concerns how Ibrahim, who has for a long time pent up a burning desire to line up his soldiers against European battalions, will take the untimely arrival of the French. This business has been dealt with by Paris (at least according to us, the other 'Egyptians') in the usual way, that is to say without insight and without a well-studied objective. – The only real consequence will be that France will have compromised itself with the Sultan, benefiting the Russians and the shiftiness of the British, who will side with the Turks if the Russians aren't halted by the Turkish desperation. Beyond that, General Maison arrived in Greece with instructions drawn up by imbeciles in his pocket. According to their terms, disembarkation should take place on the islands of Sapience, where there is not a drop of water and one can barely arrange a front of three companies. It will be interesting to see what follows. In a few days we will know whether Ibrahim has complied with a treaty that our side is not fulfilling in any way. It is hoped that he will yield to the circumstances. The Sultan has ordered Egyptian troops to go to Roumelie – and they may, for the moment, coast towards Egypt – it is a delicate game for the Pasha! Enough of global politics! I will come to my own world now.

I have had to muster all my political acumen here (all this is absolutely confidential). You will have seen from the letter of M. Drovetti, dated from the camp in Gemiale, that the reasons for delaying my voyage to Egypt were exaggerated. All of that was, in essence, based on no more than personal interest. The dealers in antiquities all squirmed when they heard about my arrival in Egypt for the purpose of doing excavations. Their cabal hatched the moment my request for official permits for the excavations was sent out. Minister Boghoz and the Pasha were lied to, and His Highness said that he would give permission only to his friends Drovetti and Anastazy. They told me to forget about it; but I asserted via a note to the chancellor of the French consulate that, having come to Egypt with a mission to undertake research for the museums of the King, I would be obliged to inform the ministers of the King what exactly the causes were that prevented me from executing this part of my instructions; that the refusal of permits was merely the result of commercial intrigue; that having come in the King's name, sent by him and his government, it would be an affront to the task I had been charged with to refuse me permissions which had been granted to the likes of Belzoni, Passalacqua, Laborde, Rifaud, etc.;[6] that if the Pasha and his minister valued the reputation attributed to them in Europe, as guardians of the arts and sciences, this would be the one time, in granting me permission for excavations, when they could genuinely encourage and protect science, having up to now merely furthered and favoured through such permits personal interests and commercial speculation; that my searches aimed for an entirely different type of speculation in that I want no more than to be able to understand the arrangement of the objects found inside the tombs, and that all objects that I would discover were to be placed in the King's museum, which the Pasha himself had had the pleasure of gracing with a gift of forty pieces of gold jewellery. The note, to which I added a number of other thoughts, was given to Minister Boghoz to read. This action and public opinion in Alexandria, which does exist, decided the matter. My opponents feared the publicity in European newspapers with which I threatened them (without mentioning anyone), and the right permits were finally given to us today; Messrs Drovetti and Anastazy even ceded their right to search reserved locations.

The whole business has delayed the departure of my caravan to Cairo. But it is now irrevocably fixed for Sunday...

Champollion to Champollion-Figeac – 13 September 1828

My departure for Cairo has definitely been set for today. I will sail at eight o'clock and the two boats on which my caravan will travel shall touch the Nile the day after tomorrow, very early in the morning, after having gone down the whole length of the canal of Sultan Mahmoud, called the Mahmoudieh, the one on which Coste and little Florentin Masi worked. In forty-eight hours I will see the sacred river which up to now I have only drunk, and the land of Egypt I have so longed for. Alexandria is unadulterated Libya, and I left it without any regrets after having exhausted all its pleasures and received endless pleasantries, some of them sincere, from the Muselmen, at least more so than from the Christians.

I have just returned (at eight at night) from my farewell visit to the Pasha. His Highness was charming; I thanked him for the genuine protection he has granted us. He answered that as Christian princes treated their subjects with distinction he would like to do the same. We spoke about hieroglyphs and he ended up asking me for a text of the obelisks of Alexandria. I promised him this, and he will have it tomorrow, translated into Turkish by the chancellor of the French consulate.

Muhammad-Ali wanted to know just how far into Nubia I intended to push my expedition, and he assured me that we would receive due respect and welcome everywhere. I left him with great compliments which he humbly played down in an extremely likable way.

Tomorrow I will embark on my main boat and will take command. I have organised my cosmos, arranged for everyone's place on board, handed out tasks and responsibilities. All in all it is a small government which is well structured, acting on orders-of-the-day which are obeyed by everyone because everything serves a greater good. All will go well. Ricci is charged with health and provisions; Duchesne with the arsenal; Bibent with excavation, gear and instruments; L'hôte with money; Gaetano Rosellini with chattels and luggage, etc. We brought two servants and an Arab cook, two other Barbar servants; my attendant Soliman is an Arab with a beautiful face whose service is excellent.

Two sailing boats will carry us down the Nile. One is the largest *maasch* of the country and was organised by His Highness Muhammad-Ali; I named it the *Isis*. The other is a dahabiah [large Nile sailing boat] on which five people may easily be quartered; I have given its command to Duchesne in succession to Dr Raddi, who has to leave us in order to chase butterflies in the Libyan desert. This dahabiah was given the name *Athyr* [Hathor]. We will thus travel under the auspices of the two most energetic goddesses of the Egyptian pantheon. From Alexandria to Cairo we will only stop at Kerioun, the ancient Chereus of the Greeks, and at Ssa-el-Hagar, the ancient Sais. I owe these courtesies to the fatherland of the cunning Psammetichus and the brutal Apries; I will see whether any fragments remain of Siouph or Souafe, the homeland of the jovial Amasis, and, at Sais, any traces of the college to which Plato and so many of the Greek youths went to school.

My health is holding up, and the trials of the Alexandrian climate, the most treacherous of Egypt, are a good omen. Everyone is thrilled to have come along. I, for myself, am thankful for the fact that both the letter and the telegraphic dispatches arrived late. – You have to seize the first available opportunity to rectify the errors contained in the news reported by the newspapers regarding our departure.

Angelelli is not a professor, he is a very distinguished draughtsman, and M. Raddi is a professor who is known throughout Europe for his brilliant research into natural history in Brazil. – NB: redress this matter. I am starting to find the wait for news from you rather tedious. Nothing has come to us from France. Or Pariset! The telegraphic dispatch must have cramped his style. He is greatly mistaken in not joining us: we had already made his bed for him, in our *maasch*. Do tell him to come and that he will be received with open arms. The Pasha knows about the purpose of his journey, and if he is looking for the plague, the army of Ibrahim will probably bring it to him, or some equivalent.

Adieu, my dear friend. I will write from Cairo. All love to you and those on our side.

Pariset had been allowed to leave Marseilles after all. De Laborde, whom Champollion narrowly missed in Toulon, had made a point of telling ministers that Pariset was very welcome in Egypt. Despite the fact that there had not been any incidence of the plague for a few years. The Pasha was building a hospital for plague sufferers, causing Alexandrines to quip 'all we need now are a few patients.'

3.

Cairo

Egypt, at Last

From Champollion's diary

14 September 1828: The entire morning was devoted to preparations for
our journey: it is scheduled for eight o'clock in the morning, but the need
for loading fresh provisions and letting bread which was baked at night
cool off lost us a few hours. But at last, after saying my goodbyes to
Messrs Anastazy, Méchain, Rosetti and Lavison, I left the house of the
French consulate at ten o'clock with all members of the Tuscan expedition,
who had come to collect me. We lost a quarter of an hour leaving the *okel*
because the Alexandrinian donkeymen, hearing of our imminent
departure by public road, had amassed in a mob underneath our windows
and obstructed the doors of the *okel*. It was a downright battle: one would
pull me to the right, the other to the left, and in the heat of the
skirmishes I often found myself squeezed in between two donkeys and
very near to losing my breath. Finally, two French and Tuscan janissaries
underlined their public image by dealing the riotous attendants a couple
of blows with their silver-apple-headed canes and succeeded in making a
little bit of room for us, and each of us could choose our mount. Our
caravan, formed at last, set itself in motion, headed by the two janissaries
in their red robes and white turban with their drummer-major-style canes
pressed against the saddle. Arriving at the Square of the Consuls, the
cortège went up to the house of the Austrian consul [M. Acerbi], who I
wanted to salute before leaving. We resumed our route to the Arab
enclosure, and after a little while reached the Mahmoudieh canal, along
whose banks the *maasch Isis* and the dahabiah *Athyr* were tied up. I
installed myself on board the *Isis*, where I received a visit from the prophet

Tod, who stayed with us until the very last moment of departure, despite the aggravation that was overwhelming us. We set sail at last at noon, when we ended an improvised lunch prepared by my Arab domestic Soliman, who will have to be our cook for the entire voyage from Alexandria to Cairo as the incumbent, Moustapha, fell ill on the eve of our leaving. Navigating the Mahmoudieh, dug a few years ago under orders from Muhammad-Ali, who requisitioned 100,000 people from neighbouring provinces in order to carry out this immense work — these conscripts literally completed it with their hands as there were neither the tools nor utensils which would be necessary elsewhere — navigating this canal is very easy during the flood season; the only real difficulty consists of the inevitable brouhaha that follows when several *djermes* or *maasch*, joined by a cable, encounter either vessels sailing in the same fashion or those which lie motionless on the banks of the river. This public work, of overriding importance for the fresh water supply to the inhabitants of Alexandria, and secondly for commerce with the second city of Egypt, as the Pasha wants to live here while establishing Ibrahim-Pacha in Cairo, is no more than excavated dirt without any type of abutment or supporting walls, with the exception of a few *tois* of walls at the mouth of the canal near Atfeh.

The surrounding countryside is shockingly desolate, and the point where the country house of Moharrembey Atfeh, a relative of the Pasha and governor of Alexandria, was built is hardly any more cheerful, despite a few palm plantations which they call a 'garden': the canal cuts through a corridor of land between the Madieh (or the lake of Edkou) and Lake Mareotis. The bed of the latter is almost dry; it looks like a vast empty basin topped with sand. Its south-westerly end was, when we passed it, covered by the rising water, and a few islands scattered here and there seemed by an effect of light or a mirage to be hovering in mid-air. At another point on the canal we saw in the distant north the minaret of Aboukir. We passed the night at El-Kerioun.

The *Athyr*, on which Professor Raddi, Bibent, Duchesne and Bertin boarded and which was supposed to adapt itself constantly to the speed of the *Isis*, was outpaced and left a long way behind towards midnight. We noticed its delay at seven in the morning, when, advancing towards Atfeh, we were about to sail down the Nile. Despite my impatience to see this celebrated river, I ordered the *reis* of the Isis to moor and wait for the

Athyr before launching onto the Nile. We went ashore three hundred feet from the mouth of the Mahmoudieh canal, whose southern bank is crowned with casemates made of rose canes that serve as food stalls for all types of foods. – Rosellini, Lenormand and I ran to the beginning of the Mahmoudieh, and the astonishing lushness of the delta, from which we had been separated by a branch of the delta's canopy which presents even here a very imposing view, even though it is screened by an island which divides the waters, exhilarated our eyes, which had for so long been deprived of a landscape appointed with beautiful vegetation. Tamarinds, palms and sycamores, across which we saw on the left the minarets of Sendioun and to the right those of Fouah, braided the background of this vista and soared above enormous roses, whose stems filigree the two banks of the Nile at this point. We returned to the *maasch* after we had satiated ourselves with this spectacle, which reminded Lenormand on a number of points of what Holland looks like.

Seeing that the *Athyr* hadn't arrived, I commanded the *reis* of the *Isis* to enter the Nile and set sail for Fouah. The canal flows into the river opposite a low island, which strips this branch of the canopy of part of its width. Our entry into the river was difficult because the canal is very narrow and because my boat is one of the largest sailing the Nile. In order to give some rest to the sailors, I stopped the *Isis* on the left bank at six hundred *tois* to the south-east of the Mahmoudieh, facing a small village which is called Senabadeh but which the map of the Commission places too far down the Nile, inserting a village called Kafr-cherkaouy in between, of which I haven't seen any sign.

The *Athyr* at last joined us after two hours of waiting, and we went down the Nile to Fouah, where we arrived at noon. After lunch I made a tour of Fouah. This is the first example of real Egypt; it is entirely built in brownish bricks and almost all houses resemble one another. We saw a few pretty mosques and fragments of walls that are also made of brick. – Around four in the afternoon we left Fouah after waiting for a long time for the *reis* of the *Athyr*, who had taken the opportunity of our stay in the village to visit a few Almeh [girl oracles]! At four thirty we were in between the village of Schorafeh on the eastern shore and Sorenbaieh on the western one: the wind was excellent and the *maasch* advanced slowly, despite the strong current of the river, whose bed extends across its entire majestic width here. Next we saw, wedged in a little, the village of Kebrith,

called Gobaris on the map of the Commission of Egypt.

At five o'clock we were in view of the large village of Salmieh: the one which was burned down at the orders of the general heading the French army in Egypt. – Facing Salmieh is the village of Louieh, not included on the map of the Commission. – At six fifteen we saw, in the delta, the large village of Mehallet-Maleg, to the north-east of which, and at about four thousand *tois* inland, lies a land called Koum-Schabbas. In front of Mehallet-Maleg one can distinguish Kafr-Schaikh-Hassan, called K.-Scheikh-Hacein on the Commission's map.

The two banks of the canopy are during this season covered with the most beautiful greenery. The countryside of the delta and Libya is cultivated with great care, and variety abounds with trees of all species, among which the most numerous are: 1 the palm; 2 the tamarind; 3 the mulberry (*thont*); 4 the *mimosa nilotica*, called *santh* by the *fellahs*, who have thus preserved the ancient Egyptian name for this pretty tree, which derives from the word spine, and whose leaves are delicate and small and which is covered with very sharp thorns; 5 the sycamore (*goummez*); 6, but rare, the weeping willow; 7 the willow, much more common than the previous one.

It was while contemplating this beautiful countryside that I saw arranged in a straight line on the western bank of the Nile a dozen or so cows taking their chew, each one of them in their own manger made of mud, of which here a sketch of its profile. This is exactly the shape of the mangers put on the altars in front of the images of the sacred bulls Oenouphi, Mnevis and Apis.

At six fifteen we were in front of Soukhrat, which the map of the Commission calls Kourat, corrupting this name, pronounced Soumoukhrat by my *reis*, which is much more like that of Naucratis, the Greek village which is thought to have existed at this location.

Towards six thirty we observed on the eastern river, at the very edge of the riverbank, the ruins of a very sizeable stronghold, of such a refined construction compared to what we had hitherto seen that we thought we recognised a European influence: it was in fact the country house of Toussoum-Bacha, Muhammad-Ali's oldest son, destruction of which had been ordered after the death of its owner. To its side is a plantation of young palms. The surrounding countryside is gorgeous.

At seven thirty we rejoined the *Athyr*, which had taken the lead after Fouah. We found ourselves opposite Desouk. I learned that in a neighbouring village of this town situated on the eastern bank of the Nile Mr Salt, the English consul, had died a few months before. I forever regret not having met this erudite and great amateur of hieroglyphic studies in Egypt.

We passed, towards ten o'clock, in between Mehallat-abou-Aly to the east and Miniet-Salameh to the west; in the middle of this village the French battled with the Mamelukes in July 1798, the day after the Battle of Rahhmanieh, a town situated 2,400 metres farther north than Miniet-Salameh, which the river islands in front of Desouk prevent us from seeing. — During the night our small squadron sailed past the village of El-Ssafe, where lay the ancient town with a Saitic name lay which Herodotus mentions as the homeland of Pharaoh Amasis, who, after having usurped the crown from his legitimate sovereign Ouaphre [Apries], was nonetheless included in the 26th dynasty among the Saitic kings.

16 September 1828: Waking up at six thirty in the morning I found that the *Isis* and *Athyr*, which we had had towed to Desouk, had docked on the eastern bank very near a village actually called El-Menieh-Ghenagh, and not El-Menieh, in short, as the map of the Commission will have it. The latter part of the name comes from the town of that name, Ghenagh, located at two thousand *tois* farther to the south-east and wrongly

The stretche-out hills of the flooded Necropolis of Sais, seen from the Nile

identified as Ghenan by the Commission.

While waiting for the wind to swell, I walked with Rosellini to the village, where we found Dr Ricci, who was shopping for provisions, surrounded by a gaggle of half-naked women. I was mesmerised by a tall woman with a beautiful physique whose features were not at all Egyptian. She told me that Scham (Syria) was her country of origin, and that she had married a horseshoe-maker of El-Menieh-Ghenagh. Simultaneously detaching a small purse from her breast and shooing by gesturing hands the Arabs who surrounded us, she pulled from it, and showed me with a conspirational air, a small cross which she was at pains to hide from the *fellahs* who were coming near us; she gave me to understand that she was a Christian and was extremely insulted when I declined her appeal to show her my cross. I allowed Dr Ricci to give her a drug for her eyes which had started to be affected by ophthalmia.

After lunch, when the wind had started blowing a little, I ordered the *reis* to sail for Ssa-el-Haghar, as I was extremely impatient to visit the ruins of ancient Sais, the largest and most celebrated of the ancient delta cities. We could already, from El-Menieh-Ghenagh, looking south, see the remnants of the enormous enclosure that once circumscribed the magnificent monuments of this capitol. Its ruins look like stretched-out hills. At eleven o'clock we were at Kafr-Daouar, at eleven thirty in front of Mehallet-Ssa on the western bank, and opposite the large enclosed area of Sais in the east. The *reis* pulled in two strapped launches, and towards noon we went ashore on the delta in front of the village of Ssa-el-Haghar, which has retained its name and covers a section of the settlement abandoned by Necho and Psammetichus.

After our lunch, approximately at two, everyone armed himself, and we left to visit the ruins accompanied by our domestics, Muhammad and Khalil, who were joined by a cabin boy of the *Isis* who was a native of Ssa-el-Haghar, which we approached across the fields. My companions started to hunt, and the sound of gunshots upset two jackals, which decamped in a panic, right in front of us. — We didn't enter the village, which is situated on the highest part of the mound, but, going via the modern cemetery of the inhabitants of Ssa-el-Haghar, filled with numerous very recently stuccoed *tourbehs* [graves], we went in a northerly direction towards the ruins, which from afar looked like an Arab village which was recently pillaged. Yet we found an unbelievable number of pottery shards of all types, similar to those one comes across along the entire plain of the ruins of Alexandria, near the obelisks, and almost the entire Arab enclosure [of Alexandria]. Sais pottery consists for the most part of shards of ancient manufacture. Thus I gathered green and blue glazed Egyptian earthenware, a fragment with a lotus flower engraved on it, the lower part of an earthenware funerary figure [*ushabti*] decorated with hieroglyphs, and a very pretty glazed fragment portraying a lion's head. A vast space is taken up with remains of buildings made either of earthwork or Egyptian brick mixed with some straw, which seem to have served as chambers or buildings of very small proportions, and quite suitable for enclosing mummies or other funerary objects. By all appearances it was one of the necropolises of Sais. These tombs have been meticulously dug up and are so turned upside down that it is difficult to recognise their form and relationship. Nothing here resembles the catacombs of Thebes, nor the quarries of Sakkara; they are one of a kind.

After having crossed with difficulty the enormous terrain, which is uneven because it has been overturned in every way, we approached the modern cemetery on the eastern side, and we were overwhelmed by the rotten odour which escaped from it. This is very important evidence for Pariset's system against the plague. He seems to have proven beyond any doubt that flood water filters through to the cadavers interred in the *tourbehs* [graves], and that this is the cause of the horrendous infection vaulting a very large distance. — We walked thereafter to the north-east for

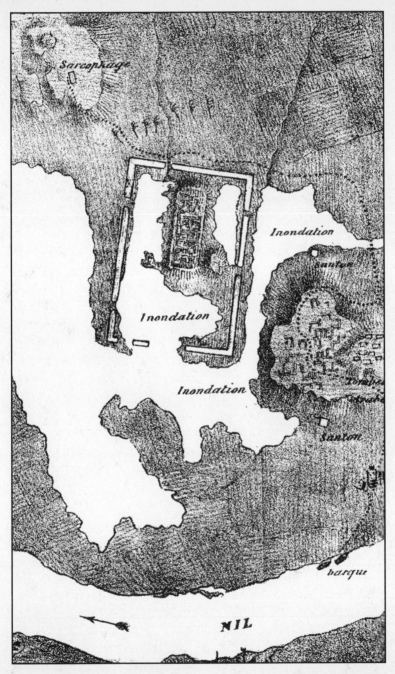

In front, right, the landing place, and left, at the top, the location of the sarcophagus

about four hundred *tois* while cutting several times through flood water, and we arrived at last, after crossing a tiny bridge, at the south-east angle of the large Egyptian enclosure which we had spotted from El-Menieh-Ghenagh. – The size of this enclosure is huge. We estimated, measuring our paces, that the length of one of the small sides was at least 1,400 feet, and the long side of the parallelogram 2,160 feet wide, which gives a circumference of 7,200 feet.

The width of the enclosing wall built in dried brick is generally about fifty-four centimetres. Its height is about eighty feet. The bricks which make up this enormous construction are sixteen inches long, seven inches wide and five inches thick. They are made of Nile mud and mixed with chaff. In various places the wall appears to be made of simple earthwork because, as the rains have distempered the surface of the wall, the joints have filled up with paste and vanished; part of its height was reduced to dust and its packed remains form considerable banks on both sides of the wall. The width of this slope, taken from the outside, was measured as one hundred and twenty feet.

The flood covered a very large part of the enclosure when I visited it. The entrance is entirely modern; a wall was built to make way for a small irrigation channel, and the aperture in the wall shows Egyptian bricks mixed with perfectly preserved hay patches. Through this opening I penetrated the enclosure, and it is impossible to describe the impression which the unfolding of the inside courtyard at such a width had on me. I saw on the left, occupying the middle over a very great distance, a suite of colossal ruins outlining all sorts of weird shapes and which, from my point of view, looked like the ruins of a palace of giants; but there is so much irregularity and so little harmony between the parts of the ruin that it is impossible to have a clear idea of its basic structure.

Having progressed to the middle of the ruins, we saw the remnants of a very wide building once divided into an infinite number of small chambers of several floors, at least to the height of the walls (eighty feet) – both connected and separated by very wide bulkheads. The whole building, which is at least as high as the enclosing wall (eighty feet), is made of dried bricks, but half the size of those which make up the enclosure. The whole site of the ruins is covered with broken pottery, among which my Barbar, Muhammad, found, at my feet, an Egyptian figurine of glazed earthenware portraying the Aegis of Neith, i.e. the head of the lion-headed goddess with a disc on her necklace, and some shards of glazed Egyptian pottery. All these slivers of pots are either shards used for bedding, mixed with bricks in the body of the bulkheads, or from large urns within the walls of each chamber; I noticed seven or eight still in place in as many of the small chambers.

To either side beyond the ruins of this enormous building are two hills reaching at least the same height as the general enclosing walls. Each of these hills supports two parallel nipple shapes. They too are lumps of dried brick mushed on the outside, and these mounds occupy the farthest points and are parallel to each other.

The entire volume of the raised chambers in a whole building measures about a thousand paces, an area which might contain an endless number [of chambers]. Altogether it seems to point to the fact that the building was once a necropolis, or rather a memnonium, that is a construction meant to preserve the mummies of the inhabitants of Sais. The two mounds beyond the ruins were two great pylons, no doubt connected by a small enclosing wall echoing the rectangular shape of the immense edifice, a veritable labyrinth of funerary chambers; the urns cooped up inside the partitions served as canopes [Egyptian vases] storing the intestines. We found the bottom of one of the jars still full of balm. (Gaetano Rosellini.)

The great courtyard has an opening (an ancient gate) in the middle of its long southerly side, towards Ssa-el-Haghar. This was the gate through which embalmed cadavers entered, the Gate of the Dead through which one went close by the other necropolis, as these ruins are also part of a memnonium whose general outline is impossible to trace. The fragments of funerary imagery we found there prove amply that these buildings are also tombs. Towards the west end of the great memnonium that is part of the courtyard there are two banks of ruins, one to the north, the other to the south. The latter, larger one is made of earthwork (or an artificial mound) on which one sees a few pieces of marble, presumably from Thebes, pink granite, grey granite and extremely attractive red sandstone. The flood waters prevented us from climbing the northern mound, which is considerably lower than the other. These two mounds might well be the location of the tombs of the Saitic kings described by Herodotus.

To the north, the tomb of Ouaphre, Apries, and the Saitic founding kings, which were to the left, he says, of the temple of Neith (Minerva).

The southerly mound was the site of the tomb of the usurper Amasis, a sumptuous building described by Herodotus, and which he says was on the right of the temple of Neith. One might reconstruct, therefore, after Herodotus's text, what the ancient layout of the large courtyard of Sais was. At roughly two hundred paces from the north-east corner of the grand enclosure were a few low mounds, formed by a sandy loose soil rubbled with dried brick. We were guided (Lenormand and I) by an old Arab, whom we asked about a sarcophagus which, according to M. Rosetti [the Tuscan consul], was part of the ruins of Sais. We did indeed find this exquisite monument at the bottom of a large crater created by excavations, still half buried in the sands, where a punishing heat suffocated us. The sarcophagus is probably nine to ten feet long. It is made of a magnificent piece of green basalt and is, on the outside, inscribed with a single line of hieroglyphs divided into two juxtaposed legends:

Words of the Temple Guardian (who is under the protection of Lord...)
O You, Saviours! Lords of Justice, etc.

The name of this high functionary of the priestly order includes the prenomen of the Saitic king Psammetichus II, which simultaneously gives an approximate date for the sarcophagus. Doubtless, excavation of these hills will reveal highly important funerary monuments. This location appears to have been a necropolis for distinguished families. The lower part of the cover of the sarcophagus still lies on the rim of the crater. The top part was presented to the imperial museum of Vienna by M. Rosetti.

Having carefully scrutinised this enclosure of Hieron, and having taken aim at a few owls, which by extreme chance we hit upon in the ruins of Sais, the mother of Athens, both cities that would put these birds to shame, we returned to the village of Ssa-el-Haghar, where we climbed up to see whether the Egyptian columns mentioned by Niebuhr were still there.

Our hunt through the poor streets of this village was in vain. Khalil, one of our domestics, was given the order to shout that anyone who had antiquities to sell should bring them to us. No one came forward; women and children fled as soon as we entered a street. But when Rosellini and I started handing out pieces of six *paras* [1 piaster = 40 *paras*], a horde of them came rushing forward and surrounded us, and we had unimaginable trouble getting rid of these fine people, who at first had thought we were Turkish soldiers and, taking fright, had hidden as quickly as possible. They showed us a few bad coins, and we returned to the *maasch* escorted by a fair chunk of the population of modern Sais. Children and little girls, both naked, didn't leave us until the very last moment.

We left the Saitic river bank at six fifteen at night; we were in between Nekleh and Goudabe at seven, and in front of Etbie on the eastern bank at seven thirty... .

17 September 1828: Waking up the next morning, we found that we had stopped on the Libyan riverbank opposite El-Dharieh because the wind, swelling from the south, came from entirely the wrong direction. My *reis* called this wind Marisi, a word derived from the Egyptian Maris, the name for Lower Egypt from which this wind hails. We took this opportunity to go for a walk in the countryside, covered with farms, and where I saw large hemp and cotton plantations. Trees of all types abound, and I saw there for the first time the fruit of the *mimosa niloteca*, the Egyptian *schonti*, in which I recognised the hieroglyph [for scented rhizome]. This fruit is called *qard* by the Arabs. – When the wind strengthened a little at four o'clock we were in front of Mit-Chahaleh, a little later at Benoufar, and at five o'clock Kafr-Zaiat. – Here the *reis* wanted to stop in order to buy grain for the crew. This village, built from Nile sediment like all the others, is the first one which reminded one of the ancient monuments of Egypt by virtue of the banks of walls and earthwork. We went through the village trying to purchase mutton, but there was none for sale. We arrived at a giant warehouse for grain and cotton which belonged to the Pasha; a building with straight walls. We left Kafr-Zaiat precisely at six o'clock to continue our route. While going through the streets of the village I quickly scribbled down the shape of the patterns that the women wore on their chins and their arms.

These tattoos are generally coloured blue. They are drawn with an instrument made up of three or four points united by strips; the skin is

 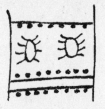

pierced until bleeding, and thus the forms of the patterns are tattooed. The pins are dipped in ink or dissolved coal powder. An Egyptian woman may have her chin painted for the modest sum of five paras. Women practise this art. Egyptian women also wear designs tattooed on their hands and arms.

Above Kafr-Zaiat we saw towards the north-east the palms and the minarets of Abiar, and further south, a little less clearly, the village of Thant. During the months of Rekeh a sizeable market takes place in this town; the ancillary purpose for those who go there is to visit the tomb of a Muslim saint called Sid-Ahmed-el-Bedaoui.

We went by Schabour at five to seven; part of this town on the western bank was carried off by the Nile waters. All of us were taken aback by the foul stench spreading from the cemetery. Another arrow for the bow of my friend Pariset. – The *maasch* dropped anchor at ten fifteen on the eastern bank at El Zairah in order to wait for the dahabiah which had lagged behind. – During the night we passed the villages of Thanoub, Amrous, Bischtameh, Koum-Scherik, one of the battlegrounds of the French army, and at six in the morning we were at Zaouiet-el-Bagleh.

18 September 1828: At six fifteen, at Attarieh, a village which eludes the Commission's map. While going past Danassour we saw in the distance on the same bank the towns of Sersena, and Ibschade, once a city of great importance and now reduced to a simple hummock. From seven to eight at Aboulkhaous in Libya, where we bought mutton. At ten past nine in the morning we were at Alkam, a site known by the battle of our army with the Mamelukes on 16 July 1798.

Nine thirty. As we approached the village of Nader, women carrying baskets of fruits, dates and pomegranates were coasting the river bank, offering us their wares. We stopped in front of an enclosure planted with trees in an orderly way, a verdant screen behind which the village lay hidden. Before we had barely touched the bank, a cascade of women and children assailed us and showed us their foodstuffs. Among this ensemble were three baladins or comedians followed by two Almeh [girl oracles], who we asked up to the bridge. One of them, graced with a pretty figure of incomparably attractive curves, carried two cymbals of copper. They sang Arab sonnets for half an hour, a sort of question-and-answer between a lover and his mistress set to a cantilena which all of us found rather attractive. The second-*reis* of our *maasch*, Ahmed-el-Raschidi, a friendly and spirited man, took our piasters and, after having moistened them with a little spit, pressed them on the cheeks of the Almeh with a great big kiss. All this made both the Muselmen and Europeans laugh. As soon as the concert was over the comedians started their routine with spasms and body movements that would have been very becoming at a satanic rite for the Goat of Mendes.

After this spectacle, Dr Ricci, who had gone to do some shopping, returned with a basket of excellent pomegranates. We then raised sail again. It was ten fifteen.

We soon went by Dimischli, which is a purely Egyptian name. It is situated on the Libyan bank. To the west, and in the delta, lies the village of Schebschir, a name which is also of Egyptian extraction, and this latter village, a perfect square, reminds one of antique cities such as Elethya. – A run-in of the soldiers with a *djerme* [type of Nile vessel].

At twelve fifteen, at Ghezaieh… and at twelve thirty we passed Therraneh. As in ancient times, it trades in sodium carbonate, which it harvests from so-called sodium carbonate lakes, which are at half a day's journey into the desert from Therraneh, where we saw hills of this pinkish-grey salt. We stopped for an hour at Zaouiet-Rezin, where the *reis* wanted to buy grain. With Lenormand and Rosellini I went into the

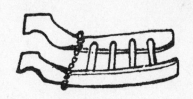

countryside where we saw *fellahs* working. Some of them were threshing corn; the device they were using was a sledge whose four cross-pieces were the axes of circular knives, or rather iron cutting wheels. This sledge is

entirely the same as the ones you may find in hieroglyphs as, for example, in the name of Herion: the only difference is the absence of the cutting wheels. On the sledge the *fellahs* fixed a wooden seat on which they sat either in order to add weight to the turning wheels or to better guide the bulls as they walked round in a circle. One of these *fellahs* left his sledge and came up to us with a submissive manner while greeting us with his hand, saying: '*Buono!* He embarked on a long speech, and the vehemence with which he punctuated his sentences told us that he had launched into a harangue intended for the converted: it was clear that he was complaining about the reign of the Pasha. 'He takes everything,' he said, while waving at the countryside and the mounds of barley that surrounded us, 'and leaves nothing for us!' All the while he plucked his tatty rags that sort of served as clothes. We gave the poor man a few piasters, which promptly produced Virgil's phrase 'you think of more than just yourselves', and, attended by two of these people, we went round the village outside the gates. In front of the mosque, shaded and spread out on a mat, the agent of the Pasha, a Turkish camaican [Ottoman official], was smoking. Shortly afterwards he had crew members of the dahabiah, natives of Zaouiet-Rezin, apprehended and thrown into gaol despite our loud protestations and the permissions from the Pasha. It was impossible to set them free: the poor devils owed money to the crown, and the Pasha and his agents show no mercy on principle when money is involved. Returning through the streets of the village along the bank of the Nile, I came across a man who carried in his hand a spindle, which is found with little variation in hieroglyphs. The cemetery of this village also gave off a foetid smell. More for Pariset. – Having left Zaouiet-Rezin at three thirty, we passed About-Nechabeh at ten to five. Here we watched the struggle for life and death between Horus and Typhon. The Libyan desert forces itself right up to the western banks of the river, leaving but a narrow border. Plants obstinately shoot up through yellowish sand, and this mixture of herbs, which is attractively lush against the barrenness of the soil (the dark earth, the gift from the Nile, has disappeared), is an unnatural and saddening sight. Vegetation is fighting the desert, but with great difficulty, and small rivulets of sand pour continuously into the Nile when the wind blows from Libya.

The *maasch* slipped by Mit-Salameh, a melancholy village seated in the desert whose huts weather the Libyan sands in dark colours. Soon night fell and we could barely see the village of Ouardan... It is the location of the ancient Letopolis (the town of the goddess Leto). Owing to a contrary wind we approached the delta banks towards eleven at night. The *maasch* dropped anchor at the village of Aschmoûn, where we stayed the night.

19 September 1828: On the 19th in the morning, while waking up, the first thing we did was leave the *maasch* to see whether we could make out the pyramids: but the sky was so clouded and the horizon so foggy that we saw nothing. Yet at seven, when the haze had lifted, we saw the great monuments to our right and, though they were eight miles away from us, we could already get a sense of their colossal size. At first we saw only the two large pyramids, and only when we went farther up the Nile, after having left Aschmoûn at eight, did we see the third one in all its magnificence. At nine fifteen, a little below the village of El-Qatah, I had a drawing made of the vista of pyramids. At ten we were opposite Meniet-el-Arous, where we moored for a moment to adjust the rigging of the vessel. One of the sailors showed me an enormous beetle with 'three' antlers: one antler, or rather a false antler, on its carapace; at either end of its carapace two horizontally placed antlers; and on its head two antlers which cross. Without any doubt, this is the Scarab.

At a quarter to two we went past Bathn-el-Baqarah (stomach of a cow), which is the point where the delta branches out into its two great rivers, the Rosetta and the Damietta. The view is breathtaking. The width of the Nile is stupendous. On the eastern side the pyramids soar above the palms. A multitude of boats, *djermes* and *maasch* sail up the Damietta branch on the right and on the left up the Rosetta branch; and others descend to Cairo. In the east lies the very picturesque village of Schorafeh, and towards noon the background of this panorama began to be dominated by Mount Mokattam, the citadel of Cairo, and the minarets of this huge capital. At three we could distinguish Cairo quite clearly. It spreads out enormously, but its mosques and houses of a smoky brown colour rather devalue the impact of its beauty. – Here the crew of the *maasch* came up to ask for bakshish [presents]. The supplicant was accompanied by two of his comrades dressed in an odd way with caps of sugared bread, beards of coarse white hemp cut in a triangle, and big moustaches, their bodies tautly dressed in tight-fitting clothing that highlighted their shapes; all of them had attached a rolled-up tail made of white drapes to themselves. Their outfit immediately reminded us of the

ancient fauns painted on antique Greek vases. With his steep cap one of
them was the spitting image of the caricature of Mercury on the famous
vase showing the love between Jupiter and Alcmene. – At three fifteen,
while the *reis* had succumbed to exhaustion (Ahmed-el-Masri is a useful
man who, until that day, had seemed to us to possess common sense and
a good head) and was asleep, the *Isis* hit the sandbank of a submerged
island near the village of Thannasch, a little above Schobra-el-Khimêh, the
stunning country house of the Pasha. This is set in beautiful gardens and
is connected to Cairo by a pretty avenue of trees in a very poor condition
which the French planted thirty years ago. Our sailors leapt into the Nile
in order to set the *maasch* free, enlisting the name of Allah and, with considerably more effect, their large and strapping shoulders. Most of these
people are built like Hercules, with spectacular physiques that resembled
newly cast bronzes when they emerged from the river and thrust forward
to tow the boat. The *maasch* was afloat again after a long half-hour of
work and effort. We resumed our voyage at four, using our grand sail as
the front mast had been broken by the northerly wind.

At four thirty we passed Embabeh, and our eyes surveyed the grounds
of the pyramids laid out before us. – At five o'clock precisely we went
ashore at the harbour of Boulaq. We beached the *maasch* and dahabiah to
the left of the customs buildings, near the old palace of Ismael-Pacha [son
of the Pasha], which is today a lyceum. Numerous boats, moored like us
to the shore, were strung along the riverbank of the Nile. The sight of
Boulaq is rather attractive thanks to the planting of several feet of mimosa
and acacia. Straight away I sent Dr Ricci to Cairo with my letters to M.
Derche, who is the French consul in the capital, and to see whether they
had thought of arranging for lodgings. An hour and a half later, M.
Youssouf Msarra, the translator of the consulate, arrived with a janissary.
I was told that M. Derche had been very ill for a few days but that they
had nonetheless rented a house for us. I delayed our general disembarkation until the next day.

20 September 1828: In the morning everything required for the transport
of our luggage was dealt with and subsequently several convoys of
donkeys and camels were loaded. Having remained on board to supervise
everything, and because I did not want to enter Cairo until the coolness
of the evening, I was fortunate to find as a pastime, at two steps away

from the *maasch*, an elegant sarcophagus of green basalt belonging to Mahmoud-Bey, the Defence Minister, in the courtyard of the customs office [now in the Louvre].[1] This monument of an excellent precision shows most of the scenes chiselled on our sarcophagus of Ramesses-Meiamoun, and a group of other perplexing ones which I copied by tracing them on paper. One among them was of great importance: it shows the transmigration scene of a lost soul in the shape of a pig, small but very detailed, of the type sculpted or painted on a tomb at Thebes and published by the Commission with many mistakes.

A visit from the brother of M. Pacho. – At five, when the translator and janissary returned with donkeys, I left for Cairo with the whole of the caravan, strutting and regularly posing *en route.* The donkeys in Cairo are much better than those in Alexandria. Taller and stronger, they have much in common, up to a point, with vigorous Arabian horses.

We went through Boulaq, whose streets are as narrow as those of Alexandria but have more style, as the majority of these houses are built in stone, and many have carved doors and windows in an antique Arab style. Its ancient mosques leave a pleasant impression and have widely different shapes. – Leaving Boulaq, we crossed countryside covered with trees of all species. Only the mounds of sand which cut through the landscape remind you that you are in Africa. We entered Cairo through the gate called Bab-el-Omara. Viewed from afar, the capital, which takes up a large part of the walls built by its founder, Caliph Moez, is an impressive sight owing to the unbelievable number of exquisite minarets set against the crisp background of the Mokattam, a barren mountain whose curves are nonetheless very picturesque.

As we cleared the gate, the great plaza of Cairo called El-Ezbekieh stretched out before our eyes. The effect of this is fantastic. It is a rectangle of impressive proportions, surrounded by tall, well-designed houses; some of them are new, among others the one of Muhammad-Bey, Defterdar [treasurer] and a relative of the Pasha, built on the site of the main quarter of the French army. The middle of this lovely square is at the moment sheathed by flood waters forming a huge basin whose edges are sprinkled with splashes of tufty trees. A massive number of people circumnavigated the Ezbekieh on horseback, or on foot, camels or donkeys; dancers of all sorts and Almeh entertained the public. You could hear cries of laughter peal from all corners of the square. The variety of clothes of all shapes and colours evoked the spirit of life and strangeness that overwhelmed our European eyes. We had arrived in Cairo at a time when it unleashes all its oriental pomp. It was the second day of the Mouled-en-Naby feast, celebrated to commemorate the birth of the Prophet [Muhammad], giving a new twist to the spectacle in front of us as a blend of physical pleasure and religious rites. Not far from a choir of Almeh, singing erotic odes or absorbed in dances under a spirit that would have put the Bacchae to shame, groups of crouching Muslim chanted praise to the Prophet or repeated with solicitation and zeal, in harmony, the names of God – milling around these devotees were Muselmen of all ages, who were striking distinctly down-to-earth poses. We came by a tent mobbed with people; I made out several dervishes, old men with impressive beards whirling around themselves and relishing the utter drunkenness caused by their spinning movement; they are called Mourghiaha (plural Maraghieheh).

Leaving Ezbekieh, we penetrated the streets of Cairo, about which we had been told so many bad things. It is true that, with the exception of the largest ones which harbour the bazaars, the streets are not wider than six to ten feet, and that daylight is virtually entirely blacked out by Moucharabieh gratings [wooden window screens]; but considering that this lack of width and light traps the coolness in the streets (even during the most scorching heat), one marvels at the stupidity of European travellers who bemoan the fact that in Cairo or Baghdad there are no large streets like those in Paris or London, without realising that these would be burning furnaces for three-quarters of the year. These streets are furthermore very clean, even though they are not paved, and completely without litter of any sort.

Cairo is truly a grand city. There is barely a street without houses built (at least at lower ground level) from handsome chiselled stone, and doors trimmed with sculpture. Mosques abound, and each of them has an individual character, either through their layout or the variety of orna-mentation and abundant arabesques which are traced on them.

The house that had been rented for me is situated in the quarter called Hosh-et-hhin, rather far away from the European neighbourhood and near the mosques called Ghame-el-Mosky and Ghame-el-Kazendher. Having installed ourselves, and received all the agents of the consulate who had come to offer their help, we went to have supper in the French quarter, where we were to take all our meals during our stay in Cairo.

After dinner, I visited Mme Rosetti, the wife of the Tuscan consul. She lives with her parents, M. and Mme Macadle, the Tuscan vice-consul. Both ladies are Levantines... We wanted to see the fireworks and nightly feast of Ezbekieh, to which we went at nine with a janissary who cleared the streets for us with his silver-topped cane, but without violence, on orders which I had given him. – The fireworks, which took place in the middle of the square, formed a sort of portico or architectural façade whose design was difficult to make out, but the whole had a pleasing effect while being mirrored in the stretched of water at the centre. I went up to a number of tents made of rich tapestries and erected at the expense of the Pasha or by private undertaking. In the first, almost a hundred Muselmen were arranged in two lines facing each other, seated and rocking the tops of their bodies rhythmically backwards and forwards and singing 'There is no god but god', adding occasionally '*Muhammed resoul Allah*' (Muhammad is the messenger of god). This drill had started in the morning, and the singers were irregularly substituted, depending on whether a zealous Muslim wanted to take their place.

The second tent vaulted over a bevy of seated Muslim who held Korans and were together reading chapters from this book, which is written in measured prose, a fact that we could hardly dispute after hearing its recitation. – An unexpected scene awaited us in the third tent: three hundred people in trance, standing while touching their elbows, rhythmically jumping while repeating the main name of God, Allah, in a toneless and deeply guttural voice, such that I had never before heard a more diabolical and grisly choir. White foam spouted on their beards, and from time to time a few of the possessed would fall, exhausted and voiceless despite the cares of the steward charged with keeping their dried-out throats moistened. I noticed something extraordinary, and that was the politeness and obvious willingness with which the Muslim made room for us, giving us the vantage point nearest to the tents. A few years before our present era, no European would have dared show up in the middle of these religious ceremonies. The hand of civilisation would move very fast here if there were a well-intentioned government presiding over the destiny of poor Egypt. But everything is consumed by a scorching totalitarian temperament.

At ten thirty we went to spend the evening with M. Botzari, an Armenian who is the Pasha's physician and is charged with the health of the country. He has an extremely pretty house in the oriental style. We were very pleasantly received by the son of the house, who brought us to the great divan. There, sitting, smoking and drinking coffee, we spent two hours listening to Arab singers who were screened from our eyes by a discreet curtain. This tempting veil, as the singers were very pretty, produced a good acoustic effect, making it appear as if the voices were coming from above. The chant of these women was a cantilena without harmony, pierced by solos whose beauty is difficult for the European ear to fathom, but which impels the Arabs to applaud while saying of the main singer, called Nefisseh (Cairo's Catalani): 'May god render your voice eternal.'

None of us particularly subscribed to that idea, but we thought it a pity that these exceptional ways of singing were so poorly performed. Under the rule of the Turks, oriental life has been suppressed to the point where the natural has become a stranger to the arts. In order to pander to its pedestrian conquerors, the artists have to push everything to extremes. It was depressing to hear at every turn the obnoxious voice of Nefisseh's husband's cutting through the chant of the Arab siren in order to applaud and encourage her at the pitch with which Bluebeard called for his wife's head. – Some of the passages in the chants of these Almeh sounded very much like our ancient French airs. – Returned at midnight.

21 September 1828: I was visited very early in the morning by M. Linant-[Bey de Bellefonds],[2] a highly distinguished traveller and draughtsman, whose drawings grace the collection of M. [William] Bankes.[3] He has completely adopted a Muslim lifestyle: forever wearing the garb of the Nizam-Ghedid and living far away from the European quarter, he has set himself up extremely impressively at the heart of Arab life and married an Abyssinian, with whom he has several children. M. Linant was joined by M. Berthier, the consulary agent of Tarsus [Greece], who had fled to Egypt in order to escape its Pasha, who wanted to kill him on receiving the first tidings from Navarino.

He delayed my daytime trawl through Cairo designed to get the right measure of this city, against which travel writers have given me such prejudices. Seated on a beautiful donkey and preceded by my janissary,

Omar, I gave him orders to show us the mosques of Thouloun [Ibn Tulun], Sultan-Hassan and El-Azhar...

Champollion to Champollion-Figeac – 27 September 1828, Cairo
On the 14th, my very good friend, I left Alexandria at the head of my squadron, a refined French frontguard sailing with all imaginable luxury on the Mahmoudieh canal, which follows the course of the ancient Alexandrian canal, but with considerably fewer twists and turns, leading directly to the Nile, passing Lake Mareotis to the right and Edkou to the left. We entered the Nile very early on the 15th, and I could understand the rapture of western Arabs when, upon leaving behind the Libyan sands of Alexandria, they enter the canopic branch [the main western branch of the Nile Delta] and are treated to the sight of the swathes of greenery of the delta, wrapped in trees of all sorts, pricked by hundreds of minarets, and numerous villages which are scattered over this blessed countryside. This panorama is truly mesmerising, and the celebrated fertility of the Egyptian land is no exaggeration...

The 20th was taken up with preparations for the departure to Cairo, and several convoys of donkeys and camels transported our beds, trunks and effects into town in order to furnish the house which had been rented in advance of our arrival. At five at night, tailed by my caravan and straddling our donkeys, which are rather prettier than those in Alexandria, we left for Cairo. The janissary of the consulate rode ahead, the translator to my right, and all my young people jigging and circling behind me; none of which seemed to put out the Arabs, who indulgently cried, 'Frenchmen!'...

A large number of mosques, some more stylish than others, covered with brilliant arabesques and crowned by graceful and rich minarets, show this capital off in an extremely imposing and varied way. I crossed it in all directions and discovered each day new ones to dazzle me. Thanks to the Thouloudine dynasty, the Fatimite caliphs, the Ayoubite sultans and the Mameluke Baharites, Cairo is still a city of a Thousand and One Nights, despite the fact that Turkish thugs have destroyed or had destroyed a large number of the most thrilling examples of Arab art and civilisation. I paid my first respects to one in the mosque of Thouloun [Ibn Thulun], a building from the ninth century, a model of chic and elegance, which I couldn't admire more, even though it is half destroyed. While I was peering at the gate, an old sheikh suggested that I enter; I eagerly accepted and, proceeding slowly through the first gate, I was abruptly stopped at the second one; you have to enter this holy place without shoes. I was wearing boots but no socks; this was a real obstacle. I took off my boots, borrowed a handkerchief from my janissary to bundle around my right foot and another one from my Nubian servant Muhammad for my left foot, and shuffled over the marble parquet of the holy courtyard; without any doubt it is the most stunning Arab monument in the whole of Egypt. The delicacy of its sculpture is unbelievable and its suite of arcaded porticoes bewitching. I won't tell you about the other mosques, nor the tombs of the caliphs and Mameluk sultans which form a suburb around the first that is even more magnificent; it would take too much time, as there is too much of ancient Egypt to be able to deal with the new.

On Monday, 22 September, I went up to the citadel to meet Habib-Effendi, the governor of Cairo and the Grand Minister of the Pasha. He received me with extreme kindness, talked at length with me about the monuments of Upper Egypt and gave me advice on how to study them at greater ease. Leaving His Excellency, I toured the citadel and found first of all an enormous piece of sandstone with a bas-relief which features King Psammetichus II and was the dedication of a propylon; I had it carefully copied. I found other scattered blocks which belonged to the same monument in Memphis, from which they were taken, and which gave me a highly interesting insight. Each of these stones, perfectly polished and cut, carries a mark which reveals under which king it was quarried; the royal legend, accompanied by the destination of the block in Memphis, is engraved in a square flat cavity. I gathered from several blocks the marks of three kings: Psammetichus II, Apries, his son, and Amasis, the successor of the latter. These three legends therefore tell us the duration of the construction of the building from which they were taken. A little farther on are the ruins of the royal palace of the famous Salahh-Eddin (Sultan Saladin), the chief of the Ayoubite dynasty. A fire ravaged its roofs four years ago, and for a few months the Pasha has been taking pleasure in destroying what remains of this grand and beautiful residence; I caught sight of a square room, the most important of the palace. More than thirty columns of pink granite still show the thick gilt-work covering their trunks, and are upright, while their enormous capitals, in Arab sculpture that rudely imitates Egyptian capitals, are piled up on the debris. These capitals, which the Arabs added to these columns (Greek or Roman), are quarried from granite taken from the ruins of Memphis, and the majority still carry traces of hieroglyphic sculpture; I even discovered on one of them, where the trunk joined the column, a bas-relief which represented King Nectanebo make an offering to the gods. During one of my walks in the citadel, where I went several times to draw Egyptian fragments, I visited the wells of Joseph, that is to say the wells which the great Saladin (Salahh-Eddin-Joussouf) had dug in the citadel, not far from the palace: a laborious work.

I also saw the Pasha's zoo, which contains a lion, two tigers and an elephant. I arrived too late to see the hippopotamus alive – the poor animal had died of sunstroke after taking its siesta without precautions – but I saw its skin impaled in Turkish fashion and suspended from the main gates of the citadel. The day before yesterday I saw Muhammad-Bey, Defterdar of the Pasha. He showed me the house he had had built in Boulaq on the Nile, and on whose walls he had by way of ornamentation framed rather attractive Egyptian bas-reliefs from Sakkara; it is a very telling action by one of the Pasha's ministers who is most well known for his opposition to reform.

I met M. Derche, our consular agent, who is dangerously ill, and among the foreigners Lord Prudhoe, M. Burton and Major Felix, all English, determined hieroglyphers who lavished their attention on me as if I were the chief of a sect. – I have tried to make several acquisitions but prices are rather high – I will starve them first before reeling in; they will be more reasonable upon my return. You and Férussac must double your efforts to make sure that the royal purse will advance funds for purchases and excavations:[4] with little I will be able to accomplish enormous things, and it would be a shame beyond repair if the government didn't profit from my stay in Egypt to enrich its museums...

I will leave tomorrow, or the day after, for Memphis; I will not return to Cairo this year. We will go ashore near Mit-Rahineh (the centre of ruins of the old city), were I will set up my base; from there I will push my reconnaissance to Sakkara, Dahschour and the whole plain of Memphis, up to the great pyramids of Gizeh, from which I hope to begin my next letter. Having swept through the site of the second capital of Egypt, I will point my hat at Thebes, where I will be from October, after having stopped for a few hours in Abydos and Dendera.

My health is still superb and better than in Europe, as I have written these seven pages in one breath, which I would have been unable to do in Paris without a headache. I am truly a newborn man. My shaved head is covered by an enormous turban. I am dressed completely like a Turk, an attractive moustache decks my mouth, and a large scimitar dangles from my hip. This clothing is very hot and is exactly what is needed in Egypt; one perspires freely, and so does everyone here.

My Arabs swear that I am everywhere mistaken for a native: in a month from now I will be able to fuse verbal

Champollion in local dress

illusion with appearances. I am getting on with my Arabic, and as I am using jargon they will soon no longer take me for a beginner.

I will stop my letter here... Greetings and tender regards to M. Dacier, love hot as the Egyptian soil to M. Dacier junior, and to all the inhabitants of rue Colbert.

I am thinking of shells for our friend Férussac and have already collected details that will not fail to interest Mme Férussac; they are about the women of Egypt. I would love to write to her about the party I threw for my young people the day after we arrived in Cairo. I ordered six Almeh or girl savants (very knowledgeable),[5] who danced and sang from six at night until two in the morning, everything in every possible good taste and appropriateness.

Goodbye, then, my dear friend. I embrace you as well as my wife and all those who support us. My regards to M. Dubois, to whom I will write imminently. Why isn't he by my side to amuse me!

Adieu, all yours

4.

Rapture and Decadence

Dendera

From Champollion's diary
30 September 1828: The entire day was taken up with preparations for our departure. We absolutely have to leave Cairo before my young people start to embrace habits which will subsequently be difficult to shed. This city which so many people dislike has cast its spell on them, and I have come to the conclusion that such a great capital, which is so new and which unites all the titillation which an oriental people offers under the government of a pasha, cannot fail to impress young uncritical minds who respond deeply to the picturesqueness of the things and people among whom they have been miraculously transported. Dr Ricci, an experienced traveller of this area, thinks of all necessary things and has taken care of all essential provisions for our voyage through Upper Egypt.

While waiting, I visited M. Linant[-Bey], who lives outside the walls in a totally oriental style as, having married an Abyssinian, he has adopted all the oriental manners. He allowed me to see his rich picture portfolios. I saw for the first time quite good sketches of the Roman antiquities of Petra. I recognised various hieroglyphic inscriptions of Sarbout-el-Qadim, which had been copied as accurately as any draughtsman might accomplish, the majority of the monuments and bas-reliefs of Naga nad Barkal, and several other points of Upper Nubia and Ethiopia. These drawings confirmed one of my beliefs concerning the monuments of Ethiopia, and I could clearly distinguish three successive styles: 1) The Egypto-Ethiopian style, that is to say the primitive Ethiopian style which is analogous to the pure Egyptian style. The temples of Barkal are an example, and carry the royal legends of Tharaca, Amonaso and even

Amenophis-Memnon, which proves that it is this pharaoh who conquered Ethiopia. 2) The Hindu-Ethiopian style, dominated by large and fat shapes, stubby, and covered with details and ornamentation which is sometimes very lavish. This style must have originated directly or indirectly among some Hindu people. This is shown beyond any doubt by the Ethiopian alphabet, which is syllabic, copied doubtless from the Hindu syllabics, as at the monuments of Naga. 3) The Arab-Ethiopian style, narrow shapes, elongated, poor and rather incorrect. This style took hold after the invasion by the Himiritic Arabs; this race ended up decimating the original Ethiopian population while preserving their customs and writing. The monuments in this style cannot be earlier than the first century.

I also found at M. Linant's the drawing of a long inscription of Pharaoh Tuthmosis IV, engraved on rock on the border of Dongola. He promised me a copy.

At about six in the evening, after the camels and donkeys were packed with all our luggage, we left Cairo and went to dine and sleep on the *maasch*, which was still at Boulaq.

1 October 1828: A few forgotten provisions and purchases that still had to be made delayed our departure until three in the afternoon. The *Isis* set sail without waiting for the *Athyr*, which I told to wait for the kavass or soldiers of the Pasha's guard who have to escort us. We coasted past the charming island of Raoudha [Rhoda], which deserves its reputation, and went by the Mequias (or Nilometer) built on its southern tip. After some difficulty caused by cangias [vessels] of the customs officers of old Cairo, we arrived at Gizeh at a quarter to three. – At five fifteen, the *maasch* went by Dier-et-tin on the Arab side, at the foot of a detached hump of the Mokattam Hills on which the Egyptian Babylon perched. According to history, Sesostris allowed Babylonian prisoners to build a small village for themselves there. The Pasha built a tiny fortress in its place.

At sunset we were opposite Thorrah, where the government stores are. The nearby mountainside (on the right bank) is pierced with quarries. On the facing bank once stood Memphis; its site is engulfed by an immense forest of palms, above which soar the tops of the pyramids of Sakkara. We arrived at seven at night at Massarah, where I ordered the *reis* to stop and drop anchor, with a view to visiting the next day the open quarries of different ages in the mountainside between this village and Thorrah farther north. A little later the *Athyr* joined us and we passed the night there with our boats attached to palms whose dates tumbled on our heads while the mooring ropes were tied up.

2 October 1828: Our donkeys, stabled in the village since the previous day, arrived without saddles and bridles, and we left at six in the morning in order to reach the foot of the mountain over farmed lands and uncultivated terrain already decked with a film of sand because they hadn't been flooded by the Nile for a few years. I made the entire journey on foot, dressed in my burnous and opening my umbrella whenever the heat of the sun became too strong. After an hour's walk we arrived at the foot of the Arab mountain range, which was pockmarked with sand mounds and piles of stone, the detritus from the quarries. By scaling these dunes and hills of sharp stones we arrived at a large quarry whose entrance, cut like a doorway and reaching a considerable height, was visible from afar; we could see it while sailing down the river, and I will christen it the central quarry. I gave each member of the expedition a different direction so that we could explore the numerous caverns to our left and right in the most effective way. Whenever someone saw an inscription or sculpture they would whistle a warning tune, and I would go over to see how important the discovery was. If the inscription was interesting I sketched it, or had it drawn if its shapes were very well articulated.

This expedition, which was burdensome owing to the very high temperature amidst the white chalky rocks which fiercely reflect the sunlight, led to the following results. In the quarries that were successively carved out of the rock to the left of the central quarry were many inscriptions traced in red and in demotic characters: the majority were on the ceiling of the quarry or in highly visible places. Repeated in large numbers in one and the same cave, several of these inscriptions are clearly related to the exploitation of the quarry itself, but others are of greater interest as they contain dates and royal names:... of the second year of King Achoris's reign[1]... the seventh year of one of the Ptolemies who, as no first name was given, must be Soter I, the founder of the dynasty:... of year four, 11... Paopi [month], of the reign of Augustus.

The quarries to the right are even more covered in demotic inscriptions, yet they also have hieroglyphics and sculptures. One of the most beautiful quarries in this direction is adorned with a stele framed by columns in an exquisite style and carrying in its upper regions three royal cartouches. It was carved out of the rock, inside and to the left of the entrance. Its fluted cornice has no ornamentation. The central cartouche, preceded by the title 'king' and followed by 'giver of life', is the first name of King Ahmosis (founder of the eighteenth Diospolitan dynasty). The second cartouche, Ahmose-Nofretari, is the queen's, his wife, as the titles principal-royal-spouse, royal-mother, lady-of-the-world-forever indicate. The third cartouche (the one to the left) is from another woman of Ahmosis's household, his sister or perhaps daughter, as the titles daughter-of-the-king and sister-of-the-king indicate. This latter title settles the question because, as the monument was sculpted while Ahmosis was alive, there was no king but him (Amenothis I did not yet rule), so the princess, who was also called Ahmose-Nofretari, was the sister of Ahmosis, emphasised by 'cherished by Ptah' and 'cherished by Atum'. This first title is inspired by nearby Memphis, and the second by the fact that Atum was the guardian deity of quarries. — Eight lines of hieroglyphs make up the inscription of the second register of the stele, and this monument is thus even more interesting as it was chiselled to commemorate the time at which the quarry was discovered. This is what the two well-preserved first lines express, while the remaining six have more or less weathered away: 'in the year 22 under the minister of the sun-born king Ahmosis these quarries were opened'.

Scrutiny of the characters that remain suggests that the stones hewn from these quarries were used for construction work in the temples of Ptah, Apis and Amenophis, doubtless in Memphis, which lies opposite the quarries. On its square base, which is supposed to buttress the stele, scenes of work in the quarry are carved, that is six bulls guided by three men and attached in pairs to a sledge on which a large square sawn chunk of rock is fastened.

On the walls of this quarry, towards the ceiling, very, very small connected steles are carved on which the figures of Ptah or lions, the emblem of this great Memphite deity, are roughly drawn.

A second large quarry also has the mark of year 22 of the same pharaoh. The stele placed on the left inside the entrance is also cut touching the rock. Its cornice is decorated with winged discs and his legend, and its colour is still visible on this inscription, which is much more disfigured than the other one. The cartouches of the first text are the same, except that Princess Ahmose-Nofretari, this time without her title of royal sister, takes that of royal-mother and the wife of the pharaoh that of divine-spouse. Word for word, this stele is a copy of the previous one.

In the tiny valley that the mountains of Tura form in between these two quarries there is a bevy of other quarries, with very few interesting inscriptions... On the wall of a neighbouring grotto the elevation of a small monolith or naos is drawn with finesse and a remarkably steady hand in red ink. Its fluted cornice is decorated with emblems of the first Hermes, flanked by cobras symbolising the two regions, and carries the cartouche first names and surnames of Psammetichus I...

Summarising, these quarries, which extend from Tura right beyond Massarah, must have been excavated across all ages. Being near the successive capitals of Egypt, Memphis, Fostat and Cairo, must have perpetuated their being mined, and even today the square stones for the pavements of Cairo houses are taken from here. The quarries first supplied the building material for Memphis and neighbouring towns. The names of Ahmosis and Psammetichus suggest that this was the case for the entire period stretching between their reigns: Acoris flags the Persian period and the names of the two Ptolemies, 'Lagides', and the inscription of year 7 of Augustus indicate Roman times.

One easily distinguishes between antique and modern quarries. The ceilings of the former are flat and marked by millions of scores made by chisels working to extract the narrowly hewn stone in such a way that it could be used for construction; there are even some of these virtually detached stones left. These ceilings are sometimes divided by large red lines accompanied by demotic words to guide the workers and mark up what needs to be done. The modern quarries are by contrast mined without any order, and their vaults are rounded and full of twisting curves.

M. Linant and a young Englishman, M. Newman, arrived on dromedaries and shared our modest lunch in the first quarry of Ahmosis. Having taken a break in that of Acoris, where our entire cavalcade was at last reunited, we took the road back to Massarah and our *maasch*, where we dined with great hunger after an extremely exhausting day. – Having barely finished their coffee, the two men said farewell and, launching forth on their dromedaries, soon disappeared out of sight in the direction of Cairo. This was at six fifteen. Not wanting to see anything else in the neighbourhood, I told the *reis* to set sail for Bedreschein, which we reached at eight thirty.

3 October 1828: I inspected, as I was waking up, a sarcophagus in porphyry granite which belonged to my dragoman, Joseph Msarra, who had had it transported from Sakkara to very near the Nile.[2] It was for someone called Petisi. The carving is not at all of choice quality, and its decorations represent minor divinities. I told the dragoman that the object did not please me at all, which put him in a bad mood, as he had counted on me for ridding himself of the thing. At six in the morning we left by donkey for Bedreschein, a village hiding in these somewhat lost lands. It is only after having passed it that the traveller discovers that he is treading on the neck of what was once a large town. You are here, in fact, already within Memphis, and the blocks of granite floating above the land, which appear amidst the sands that slowly cover them in increasing numbers, attest to the extreme sumptuousness of the buildings of this capital. – Between Bedreschein and Mit-Rahineh we found the colossus that M. Caviglia had discovered and presented to the Grand-Duke of Tuscany. This magnificently carved colossus, whose head and details I had drawn with great care, is a representation of Ramesses the Great. The material of the colossus is a very beautiful crystallised limestone. It lies with its front resting on the sand; its feet and part of the legs no longer exist... The pharaoh is coiffed in a striped *claft* [headcloth]; above it stretches the pschent [white crown], which is half destroyed. His collar has seven rings ending in a string of pearls. Two strings hold up a rich breastplate whose ridge carries a string of disc cobras with their heads crowned by solar discs. At the heart of the breastplate, worked in low relief, are the first name of Ramesses the Great protected by two divinities on foot, Ptah and his wife the great lion-headed goddess, the two principal deities of Memphis...

Its head is line for line, though in larger proportions, an exact copy of the head of the small colossus of Ramesses the Great in the museum of Turin, its most stunning exhibit. This perfect resemblance offers proof that the two statues are true portraits of the Egyptian conqueror. The colossus, near which there are several foundations of large blocks of limestone, was most likely placed before a large gate, and must have been a counterpart to a second one of the same proportions. We organised for this reason a number of excavations in the presumptive area, but there may not be enough time to harvest the fruits of these searches. This place is nonetheless amazingly interesting, as it is likely that we are within the enclosure that circled the principal sacred buildings of Memphis. The rumps of two very long hills stretch out in parallel from the middle to the north: one west of the Nile and Bedreschein — the other, farther west, saddling the village of Mit-Rahineh. I think these hills are the crushed

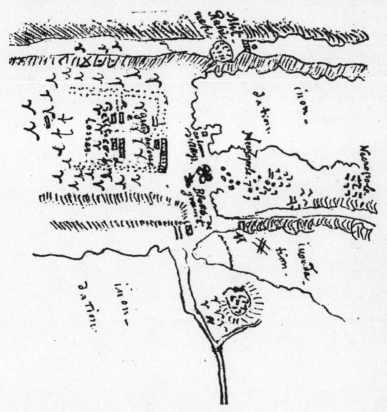

Mit-Rahineh lies in the middle (top); to the left two colossi are marked in the middle of a palm grove and opposite a necropolis which both lie in between the hills Champollion mentions. In between right against the flood line lies the column of Hathor.

remnants of this enormous dried-brick compound — dissolving and caving in under the rain and flood waters which today still submerge a good part of the area in between the parallel walls that are nowadays clumped with palms...

I went carefully past the eastern flank of the hill to the north of the great colossus, and I noticed ample remains of small buildings or chambers and corridors built from small dried brick, as in the necropolis of Sais. Infinite shards of pottery, equally reminiscent of Sais, pointed to the use of these edifices. The debris of funerary figurines and bitumen vases which one finds here removes all doubt in this respect. There is another necropolis farther north, which I visited on my way to Sakkara; it is the continuation of this one. These walls of dried brick are strewn with blocks of pink granite, sandstone and white limestone which seem to have belonged to more elaborate buildings decorated with sculptures. We lunched on Arab bread, fresh dates and water, seated in the shade of cabins made from rose stems and palm leaves. At night we returned to dine more substantially at the *maasch*, where we went to sleep.

4 October 1828: Very early in the morning, while the tents and all other necessary things were packed for an expedition of at least eight days, I went back to Bedreschein and Mit-Rahineh. I was once more overwhelmed by the craftsmanship of the colossus, and I felt instinctively deeply moved by the impressions of the first important Egyptian sculpture that fate had placed before my eyes.

Lying before this enormous face, which is so harmonious that its expression is nothing but solicitous and suave, I let myself be overpowered by this lofty heroic statue, and smiled with pity on the memory of the mean opinions and miserly idea that we, educated 'critics' of the arts, had and still have of Egyptian art. Any impartial viewer will remember the horror mixed with repulsion he feels, as I did in Rome, before any one of the enormous heads of the emperors stored at the Capitol or elsewhere; I wish he could compare this feeling with the one that would engulf him in front of an Egyptian colossus. He would see straight away that the Egyptians understood exactly how to use art for objects larger than life, for an art that is monumental – the vital ingredient of their architecture. Every over-refined detail on a grand scale is a mistake, and the artist who is sculpting a monumental statue but does not possess the Egyptian sensibility for expressing only what is strictly necessary, which does in no way mean an exclusion of finesse, will always produce monstrosities, a porcine caricature like one of those imperial heads. The sculpture of two small pink granite colossi placed near by shows far less poise than this limestone giant. They were decorations for a gate or a pylon. One of these colossi is in a rather fine state, but the more westerly one was brutally chopped up, and one can barely make out its shapes.

To the north of the giant colossus, on a sort of hillock rising above the flood level, I found a small column of limestone with the four-headed capital of Hathor carved simply, in a very severe style. Its trunk disappears almost two-thirds into the soil; I have no idea whether this column is still in its original place or whether some dealer had it moved and dropped on that spot. The local people weren't able to tell me one way or another. Hathor, the wife of Ptah, must have had numerous ones like these in Memphis, and, leaving

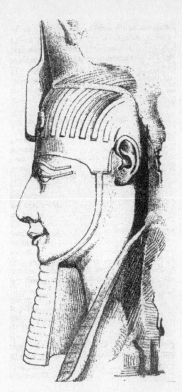

Memphis colossus of Ramesses II

aside the temple of Aphrodite, I have become convinced that on the eastern side of the rubble hill of the sacred enclosure there was a rather important monument dedicated to Ptah and the goddess Hathor. Excavations started by M. Caviglia, which I continued for two days, have brought to light blocks of pink granite in the shape of a pilaster which look like two coupled and connected columns, stamped along their entire separated twin length with titles and legends of Ramesses the Great, ending in the two dedicatory formulae loved-by-Ptah, loved-by-Hathor. I am certain that if the excavations pressed on vigorously at this location (and in a month other than October) they would lead to the discovery of some extraordinarily important building: what I see here is quite exceptional from an architectural point of view.

At three I had to start thinking again about our departure for Sakkara, where our caravan of seven camels loaded with tents, boxes and things ought to have arrived already under the guidance of Dr Ricci, who is choosing the site where we shall be camping. The direct road was closed by the extensive flood waters lapping over the countryside. We had to push our donkeys into the forest of palms which covers the dilapidated enclosure on the Bedreschein side, and march for an hour from south to north; it was during this long detour that I once again crossed the necropolis of dried brick which lunges far towards the north and often reveals a peculiar arrangement of small brick walls enclosing construction rubble of limestone and, even more often, of all sorts of granite. I quite lost track of all these beddings.

At last we cleared the palm forest and, turning east after crossing a bridge, we went down a road which led us, after another hour of extravagant detours that were impossible to cut short as flood water rose on both sides of the road, to the neighbourhood of Sakkara. Exactly at this point, where the road turns into the desert and a small wood of palms is girded by a copse of perfumed *santh* (the Egyptian acacia of the ancients), our tents had been erected; two for the masters and a third for the servants. The remainder of the day was spent on interior arrangements. We paid the owner of the field where we were camping, and his three sons, to patrol and keep a watchful eye at night. Our neighbours, the inhabitants of Sakkara, enjoy an excellent reputation for deserving such nocturnal vigil.

5 October 1828: The previous night I made a reconnaissance of the pyramid of five degrees, called Medarrag by the Arabs, which rises above the hills to the north-west of our camp, poised between the desert sands of Africa and the extremities of cultivated farmland. I rushed to see what is called the plain of the mummies, a vast cemetery that devoured generations of the people who successively lived in Memphis: a local called Mansour served as our guide. Leaving the camp, we entered the desert and walked towards the Libyan mountains, which are everywhere surrounded by sand. Our poor donkeys had a tough time clearing the ever so slight incline that leads to the infinite plain of the desert. The sands parted under their feet, and at every turn mount and rider risked rolling on top of each other. At last our guide halted near the summit of the

incline to show us an antique tomb. I followed Mansour, who had a candle, crawling on my stomach, and found myself in a square room clad with beautiful carved freestone, but without any trace of paint. It was the tomb of a royal scribe or Memphite chief teacher called Amenemet. The entire decoration of this cave was purely religious. The deceased revered Osiris, Sokra and, above all, the two Memphite deities Phtah and Hathor. I searched in vain for a royal cartouche which would tell me the date of these carvings. All I could find was a very lightly drawn Greek inscription which said that the insults of an enemy often require the advice of a friend: this elegant saying is unfortunately drawn on top of the Egyptian sculptures, and as a result rather modern by comparison. The workmanship of the tomb belongs to an accomplished age, even though it is a little plump and overfed, which is in any case the Memphite style.

We managed to scale the hill and, having at last reached the top of the plateau, we could take in the devastation that centuries have wreaked on the graves of the Memphites. Just think of an immense flat expanse through which pyramids push up, pockmarked with tiny mountlets of sand covered with bits of antique pottery, swaddling rags of mummies, broken and desiccated bones, Egyptian skulls blanched by the morning dew of the desert, and any kind of rubbish you can think of. At every instant one comes across, at one's feet, either a dried-brick wall, or the opening of a square shaft clad in dazzling freestone but filled in with the sand that the Arabs dig up as they search them. All these mountlets are the result of the hunts for mummies and antiquities, and the number of the tunnels or tombs of Sakkara must be gigantic if you consider that the sand that is blown about covers up several other openings.

You would be mistaken if you thought that these shafts led to sculpted chambers; this is actually very rare. It was more usual to build, on the opening of the shaft or very near by, one or more rooms decorated with sculptures serving as chapels for the family vault or catacomb, enclosing the bodies of an entire family. I persuaded myself of this conclusion by visiting several tombs that are still very well preserved...

One of the most exciting ones, and the first which I had copied in detail, is a little to the north of the Medarrag pyramid. The following sketch gives an idea of the arrangement of its L-shaped rooms. The construction of this tomb, or rather vestibule of the tomb, struck me as extremely accomplished. The carving that decorates it is likewise highly skilled, but without being exceptionally attractive. You will read only one proper name here, the one of the head of the family who paid for the monument. His name was Menofre or Menofe, whose principal title indicates that he was an officer in charge of parts of the royal hairdressing salon. Other epithets such as 'loving-his-master', adoring-his-master', which are also attached to Menofre, are like the title 'one of the friends of the king' of the Egyptian Ptolemaic officers, and prove the high antiquity of this sort of association. The deceased was, as a 'royal priest', moreover, a member of the ecclesiastical élite, and his name is always preceded by the [hieroglyphic] sign for a priest. I was ecstatic to find among the reliefs the full name of the pharaoh at whose court Menofre lived. But the proper name of this monarch, Osse, Asso, Aseso [Djedkare, Isesi], belongs to a dynasty [the fifth] whose successive names, the abbreviators of Manetho[3] did not deign to give us, which means that the era of the tomb and its author remain rather clouded, though its most essential details are now available...

You enter Menofre's crypt through the forced opening (F) in a dilapidated wall. The first room (A), open to the sky, is fairly narrow, and the majority of the statues that embellished it have been stolen or destroyed. Only on the wall marked (a) [to the right of the entrance] are they still there, and these represent people of both sexes walking to the door of the chamber (D), carrying offerings of all kinds, or perhaps produce from the lands belonging to their master, Menofre. Among these people working in the house of this Memphite lord, several lead superb white and red, white or black bulls, and two of these animals are marked on their left thigh with a huge sign drawn in black with the characters 'royal household' and the numbers 43 and 96, which shows that the grand houses of Egypt gave their cattle numbers. At a guess, these numbers represent the total number of animals of a particular colour.

Above the backs of the animals is carved the word for bull. They are on a leash, and each one of them has a collar that ends in an ornament in the shape of a lotus flower. On the wall there are also twelve walking women who carry large baskets or vases on their heads which contain stalks full of dates, bananas, figs and other fruits or foodstuffs. Dressed exactly the same, these svelte-waisted women carry stems of lotus flowers, clutch geese by their wings, hold calves in their arms or on a leash, or a bouquet of flowers with their left hand (with their right they steady their

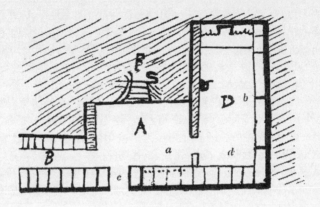

Sketch of the tomb of Menofre

baskets). Another one leads a small gazelle with a leash fastened to the left
hind hoof of the animal.

The inside of the longest chamber (D), whose ceiling of broad stones
is impeccably preserved, is much more varied in its sculptures. The wall
farthest from the entrance (b) is divided into three horizontal parts, and
is almost a natural history display. Leaving aside a few extraordinarily well-
carved bulls, led by a young man carrying straw to feed them, and the
inscription 'the excellent cow' chiselled above the back of one of the
victims, I focused mostly on a series of several types of goats and gazelles
executed with sophisticated care, each with its name inscribed in well-
preserved hieroglyphs...

This series of desert quadrupeds ends with a man carrying in each
hand, holding them by their ears, two hares – a type of rodent which is
so common on monuments, but whose name the sculptor has sadly left
out. – An equally thrilling series is depicted on the second horizontal
section. This is a flock of birds in front of which are heron-like waders –
storks or cranes, followed by several types of geese, a sort of penguin,
and a turtledove whose name is crisply carved and which up to now I
thought referred only to a sort of martin. In Paris I will easily be able to
determine what birds they are, as all their hieroglyphs are available.

The entire wall (c) is taken up with a long bas-relief showing men
cutting the throats of bulls and slaughtering them. The flow and gestures
of their poses made me decide I had to possess an exact drawing of them;

above, there are several people carrying offerings. – On one of these walls (e) is a half-sculpted scene of two men milking a cow, and this is represented in hieroglyphs by exact signs for milk followed by an additional component on its closing sign, a vase, which shows milk falling into its neck. – Men working in the kitchen are drawn but weren't finished on the top part of the same wall. One of the cooks draws some sort of small ball from a deep vessel which he puts on the fire, while the other kindles the fire with a fan which he holds in his right hand.

The far end of the longest room (D), taken up by a bench, was decorated with one of those steles in the shape of repeating gates [false doors] which chase inside each other, and strewn with the titles of the deceased Menofre. On the left and on the right of this stele I found the two inscriptions from which I took the royal first and family name already mentioned.

Champollion to Champollion-Figeac – 5 October 1828,
from my camp in Sakkara

I wrote to you, my dearest friend, [from Cairo], where I stayed till the night of the 30th, and that all of us slept on the *maasch* in order to weigh anchor early in the morning to reach the site of Memphis. On 1 October we spent the night in front of the village of Massarah on the eastern bank of the Nile, and the next day, at six in the morning, we chased through the plain in order to visit the quarries I wanted to see, because Memphis, set on the opposite bank, right in their view, must have come spawned from their vast wings. This was an extremely rough journey, but I managed to see almost one by one all the grottos pierced into the slopes of Mount Tura...

Returning at night to our boats, like Greeks preparing their assault on Troy, but with more luck as we brought back some of our spoils, I ordered the *maasch* to set sail for Bedreschein, a village nestling a little way back on the western bank of the Nile. The next morning we left, early, for the gigantic forest of date-palms which covers the site of Memphis: passing Bedreschein, which is fifteen minutes inland, you can see that you are crossing ancient land belonging to an important city from the blocks of granite that are scattered across the plain, and those which still tear through sands that will not hold back from covering them for ever...

We saw the giant colossus which M. Caviglia excavated. I jumped at the opportunity to examine this monument of which I had heard so much, and I have to say that I was pleasantly surprised to find this magnificent piece of Egyptian sculpture. This colossus, which has lost part of its legs, is no less than thirty-five and a half feet long... [It] is by no means on its own: if I were to get extra money for wide-ranging excavations at Memphis I could respond in kind by populating the Louvre with statues of the richest materials and crucial importance. Do push this request and frame it with lots of loud indignant noises to convince the doubters...

On 4 October I camped at Sakkara as we have two pretty tents and one for the servants. Chosen in advance, seven or eight Bedouins serve every evening as our night watch and as our agents during the daytime: they are wonderful, if you treat them like humans.

Here at Sakkara I visited the plain of the mummies, the ancient cemetery of Memphis, studded with defiled tombs and pyramids. This place is, thanks to the rapacious brutality of dealers in antiquities, almost useless for studying: tombs decorated with statues are for the most part pillaged or filled in again after having been plundered. This wasteland is a ghastly series of sand mounds produced by digging and disturbing, showered with bones, skulls and debris of the ancient generations. Only two tombs galvanised our attention; they were the dividend of my decision to set up my camp on these bleak grounds. In one of these I found a series of birds stunningly sculpted on the walls, accompanied by their hieroglyphic names, five species of gazelles with their names, and a few domestic scenes such as milking cows and two cooks doing their handiwork.

From Champollion's diary

6 October 1828: I returned very early in the morning to the plateau of tombs in order to hand out to my draughtsmen the work to be done on the tomb of Menofre; after that I visited to the north of the Medarrag pyramid a tomb which must have been of supreme interest before modern thugs plundered it. This monument was excavated at the expense of Muhammad-Bey, Defterdar and a relative of the Pasha, known in Egypt for the cupidity and extreme cruelty of his character. This tomb, of a royal and legal scribe called Raases, only has sculpture on its architraves and pillars supporting the main chamber. All the walls of this room were once

covered with paintings of farming and domestic scenes; but today it is difficult to make out clearly the separate parts of this host of scenes. Coloured statues of offering-bearers and panoramas decorated a second room of this tomb. The majority of these exceptional bas-reliefs are the ones I saw as decoration in the house that Muhammad-Bey had build at enormous expense between Boulaq and old Cairo.

Returning to the camp, I was visited by Sheikh Muhammad, the agent of the Pasha in Sakkara, who is in charge of collecting taxes and exploiting the countryside for His Highness. I invited him to dinner, which he gracefully accepted.

7 October 1828: All morning from seven o'clock I stayed in my tent to deal with my European correspondence. At three a messenger from Mansour, dispatched with the promise of a bakshish of four thalers [Egyptian currency] to find an unspoilt site on the plateau of Sakkara, arrived to tell that his divining had been successful and he was only waiting for us before he would start digging. We mounted our donkeys and hurried into the desert as quickly as possible. When we got to the excavation site I saw at once that this was a peripheral and long-dug-over area. In no doubt that the Sakkariote was deceiving us, I gave him a piece of my mind, sending him back while sneering that he must think we were idiots. So I went to the large tomb which M. Jumel discovered and excavated. This stunning monument, consisting of several rooms and part of numerous huge excavations of several trenches, is with few exceptions illustrated with a number of chapters from the great Book of the Dead, which vastly diminishes the value of his research. Only the vault of the large room is worth paying some attention to. It was once covered in bas-reliefs of the ten hours of the day and the ten hours of the night, symbolised by women carrying a star on their heads. The ten daytime hours shelter under the left side of the vault, and the hours of the night to the right. — The idea of hour is expressed by a group of hieroglyphs in which you can recognise the Coptic word for 'hour'. And the star in this group stands for any division of time. All these hours have their own proper name in Egyptian. But only one of these names is still distinguish-able in Jumel's tomb. I am making a note of them in the hope that I will be able to complete the list in some tomb in Thebes.

The Great Sphinx

The bas-reliefs, which represent the adoration of other hours of the day and night by the deceased, were destroyed or removed a few years ago. I had one of the two large lists of offerings which cover two entire walls of this room copied... At night I returned to the camp, where Sheikh Muhammad of Sakkara was waiting; he honoured our dinner with his presence.

8 October 1828: Starting in the morning we packed our tents and seven or eight camels which had arrived from Sakkara were loaded with our luggage: twenty donkeys had come to carry helpers, masters and their servants. At seven in the morning we were on our way to the magnificent pyramids of Gizeh, which we had to see before leaving for Said. We climbed the plateau of the pyramids of Sakkara and crossed the entire plain of the mummies, leaving the Medarrag and the tomb of Menofre to our left. We went down again near the village of Abousir, the ancient burgh of Bousiris, where the men who are used to scale the pyramids live. Not far away from this village, which we left to our right, lie, on the heights of the Libyan plain, great dilapidated pyramids whose mass is nonetheless still enormously imposing. Seen from a certain angle, they

look like a huddle of three tall, rocky peaks, around whose soaring summits several types of birds of prey glide ceaselessly. The one that is closest to the farmland of the plain still has its rampart, made of colossal pieces of limestone, whose outline you can trace from a considerable distance. We made little progress for three hours, making several detours because the flood water was encroaching further on the Libyan mountains.

The ground here, covered with succulents and wispy grass, teemed with small toads, forming entire legions near the flooded waterline. After crossing a village, which was probably El-Haranyeh on the Commission's map, we arrived, harassed and exhausted, both our donkeys and we men, under the shadow of a few sycamores shooting up a short distance from the Great Sphinx.

Revived by a short rest, I ran to the monument which, despite the damage it has suffered, still gives a good impression of its sculpture. Its collar is completely gone, but Denon's observation on the softness, or rather morbidezza, of its lower lip is still spot on. I would like to have dug out the sands which cover the inscription of Tuthmosis IV carved on its chest; but the Arabs who had rushed down to throng around us from the heights that crown the pyramids said that it would take forty men and eight days to complete the work. I had to let it go, and I turned to the great pyramid.

Like me, anyone will be astounded by the fact that the impression this gigantic building makes diminishes the closer one gets to it. I felt as if I myself were being humiliated, gazing from fifty yards, without any surprise, at this building whose measurements alone give a sense of its immense size. It seems to lower itself the closer one gets, and the stones that make up its bulk seem no more than bricks of a minute size. You simply have to touch the building with your hands in order to feel at last the enormity of its materials and the enormity of the bulk that your eye is taking in. At a distance of ten yards, the intoxication takes hold again, and the great pyramid seems no more than a vulgar construction. You really regret having come close to it. The fresh intensity of the stone gives the impression of it being under construction, and not for a moment what you imagine when thinking of one of the most ancient monuments erected by man.

A view of the entire plain

We went to set up camp near the entrance of the causeway, which goes down to the great pyramid. There we were given a frugal lunch of dates, water and moist bread by the Bedouins. A little later our repast was made a little more sumptuous by the arrival of our camels. We unpacked some roast mutton, and brandy mixed with water was just the invigorating drink we needed. Immediately after lunch I let an Arab guide me to a sculpted and painted tomb aligned with the western façade of the second pyramid and in the middle of the first. I found very interesting sculptures, and I decided to have them painted so that they would form the centrepiece of our treasure trove of habits and customs. The same night we started copying them with immense care.

Our camp was set up on the eastern inclination of the plain of the pyramids, on the side which looks over Cairo. Only my tent was erected – the majority of my young people preferred to move their beds to a series of tombs carved out of the mountain flank, or to a house belonging to Caviglia, built at the expense of a tomb.

For unknown reasons there are no entries for 9 and 10 October about the sphinx in Champollion's diaries. However, Nestor L'hôte, one of the French draughtsmen of the expedition (whose permanent job was with Custom's & Excise, but who had been one of the first to write to Champollion about joining), wrote:

... The sphinx retains on its head, on the areas near its ears, the reddish-brown colour with which the Egyptians used to paint the skin colour of their countrymen. We debated the fact that the physiognomy of its face resembled that of an African. It does contain African features, but ultimately it is much less close to what one imagines to be typically black [traits] because one has to take into account its broken nose, whose absence seems to enforce that appearance.

We went back to see the sphinx. This monument, which we know to be a symbolic creature with a lion's body and a human head, is covered up to its shoulders in the sands across which one is able to trace its back and buttocks. Its neck and part of its breast are exposed as a result of the excavation which an Englishman undertook a few years ago.[4] It is said that under the sphinx lie the façade and entrance of a small temple or chapel in the shape of a monolithic altar. If this is true, and I have no reason to doubt it, the following [sketch] would show the shape of the complete monument. This arrangement tallies with the one the ancient [Egyptians] gave to their monuments of the same type and figure on the bas-reliefs of Thebes and in collections. The sphinx was the emblem of wisdom  joined with might, an absolutely essential attribute for the divinity accorded to the pharaohs, who were the embodiment of the deities on earth. The animal with a human head would have the characteristics of the god, that is to say the deified king...

Champollion to Champollion-Figeac – 8 October 1828,
from my camp at the feet of the pyramids of Gizeh

I moved my camp and penates [household gods] into the shade of the pyramids, leaving Sakkara yesterday in order to visit one of the wonders of the world, after seven camels and twenty donkeys carried us and our luggage across the desert which separates the southern pyramids from those of Gizeh, the most famous of all, and which I had to see before leaving for Upper Egypt... There is little to do here, and as soon as they have copied a few domestic scenes, carved in a neighbouring tomb by the second pyramid, I will return to our boats, which will take us to Gizeh, and we will be whisked by our sails towards Upper Egypt, my real destiny. Thebes lies there, and we will be reaching it late already.

Father Bibent, who has been totally useless, except for creating trouble among us, will leave the expedition. He will return to Europe: may God be on his side![5]

Except for a little travel tiredness, I am doing very well. So are you, I hope. I can only assume that that's the case, for I still haven't received anything from Europe.

— Adieu, my dear friend...

From Champollion's diary

20 October: I woke up at Minieh-ebn-Khasim, which the *maasch* had reached at midnight. As I had to do some shopping, I and one of the kavass [guards] joined a group of our people who were purchasing groceries. There is nothing worth observing in Minieh. It is a large village which looks like all the others... Hassan Aga, our senior kavass, who knows this area, brought us to a gigantic cotton mill which the Pasha established in a Louis XV-style building containing vast rooms filled with European machinery propelled by bulls and operated by men, children, women and young girls. They showed us cotton samples of rather well-made and extremely smooth cotton.

When all of us were back on board and the groceries had been purchased, I gave order to set sail for Saouadeh, where the *Description de l'Egypte* signalled that a number of antiquities would be waiting for us. Having gone ashore and sent for a local to guide us, we proceeded on foot to the Arab mountainside. There a sort of limestone breastwork presented itself, and our guide gestured that we should enter through a modest door, which looked as if it belonged to a tomb. Very soon we were in full sunlight again, and found ourselves in a small courtyard cut out of the rock and surrounded by a Doric triglyphed cornice with capitals that still carried the architrave, though the trunks, which were also carved out of rock, are smashed and no longer exist. It was a tomb in the Graeco-Roman style, and without doubt from a good era.

Under the northern portico several square cavities are driven into the rock, and they seem to have served as resting places for sarcophagi. Nowadays you can see the tombs of two Coptic priests. – Its eastern side, divided into two parts by a wall of dried brick, is today a church. Its priest did it proud, surrounded by women and children, as Saouadeh is the cemetery of the Copts in the surrounding area. We thanked M. Priest with eight piast[er]s and headed straight for the bank of the Nile, where I had told the *maasch* to pick us up. While we sat in the shade of a palm, waiting for the boat to reach the shore, the priest and a young vicar, grateful for our gift, came down to give us dried dates, which we readily accepted as they were excellent.

On board the *maasch*, I had it set sail for Zaouiet-el-Maietin, where we knew there were a number of Egyptian caves. Having covered the distance, we had lunch and left for the village straight away after coffee, in order to go to the foot of the Arab mountains to the south. Our guide made us cross a cemetery to which they still ship the dead of Minieh Muslims; the location of Zaouiet-el-Maietin (the orator of death) seems to have been an antique haven for the dead of the Heptanomide, a derivation of the name Hermopolite – I mean the cities of that name situated on the right bank of the river, such as Minieh (Ibcum). The left bank of the river, where the Nile herself bathes the toes of the mountains, is generally so barren that farming couldn't establish itself, with the result that they had to sacrifice it to crypts. This explains the cortège of Egyptian caverns which you will find here over a considerable distance, from Souadeh to beyond Antinoe. This motivation (the dryness of the soil) was so compelling that it seems to have negated the usual principle followed by the ancient Egyptians, of positioning their cemeteries on the western bank of the Nile, because of the equation between the idea of the underworld (the domicile of the dead) and the west (Amenti).

Solve problem: find the text with the name of [Pepi].[6]

21 October 1828: More inspection and drawing of tombs.

22 October 1828: I finished the compendium of a tomb which will be cited and, having nothing else to quarry from these old tombs, we returned to our *maasch*, which was anchored at the small village which takes its name, Koum-el-Ahmar, the red mound or tee, from the infinite number of

shards of Egyptian pottery that cover its entire slope from the Nile right up to the area of the deserted crypts. On this soil there are the remains of tiny dried-brick buildings dating back to a necropolis for ordinary people, while the rich had their tombs cut out of the massive limestone rock that wreathes the mountains.

While we were having dinner, I directed the boat to Beni-Hassan-el-Qadim, which we reached at midnight, spirited away, so to speak, by a gasp of wind as the *maasch* thrust through the current at a staggering speed.

23 October 1828: In the early morning a few of our young people went up to the grottoes that you can see in the mountainside, about a twenty-minute climb from where our boats were moored ...

24 October 1828: Staying at the crypts of Beni-Hassan-el-Qadim. Our day was divided up as follows: at sunrise we went up to the grottoes after a light breakfast. At noon lunch was brought up by our crew. – The tombs of Rotei, Menotheph and Nebotheph were our suite of dining rooms. The latter was particularly sensational because through the columns of its elegant portico we looked out over the partly lush and partly flooded plains of stunning Heptanomide. We collected an invaluable haul of tableaux of civil and domestic life, arts and professions, animals of all kinds, drills and costumes of the military caste, which I edited on location, almost always from the top of a ladder or in else in terribly uncomfortable poses. That is why my writing is so bad and the details so rough. After we had finished our business among the caverns of Beni-Hassan-el-Qadim, I terminated it by sailing to Beni-Hassan-el-Amar, where we arrived at eleven at night to anchor in a sideshoot of the Nile, in the middle of banks so thronged with palms that this area looked like a lake surrounded by plantations. The village is concealed behind the palm leaves; it is called Beni-Hassan-built-anew because it is a town that was rebuilt after the fire and sacking of Ben-Hassan – which is today nicknamed el-Qadim (the old) – on the orders of Ibrahim-Pacha when he wanted to exterminate a lair of brigands: the countryside is today as safe as the rest of Egypt.

6 November 1828: I ordered the *maasch* to be secured near the village in order to visit the bizarre monuments which are said to be up in the

mountains. So we left early in the morning, on foot, aiming to the east, to the Arab mountains and towards the cleft of a valley we saw before us. Quickly leaving the farmed countryside, we entered the desert, and, after a walk of twenty minutes, we were led to the right (north) of the ravine, or 'Ouadi', which runs from the valley; there were two fields with an unbelievable number of cat mummies, wrapped individually or a few together in simple matted fabric. – We returned to the road, towards the valley, walking on the left side of the Ouadi, and a little later we came to the entrance of the valley, which is extremely pretty, even though it is no more than a grand spectacle of drought and dryness. It is pure desert, walls of steep rocks, sieved on the right by numerous caves and wells carved out for mummies of cats and other quadrupeds rather than humans.

The mountain that forms the left side of the valley is also punctured with a number of caves, but these are of no interest whatsoever. Those on the left have no sculpture or inscriptions, except for the gate of a huge cat tomb which was decorated in the reign of Alexander IV, the son of Alexander the Great, that is 317 to 297 BC.

Negotiating a rock that juts out into the valley from these grottoes and from this side of the mountain, you travel only a short distance before you find a large cavity supported by eight largely destroyed pillars, decorated with painted sculptures and enormous hieroglyphic inscriptions. This is a temple dedicated to the goddess Pascht (Bubastis), decoration of which started during the reign of Tuthmosis IV and continued under his successor, Pharaoh Menephta, in whose name, here as elsewhere, they erased a figure which is still clearly visible in the last cartouche to the left of the frieze which decorates the western wall of the hallway. This grotto is none other than the cave of Diana (Bubastis), the name which ancient geographers gave to a location now occupied by one of the Ben-Hassans of today. The entire day was spent drawing the bas-reliefs and inscriptions of this sacred place, and unwrapping a horde of mummies of cats and dogs. I am convinced that all the holes and cavities made in this mountainside have no other goal than to be a depot for the conservation of the mummies of the animal dedicated to Bubastis, the cat, which you find here in such abundance. The back of the valley, between Ouadi and the cave of Pascht, is yet another necropolis of cats, arranged in beds and folded in matted fabric, in contrast to the cats of an elevated rank, which were placed in the temple of Alexander, whose corridors are lumbered with the mummified bones of this species of creature. We returned to the *maasch* only at nightfall, and after dinner we left for Antinoe, where we arrived at night.

Champollion to Champollion-Figeac — 5 November 1828, Beni-Hassan (below Minieh), at night

Man proposes, my dearest friend, and God disposes. I expected to be in Thebes on the 1st of November: and look, it is 5 November and I am still in Beni-Hassan. All this is the fault of wonderful Jomard, who, in describing the cave tombs of this area, gave such a flimsy idea of them with his tiny, inexact drawings, and his even more questionable phrases, that I counted on dealing with these grottoes in a day; but they have devoured fifteen of them without my feeling in the slightest that they have wasted my time. I should, in any case, return to where I left off.

My last letter was dated from the great pyramids, where I camped for three days, though not for those colossal hulks which make so little impression the closer one gets, but for the inspection and filleting of the funerary tombs carved into the mountain walls. One of them, belonging to a certain Eimai, threw up a series of bas-reliefs that were extremely exciting in terms of what we know of the arts and crafts of ancient Egypt, and I must give very special care to the investigation of this type of monument, which is as much a part of history as the panoramic battle scenes of the palaces in Thebes, which I haven't yet seen, but which fill me with dreams every night. I found several tombs of the princes and grand dignitaries around the pyramids, but few inscriptions of very great interest...

We sailed for Lower Egypt, but it wasn't until 20 October, having survived the crushing boredom of placid water and a complete absence of northerly wind, that we arrived in Minieh, which I made everyone leave immediately, after a visit to a cotton mill operated with European machines and after some purchases of essentials. We headed towards Saouadeh to see a Greek cave with a Doric order, which is not badly described by Jomard...

In order to check out what was there, some of our young people had left at the crack of dawn for the nearby grottoes, reporting back to me that absolutely nothing at all was there, as all the paintings had been almost completely defaced. I nevertheless went up at sunrise to visit their caves, and I was pleasantly surprised to find a staggering series of paintings which were models of perfection in even their smallest details, if you wetted them with a sponge and wiped away the crust of fine dust that covered them. We got to work immediately, and by the grace of our ladders and the glorious sponge, the most exquisite triumph that human talent might produce laid itself open to our eyes in a series of murals that couldn't be more thrilling, all dealing with ordinary life, crafts and professions, and, a novelty, with the military classes. In the first two caves my catch was breathtaking, and this while an even richer prize was waiting for me in the two tombs farther to the north; these two caves, whose architecture and a few details of the interior are botched in Jomard['s drawing], are curious (as are several smaller neighbouring caverns) in that the doorway of the tomb is preceded by a carved portico touching the rock, and is formed by columns which look to be in the Greek Doric style of Sicily or Italy, to the point that you will be deceived by them at first glance. They are fluted, with a rounded base, and practically all of elegant proportions. The interior of the two farther caves was, or rather is, still supported by similar columns: we all agreed that we had discovered the original of the ancient Doric style, and I will affirm this without a hint of hesitation in putting forward my opinion, like Jomard when applying [the terms] Corinthian and Ionic to buildings from the time of the emperors, because these two caves, more heavenly than any, are dated and belong to the reign of Osortasen [Senusret I], the second king of the twenty-third (Tanite) dynasty, and so go back to the ninth century BC.[7] I will add to this that the more gorgeous of the two porticoes, still intact and belonging to the tomb of Nebothph [Khnumhotep II, no. 3], a chief administrator of the eastern territories of Heptanomide, is made up of columns without a base, like at Paestum and in all the magnificent Greek Doric temples.

The paintings of the tomb of Nebothph are really gouaches, all finesse and illustrative poise, which is highly remarkable: they are the most brilliant I have seen to date. The animals, mammals, birds and fish are painted with such delicacy and realism that the copies I made of them are like the coloured engravings of today's accomplished works of natural history: we will need the full complement of the fourteen witnesses who saw them to convince people in Europe of the accuracy of our drawings,

View from Beni-Hassan's proto-Doric columns

which couldn't be more exact.

In this cave I also found a scene of the greatest importance. It shows fifteen prisoners, men, women or children, taken hostage by one of the sons of Nebothph and presented to this chief by a royal scribe, who at the same time hands him a leaf of papyrus on which the date of the capture is set out, as well as the number of prisoners, which was thirty-seven. These large and very singular-looking captives, mostly with aquiline noses, were white as compared with the Egyptians, as their bodies were painted in a yellowish-red tint in order to imitate what we would call skin colour. The men and women are dressed in rich delicate weaves, painted (particularly on the women) as if they were tunics, like those of Greek ladies on vases of the old style: the tunic, hairstyle and shoes of the female captives of Beni-Hassan resemble all those of the Greeks on the antique vases, and I recognised on one of their robes the waved ornamentation that is so typical of the adjective 'Greek', which is coloured in red, blue and black and drawn vertically. These details will tickle the curiosity and ignite the interest of our archaeologists and that of our friend Dubois, who I wish today more than ever were here by my side, as our knowledge of the development of art in Egypt is finding utterly authentic evidence. The male prisoners, with their pointed beards, are armed with bows and lances, and one of them holds in his hand a Greek lyre. Are these Greeks? I do strongly believe they are, but more like Ionian Greeks, or a people from Asia Minor, neighbours of the Ionian Greeks, who shared their customs and manners; Greeks of the ninth century BC, realistically portrayed by Egyptian hands. I had this long scene copied with Jansenist rigour; there isn't a stroke of paint which isn't in the original.

The fifteen days in Beni-Hassan were monotonous but productive. At sunrise we would go up to the caves for drawing, colouring and writing, sacrificing at most an hour to a modest lunch, which was brought to us from the boats, sitting on the sand in the grand room of the hypogean from which, through primitive Doric columns, we overlooked the over-whelming plains of Heptanomide. Only the setting sun, quite a spectacle in this area, sounded our retreat: we would go back to the boat for supper, sleep and a repeat performance the next morning.

This tomb life has resulted in a portfolio of perfectly executed drawings of absolute accuracy which already exceeds the three hundred mark. I dare say that even with no more than these riches my voyage to

View of the tomb (in *l'Égypte ancienne*, 1839, by Champollion-Figeac)

Egypt is already more complete and productive than all of the papers of the Commission, including those on architecture, with which I am not concerned except in places that are unknown or haven't yet been visited. Here, then, a little sketch of my conquests: this summary is divided by subject in alphabetical order, as in my travel portfolio, so as to have at my fingertips all the drawings that have been done and to be able to compare them with new monuments of the same type.

1. Agriculture, all with explanatory hieroglyphics, as with the scenes below...

2. Arts and crafts...

3. Military caste. Education of the military classes and all their gymnastic exercises, in more than two hundred images which capture the methods and means two skilful warriors might have deployed while attacking, defending, retreating, advancing, standing, pushing down, etc.; you will be able to judge from this whether Egyptian art only portrayed people in profile, legs together and arms clinging to their hips. I have in particular copied a peculiar series of nude soldiers; and over sixty figures representing soldiers of all armies and ranks, guerrilla warfare, the tortoise formation and ram, military expeditions, a bat-

tleground, and the preparations for a military meal; and moreover the manufacture of lances, javelins, bows, arrows, maces, battle-axes, etc.
4. Music, song and dance...
5. Livestock...
6. Portraits of kings... A foundation stone for an iconographic gallery which will contain the portraits of the Egyptian kings and grand dignitaries. This portfolio will be completed in Thebes.
7. Sports, games and entertainment. You will recognise mora, drawing straws, blindfolding, mail, pegs stuck in the ground, various hearty sports: wild-animal hunts, a scene of a large desert hunt featuring fifteen to twenty mammals in which the game is either carried dead or taken alive; several tableaux show hunting birds with a net; one of these is very large and gouached with all the colour and bustle of the original; finally, enlarged drawings of various bird traps; these hunt accessories are painted on their own in some caves...
8. Private law. I grouped some fifteen pictures of bas-reliefs showing offences committed by servants under this title ...

6 November 1828, Antinoe-el-Tell

These are my commentaries which I edited on location: almost all of them poorly written or badly drawn legends with respect to their shape (but always accurate), as they were made from the top of a ladder and in rather unpleasant positions. – When our work ended at night, I ordered the boat to go to Beni-Hassan-el-Amar, where we arrived in the middle of the night.

From 8 November 1828, before Monfalouth

9. Private life...
10. Historical monuments...
11. Religious monuments...
12. Travel by boat...

These are up to now my conquests and spoils. It's a good start. I hope to complete and steadily increase these various groups, as I have not, so to speak, yet seen any Egyptian monument; the great buildings won't really start until Abydos, and I won't be there for another ten days.

With a lump in my throat I slipped past Aschmounein, mourning its splendid portico which the thugs recently sacked. Yesterday, Antinoe was little more than a boneyard; all its buildings had only very recently been disembowelled, and no more remains other than a few granite colonnades which Egypt's Visigoths weren't been able to sink their teeth into.

I was comforted a little about the loss of these landmarks by the discovery of one extremely interesting example which no one has ever mentioned, not even Jomard, who spent a long time in this area. We saw in a neglected valley in the Arab mountainside, opposite Beni-Hassan-el-Amar, a little temple chiselled out of the rock whose decoration had been started by Tuthmosis IV and was continued by the Mandouei of the eighteenth dynasty. The temple, covered in coloured bas-reliefs, is dedicated to the goddess Pascht or Pepascht [Bastet]... the Diana of the Romans [Bubastis of the Greeks]. Geographers, Jomard himself included, put the *speos-artemidos* (Diana's grotto) at Beni-Hassan, and they are right, because I just found the temple carved out of the rock (the speos of the goddess)... In front of the temple, buried in the sand, is a reef of cat mummies rolled in mats and mixed with a few dogs; farther on, between the valley and the Nile in a desert plain, are two enormous depots of wrapped-up mummies of cats covered by two feet of sand.

Tonight I will arrive in Siouth (Lycopolis), and tomorrow I will give this letter to the local authorities so that they can send it to Cairo, from there to Alexandria, and from there at last to Europe; may they have more luck than yours! I will say testily that I haven't seen a word from either you or my wife since leaving Toulon; imagine my disappointment, as Rosellini received a bunch in the last few days and not even a shadow of one for me. I don't know what cretinous dervish is fingering my correspondence but I am lost to find reasons for this delay.[8] – My health is holding out, and I hope that the excellent Theban air will ensure the continuation of this wellbeing. Do give me news about my wife, who I will write to from Thebes. My regards to our great M. Dacier, my love to all his friends and to all of those who still remember me. Embrace my friends Dubois, Duguet and Teuillet. I am as always and for ever entirely yours with my heart and soul. Adieu.

From Champollion's diary

7 November 1828: When we woke up, we hurried ashore to get past the dotted palms of the village of Chaikh-Abade, and rush to the ruins of Antinoe. Nowadays it is no more than a series of heaps of rubble sheathed with pottery shards of all kinds... I bought a head of Ramesses the Great for the modest sum of one piast[ers] (seven sous), including transport of

this small hulk to my *maasch*. My dragoman arranged this bargain; I would have been too ashamed to agree to it. I paid the carriage fee on top of the price given for the object...

Towards sunset I stopped at El-Tell, the destroyed village whose plan and description are noted by the Commission, but which the Englishman Wilkinson believes he discovered and engraved for the first time... 9 We inspected the whole site of the village, whose main roads, long and wide, are easily made out. The construction, which Jomard believes was once a granary, seemed to me clearly to have been the foundation of a religious building, the base of a temple with two pylons and two courtyards of dried brick, in short a temple built of sandstone. What is left of this stone, mixed with black and pink granite, covers an extremely large area in the shape of a square aligned with the two pylons. I myself found in the middle of this detritus an alabaster fragment, beautifully polished, which belonged to an Egyptian statue.

We left El-Tell the same night, and very early in the morning of 8 November we were in front of Tarout-es-Scherif. Later in the morning we went by the long and dangerous mountainside of Djebel-Aboufeda, perforated with grottoes, which I put down for a visit upon our return from the Second Cataract, in order not to let the right season for going up the Nile slip by. It was here, in front of this cursed mountain, that, while the *Athyr* was fastened to the *Isis* in full sail in order to drop off Messrs Duchesne, Lehoux and Bertin for lunch, M. Bertin fell into the Nile, whose current is awesome at this point. Only his great presence of mind saved his life, and his talent for swimming, which made him pluck from the air a rope thrown from the boat of our kavass [guards]. This catastrophe, which happened before my eyes, made me sick with apprehension: it would have been ghastly for me to return to France with a member missing and to have lost him in such an accident.

In the afternoon we went by Monfalouth (the scenery of wild Egyptian donkeys) and next we grounded before Mangabad (the vase factory of the Copts). Having set ourselves free with great difficulty, we moved on for a few miles and then spent part of the night very near Osiouth [Assiut].

9 November 1828: We woke up in the morning before the small harbour of Osiouth, the [Saout] of the Egyptians and Lycopolis of the Greeks. I wanted to see the caves and tombs of this ancient city, and we decided

to stay here for the entire day. Donkeys were ordered to bring us to the city, which is about twenty minutes away from the river...

The tombs of Lycopolis seem to have been much more splendid than the tombs of Heptanomide. They are certainly on a more colossal scale, though all destroyed, and you will see only the skeletons of tombs, whose surfaces are all made of sandstone, once carved and now either stripped by ungodly hands or mutilated by childish ones. I had only a rank of soldiers on the south wall of the main tomb copied. – On our way to the caves, they guided us through the cemetery of modern Osiouth, which stretches itself out over the final incline of the mountain, whose flanks billet so many ancient Egyptian mummies. This cemetery, made up of pretty little structures completely bleached by the sun, looks like a charming Lilliputian village. On our return, I went to the village for a long bath where, after a little rest which we greatly needed after climbing the mountain on foot, either in a long robe or Mameluke dress, they served a dinner of small chunks of mutton stuffed in a hot paté-like *godiveau* [pastry], a bowl of sour milk to ladle over the meat, and succulent watermelon. The pseudo-*godiveaux* were delicious, and we sang their praises to the point of ordering a second helping. After dinner we paid a visit to the Bey, the factotum of Scherif-Bey-Kiaya, for whom Habib-Effendi had given us letters of introduction, which we passed on to his lieutenant. We went back to the *maasch*, where we went to sleep.

10 November 1828: Leaving Osiouth in the morning, we arrived at the height of the large town of El-Qatui, which is called Matia on the Commission's map, and we had to make a stop-over there as all of sudden the wind ceased to blow. Here my Barbar Muhammad looked up his father, who manufactures beer, which he wanted to treat me to, but of which I did not drink a sip. At one we sailed off again, only to stop well before nightfall at some distance from Qauou-el-Kebir. – We went by this ancient site of Antaepolis without going ashore because it was easy to see that not a scrap was left of the handsome portico described by the Commission. Three years ago, the Nile swallowed up this beautiful monument, and we glided over its shrouded debris on the bottom of the river. We spent the day at Scheik-el-Haridi, famous for Paul Lucas's demon Asmodeus.[10] We had to try to make the best of a few gusts of wind and, as we had lost all hope of reaching Akhmin safely because of nightfall, we

moored the *maasch* at a village that will remain nameless to spend the night and repair the *Isis*, in whose hull a big hole had opened up. – After dinner, Lenormand, L'hôte, Rosellini and a few others joined a musical soirée given by Muhammad-Bey, the Mamour of Said, whose parlous state of health had caused him to build a house near the village of Saouadgi, where the air is excellent. I declined the invitation under the pretext of being exhausted, disregarding the name and rank of this energetic Amphitryon. Those who did attend his party returned chanting praise of the light-hearted manners and care of this Turkish chief. The next morning brought us six sheep, 150 chickens, 200 melons or watermelons, etc., etc., as a present from the Bey: not wanting to seem lacking in grace, we sent him a case of St George's wine, in the full knowledge that this would be well received, as my companions had been astounded by the quantities of spirits and wine he had drunk during the dinner he had given them at one in the morning. They told me that he would be coming himself; I delayed our departure by an hour, but, as he didn't show up, ignoring again the importance of this person, whose playfulness and Bacchic tastes were all we knew about him, decided to set sail (on 12 December) for Akhmin, where we arrived after an hour's sailing; the crew was divided in two, one half executing the manoeuvres, the other scooping the water out of the hull, as there were no workers in Saouadgi who were able to close the hole in our *maasch*. Going ashore at Akhmin, the old Panoplis, we walked to the city, cutting through the town and seeing *en passant* two pretty mosques, to head north, where the Commission noted a number of ruined temples. They were in virtually the same state in which M. Saint-Genis saw them.

To the north, and in a shallow filled by flood waters, are a number of large sandstone formations without sculptures, except for one block in the middle of the basin which shows on one of its façades a sculpted relief of a king in an adoration scene. I sent for four long boards from the *maasch* to make flying bridges from one formation to the next, in order to get right up to the carved stone and discover the royal legend and the name of the adored deity. This operation succeeded with the aid of the boards and three of our sailors, who threw themselves nude into the water in order to fix and move the bridges. A sizeable throng of people framed the banks of the lake, along which palms and very tufty trees were draped. Taken all together, it was rather an operatic spectacle as observed from the sculptured hulk, where I had effortlessly arrived. There I discovered that the worshipping king was Ptolemaeus Alexander, and that the subject of his adoration was Amen-Hor-Amon-Generation, who the Greeks call Pan, and whose statue is accurately described by Etienne de Byzance, re Panopolis. – This bas-relief is ample reason to continue contemplating the god worshipped in that city, his rank and appearance...

Returning to the *maasch*, I found the cangia [vessel], horse, son, seraph and musicians of Muhammad-Bey, sent by their master in pursuit of us, with a very polite letter articulating his mortification and disappointment that I had left without waiting for his visit, that he had agreed with my companions that he would come and meet me in the morning, that we would have lunch with him and spend a day with entertainments, and that after dinner we would take leave of each other. His envoys insisted that we return to Saouadgi, and that the Bey would be unwell if we refused. After some toing and froing and long indecision, I decided to surrender to the pleas of the seraph and his cacheff [local governor], and told the *reis* to return to Saouadgi as soon as the *Isis* was in full repair. *En route*, we put on our military Mameluke costumes. The Bey's cangia went ahead of us: he announced our imminent arrival, and, setting foot on the riverbank, I found the Bey's staff headed by his major-domo, who showed me the way to the apartments of the Bey. He was in his harem, and begged us to wait in his divan, where we were served strong pipes and sugared coffee, a kindness which several of us thought exceedingly friendly.

When he arrived, Muhammad soon assumed, after a lively round of compliments between him and me, a teasing tone, and chided us good-naturedly for our departure in the morning. I informed him of our permissions, as in the interval we had heard that we would have to talk to one of the most important chiefs of Upper Egypt. A second later, one of our servants carried in a cabinet with a crystal serving tray as a token of our appreciation for his great help.

The conversation soon resumed its air of pleasantries and, during the three hours which went by before dinner, our pipes were filled at least six times, and bottles with brandy went round every ten minutes. I was determined only to wet my lips with this treacherous liqueur. But nothing of the sort applied to our Amphitryon, who downed his glasses filled to the brim like a man who has followed this career for forty years; the Bey is quite old but all the same fairly tough, despite a sort of asthma which flourishes under his abuse of brandy. He sent for two Greek house musicians, who played and sang Turkish songs, one on something like an eight-string theorbo and the other on a twenty-four-string violin. The first one was about seventy, and I will leave to your imagination what honeyed voice we heard. This junior was trumped by an Arab singer with a white beard who we thought was at least eighty. The ancient swan took off and crooned several Arab lamentsat full steam and with all his might .

Our Armenian dragoman, who lived in Constantinople for a long time and was a fresh arrival from the Turkish capital, wanted to show off his talent, and, grabbing his flute, which he plays well, bowled over the Bey and his people with a few good European pieces, but most of all by playing more than superbly a very slow and extremely melancholic Turkish air. Next the flute, theorbo and violin joined together for a concert that wasn't at all bad. The two Greek musicians spontaneously started to play the tune of 'Marlborough Goes off to War', which our young people had sung at supper last night to the delight of the Turkish and Arab congregation. This song amused everyone, winners and losers, Turks and Arabs. The Marseillaise also found a perfect reception, and they loved the chorus of *Masaniello*, the new Paris opera: 'Amis, la matinée est belle!'

At last supper was served. I was asked to wash, as were my travel companions: I wiped my hands with an embroidered serviette of coloured silk; each had his own for this cleansing operation. As we sat on the edges of the divan, our legs hanging down to create more space, two small tables or guéridons were laid on which some twenty different dishes were placed in succession, not counting the anchovies, salads and other restoratives which remained on the table throughout and in the centre of which the more substantial courses were put. These plates were modest, except for the first one, a small, completely stuffed sheep that tasted excellent. Dinner was concluded with melons and watermelons. I have never eaten such exquisite melon. Wine circulated in small quantities but frequently, and the Bey, a true philosopher, never refuses a glass and always hands it back emptied.

I proposed a toast to the King of France, the Pasha and Ibrahim-Pacha: all this was enthusiastically received by Muhammad, who swore on his grand scimitar that the friendship between France, the Sultan and Egypt was so true that it could never end. I received nothing but his protestations of affection. He laid on a show of sailor acrobatics, and his musicians accompanied dancers of various types, first Arab ones, then by contrast Almehs, followed by Turkish dances and ending with Greek ones. These thrilled us beyond anything else: they reminded me of the Dedalus of the Athenians. At one in the morning we took our leave from the Bey at last. That evening he had given me a collar with a red jasper intaglio of Helios and Selene's busts, of Greek make, though rather crude.

Having left Saouadgi very early on, we sailed by Akhmin, where we stopped for fifteen minutes to take on board yet more presents from Muhammad-Aga: from there we set sail for Menschief-el-Neide, where ancient Ptolemaos is supposed to have been. After lunch we sped past a mountainside, escarped and trimmed with caves, called Djebel-el-Asserat, and it was there, while passing the mountain and the islands called Gheziret-Benou-Qas, that we saw crocodiles for the first time; I saw four of them, three of which were very large, grouped on the sand and attended by a black-and-white bird called the Dominican. This is perhaps the trochilus. A little later we went ashore at Girge, only recently the capital of Upper Egypt, though it has lost all its importance: it is half deserted. On shore we were welcomed by the honourable M. Piccinini from Lucca, who is in charge of M. d'Anastazy's excavations and, following the orders of his master, had come to put himself at our disposal. We made a visit to Father Davielle di Procida, at the [Capuchins'] convent of the Propaganda. This Neapolitan is the father superior of five convents: of Tahta, Akhmin, Girge, Fardjiouth and Nagade, in whose convents there are one or at most two clerics. There is only one in Girge, and he is a Copt taught by the Propaganda. Intrigued to know how Coptic was read in Egypt, I asked the father to recite a page from his missal, which he went to look for with good grace. I realised immediately that he was uncertain of the letters and that he often mistook 'f's for 'n's. We left the fathers somewhat late, beckoned by our supper, which was followed by dance and songs of the Girge Almehs.

Champollion to Champollion-Figeac – 24 November 1828,
Thebes[Dendera]

My last letter, my dear friend, dated from Beni-Hassan, and terminating descending down the Nile while concluding at Osiouth, must have left on the 10th or 12th of this month... May God will them to arrive more promptly than the ones which were addressed to me by you as. since my departure from France. I didn't even get one! – Not even the ones Pariset took with him and which he undoubtedly left at the French consulate. Only yesterday, and from the mouth of a British naval captain who was venting his spleen regarding Egypt, did I hear that Pariset had also arrived here and that he is at the moment in Cairo. I am Egypt's captive – she is my be-all, and I seek from her my consolations as I don't receive any from Europe. It isn't the rest of you I am accusing – it is beyond any doubt that you are thinking of me, and are writing often…. but your kind thoughts aren't reaching me. If this were otherwise, and I could be at rest about the good health of everyone I cherish, I would be the happiest of men: as at last I am at the heart of ancient Egypt and its most supreme wonders are only a few yards away from me. – Here is first of all the rest of my itinerary.

On 10 November I left Osiouth after having visited the caverns which are impeccably described by Jollois and Devilliers, whose extreme precision I admire daily. On the 11th, in the morning, we went to Qauo-el-Kebir (Antaeopolis) and my *maasch* hurried over the site of the temple which the Nile has gobbled up completely without leaving the slightest souvenir. A few ruins (of Panopolis) at Akhmin were visited by me on the 12th, and I was rather exhilarated to discover a carved block giving me the date of the temple, which belongs to Ptolemaeus Philopater, and the image of Pan, who is none other than Amon-Generator, as I have argued before.

The following afternoon and night we spent at a feast, ball, acrobatics and concert, with one of the commanders of Upper Egypt, Mohammed-Aga, who sent his cangia, people and horse to bring me and my companions to Saouadgi, which I had left in the morning and to which I had to go back in order not to be disrespectful towards this good man, a bon vivant and excellent companion who raises his glass with skill and breathes nothing but happiness and pleasures…

We left on the morning of the 13th, weighed down by the gifts of this fine Ottoman. In the afternoon, we went by Ptolemais, where nothing remarkable remains. At four, spiriting past the Djebel-el-Asserat, we saw the first crocodiles: there were four of them, sleeping on a sandbank, a flock of birds whirling around them. I have no idea whether among them was the trochilus [humming bird] of our friend Geoffroy-Saint-Hilaire [one of Napoleon's savants]. A little later we left for Girge. The wind was weak on the 15th and we made little headway. But our new friends the crocodiles seemed to want to compensate us for it; I counted twenty-one huddled on the same island, and a salute of gunshots, fired from quite near by, resulted in no more than the dispersal of this devilish conclave. They threw themselves into the Nile, and we lost fifteen minutes setting loose our *maasch*, which had come too close to the sandbank.

On the evening of the 16th we at last arrived in Dendera. The moonlight was sparklingly clear and we were but an hour away from the temples: could we resist the temptation? Even the coldest fish would have said yes![iii] Supper and immediate departure were arranged in a moment: alone and without guides, but armed to the teeth, we started crossing the fields, assuming that the temples were in a beeline from our *maasch*. So we strode on for an hour and a half, singing marches from the most recent operas, without finding anything. At last we came across a man; we called out for him and, taking us for Bedouins, he decamped as fast as he could, for, dressed like orientals and wearing a wide white burnous with a hood, we looked, to Egyptians, like a tribe of nomads, while without any hesitation a European would have taken us for a group of Chartreuse guerrilla monks, armed with guns, sabres and pistols.

The fugitive was brought before me and, placing him between four people and a corporal, I ordered him to lead us to the temples. This poor devil, who was at first little at ease, showed us the right way and ended up walking without duress: skinny, dried out, black, covered in old rags, he was a walking mummy, but he was an excellent guide and we treated him as such. At last the temples heaved into view. I won't try to describe the impression that the great propylon made on us, and above all the portico of the grand temple. It is quite possible to survey it, but to translate the idea of it, that is inconceivable. It is a unity of grace and majesty of the highest order. We stayed there in ecstasy for two hours, running down the great halls with our poor torches, trying to read the external inscriptions in the moonlight. We didn't return to the *maasch* until three in the morning, only to go back to the temples at seven o'clock. There we spent all day of the 17th. What was spectacular in the brightness of the moon was even more so when the rays of the sunlight chiselled out all the details. I saw that I had before me a masterpiece of architecture covered with sculpture in a poor style. I disagree with the Commission, the bas-reliefs of Dendera are detestable and they couldn't be anything else: they are from a time of decadence. Sculpture was already affected, but its architecture, which is less subject to shifts as it is an art of proportions, continued to be worthy of the gods of Egypt and the admiration of the ages. These are the periods of its decorations: the most ancient part is the external wall, on the extremity of the temple where the colossal sculptures of Cleopatra and her son Ptolemaeus-Caesar can be found. The upper bas-reliefs are from the time of Emperor Augustus, as are the external walls lateral to the naos, with the exception of a few small sections which date back to Nero. The pronaos is completely covered with the imperial legends of Tiberius, Caius [Caligula], Claudius and Nero, but on the entire inside of the naos, as well as the chambers and buildings on the terrace of the temple, there isn't one sculpted cartouche: all are empty and none of them were erased. The most amusing of all this, *risum teneatis, amici!* [don't laugh], is that the part of the famous circular zodiac with the cartouche is still in situ, and that, like the rest of the interior of the temple, it is empty and has never been touched by the tapping of chisel. It was the members of the Commission who added the word 'Autocrator', thinking that they had forgotten to draw the legend which never existed: that is called handing over the whip to be flogged. Other than that, Jomard shouldn't jump for joy because the cartouche of the zodiac is empty and contains no name; the carvings of this apartment, like those on the inside of the temple, are nauseating, most awful in style, and cannot go back further than Trajan or Anthony [Antoninus Pius]. They look like those on the south-eastern propylon, which is by this last emperor and which, being dedicated to Isis, lead to the temple of this goddess, located behind the great temple which — contrary to the Commission — is the temple of Hathor (Venus), as the thousand and one dedications with which it is powdered say, and not the temple of Isis. The great propylon is plastered with images of the Emperors Domitian and Trajan. As for Typhonium, it was decorated under Trajan, Hadrian and Antoninus Pius.

The Dendera Zodiac was one of the most controversial debating points of the early nineteenth century while hieroglyphs continued to be undecipherable. Zodiacs were seen as a new exciting key, not only to the chronology of ancient Egypt but also to that of the creation of the world, as it was thought that the position of the stars might give a clue to their

The Dendera Zodiac

chronology. Jomard, for example, was one of the scientists who claimed that the Zodiac was much older than the 6,000 years which the bible put forward as the time of creation. In January 1821 Jean Baptiste Lelorrain (commissioned by the collector Sébastian Saulnier) cut the stone from the ceiling of the Temple of Hathor in three weeks. He was operating in secrecy because Bernardino Drovetti and Henry Salt had tacitly designated the western bank as British. In January 1822 the Zodiac was put on display in Paris where people queued for hours to see it. Champollion thought the Zodiac was not much older than the Roman period. He used the Zodiac help him understand the use of determinants better. He was, however, outraged about the fact that it had been sawn from the temple ceiling.

Extract from an anonymous letter which Champollion wrote in October 1821 to the Revue encyclopédique: 'We applaud the patriotic sentiments that decreed this audacious project of our two compatriots, which was so skilfully and triumphantly brought to an end. France has done so much towards unveiling the antiquities of Egypt that it has a strong claim to some of its most precious works; she should likewise take pleasure in being able to show foreigners a monument which compensates for the loss of the Rosetta Stone and the other pieces which the Commission of Egypt had gathered with so much care. While congratulating Messrs. Saulnier and Lelorrain with the fact that the circular zodiac of the temple of Dendera will be transported from the banks of the Nile to the shores of the Seine, and not those of the Thames, we would nonetheless like to offer a defence for the expression of some regret that the this magnificent temple was dispossessed of one of its most beautiful ornaments; we ask ourselves whether our ardent compatriots weren't suffering from an excess of otherwise noble and generous sentiments. Absorbed by the desire to honour their fatherland, did they consider all the consequences of their undertaking? Here we are not dealing with statues, detached stones, obelisks even, or so many other monoliths which conquerors and visitors have taken from Egypt over twenty-three centuries. This is an exceptional building, intact until now, whose demolition of sorts has now begun. Where Persians, Greeks, Romans or Arabs have disfigured the temples of Egypt, we are far from able to excuse them; but we must take heed of either blind fanaticism or the terrible scourge of war. Why imitate them in peacetime? Would we in France dare to take Lord Elgin's example as our lead? Emphatically, no...'

The morning of the 18th I left the *maasch* and hurried to visit the ruins of Coptos (Kefth); nothing is left in one piece. The temples were destroyed by the Christians, who used the materials to build a large church on the ruins and in which you will find numerous portions of Egyptian bas-reliefs. I recognised the royal cartouches of Nectanebo, Augustus, Claudius and Trajan, and farther on a few stones of a small building erected under the Ptolemies. Hence the village of Coptos consists of few monuments of a high antiquity, judging by what is presently visible on the surface.

The ruins of Qous (Apollinopolis parva), which I reached the next morning of the 19th, were much more interesting, even though of its antiquities only a half-buried propylon has survived. This propylon is dedicated to the god Aroeris, sculpted on all façades, whose images are adored on the façade looking out over the Nile, that is the most important side, and were carved earliest by Cleopatra Cocce, who has the surname the-goddess-Philometor, and her son Soter II, who also styles himself Philometor. Yet the façade on the backside of the propylon, the one which faces the temple, covered with reliefs and finished with great finesse, shows all over the legends of Ptolemaeus Alexander in all letters, which proves that his death followed his mother's over a considerable time. He also assumed the surname Philometer...

Late in the morning of 20 November, bored with teasing us for two days and banning us from entering the sanctuary, the wind finally consented to letting me escape to Thebes! This name already loomed very large in my mind: but it has become colossal ever since I went through the ruins of this capital city, this mother of all cities. For four entire days I encountered surprise after surprise. On the first tour I visited the palace of Kourna, the colossus of the Memnonium [Ramesseum] and the supposed tomb of Osymandyas, which is covered with nothing else but the cartouches of Ramesses the Great and of two of his successors. The name of this palace is written on all its sides: the Egyptians called it the Rhameseion in the same way that they called the Memnonium 'Amenopheum', and the palace of Kourna 'Mandoueion'. The supposed colossus of Osymandyas is an attractive colossus of Ramesses the Great.

The second day was entirely taken up with Medinet-Habu, the surprising union of buildings where I found the propylons of Antinous, Hadrian and the Ptolemies, a building by Nectanebo, another by the Ethiopian Tharaca, a small palace of Tuthmosis III (Moeris), and finally the enormous and gigantic palace of Ramesses-Meiamoun [Ramesses III] covered with historical bas-reliefs.

On the third day, I went to see the old Theban kings in their mausoleums, or rather their palace chiselled from the mountain at Biban-el-Molouk [Valley of the Kings]. From morning till evening, I allowed myself to roam through the enfilades of apartments sheathed in sculptures and paintings which are mostly astonishingly fresh. There, on the go, I learned things which are of huge interest to history. I saw the tomb of a king whose image and cartouche had been defaced from top to toe, except for the sections with images of the queen his mother, and those of his wife, which were meticuloulsy avoided, as were their legends. He was undoubtedly a king who was condemned after his death. I also saw a second one of a king from one of the most ancient eras being impudently trespassed upon by a king of the nineteenth dynasty, who had all old cartouches resurfaced with stucco in order to insert his own and thus usurp the bas-reliefs and inscriptions traced for one of his predecessors. One has to praise, though, this intruder for the fact that he had a second room carved out in which to rest his sarcophagus in order not to disturb his ancestor. With the exception of that one, all the others belong to the kings of the eighteenth and nineteenth or twentieth dynasties [about 1500 B.C. − 1000 BC]: but neither the tomb of Sesostris, nor the tomb of Moeris, is there. I won't even talk to you about the series of small temples and structures dispersed in the middle of these magnificent things…

The fourth day (yesterday, the 23rd) I left the left bank in order to visit the eastern side of Thebes. I saw first of all Luxor, a vast palace, ushered in by two obelisks of almost forty-five feet, pink granite of one piece, done in exquisite workmanship, chaperoned by four colossi of the same material and of a height of about thirty feet, as they are buried up to their chests. All this, too, is by Ramesses the Great. The other parts of the palace are by the Mandouei kings, Horus and Amenophis-Memnon, apart from some reparations and additions by the Ethiopian Sabacon and several Ptolemies, including a sanctuary entirely built from granite by Alexander, the son of the conqueror. Last I went to the palace, or rather the city of monuments, of Karnak. There the full pharaonic splendour put itself on display for me, all that man could think of executed on the grandest scale. All that I had seen in Thebes, everything that I had admired with enthusiasm on the left bank, seemed mediocre in comparison with the gigantic conception that surrounded me. I will contain my urge to describe any of it; because one of two things will happen; either my impressions will convey only a thousandth of what ought to be said when describing these objects, or rather, if I draw a contour sketch of them, or an extremely sober one, I will be taken for an enthusiast, not to put too fine a point on it − a fool. It is enough to conclude that we in Europe are no more than Lilliputians and that no other ancient or modern people has achieved a level of architecture that is so sublime, so large, so grandiose as the ancient Egyptians did; they created men of a hundred feet high while we reach at most five feet eight inches. In Europe artistic inspiration that rises above our doorposts stops in midair, tumbling helplessly before the one hundred and forty columns of the hypostyle hall of Karnak.

In this astonishing palace I was engrossed by the portraits of, for the most part, old pharaohs known by their grand actions; these are portraits as they ought to be done. Portrayed hundreds of times on the interior and exterior walls, each one of them possesses his own distinct appearance, which has little in common with that of their successors and predecessors. There, in colossal panoramas of a truly great and heroic style, more accomplished than what one would think possible in Europe, you will see Mandouei fighting the enemies of Egypt and returning triumphantly: farther on the campaigns of Ramesses-Sesostris; elsewhere Sesonchis [Seshonq], dragging before the feet of the Theban trinity

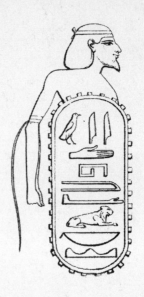

Bas-relief from Karnak celebrating Seshonq's victory over Judea

(Amon, Muth and Khons) the chiefs of over thirty vanquished nations, among whom I found, as I ought to, the Ioudahamalek, the kingdom of the Jews or Juda in complete letters. That is a gloss to add to the first chapter of the first Kings, which relates in fact the arrival of Sesonchis in Jerusalem and his success. So the identity we have established between the Egyptian Scheschonk, Manetho's Sesonchis and the Sesac or Scheschok of the Bible is confirmed in a most satisfying way.[12] I found an avalanche of buildings of all eras around the palais in Karnak, and when I return from the Second Cataract, for which I will sail tomorrow, I will stay for five or six months in Thebes. I expect an enormous harvest of historical facts as, while walking through Thebes without seeing even one of the thousands of caves which dot the Libyan mountainside, as I did four days ago, I have already amassed extremely important documents.

Thus, I am certain that the entire sequence of the eighteenth dynasty will need to be redrawn from... the cartouche of Ousirei or Mandouei. I saw two royal lists, one in the palace of Ramesses the Great and the other in the palace of Medinet-Habu, with the succession of the kings from Amenophis-Memnon up to the sixth successor of Ramesses the Great. So from Sesostris the kings are as follows: [Merenptah, Seti II, Setnakhte, Ramesses III, Ramesses VIII, and Ramesses VI].[13] Moreover there are, judging by the monuments, a lot more Ramesses forming the twentieth dynasty. As a result Huyot[14] caused me to make a mistake, by taking for very old monuments those with the cartouche [of Seti II]. I saw them: they are of a later era than Sesostris. — Meiamoun-Ramesses, instead of being the grandfather of Ramesses the Great, is his fourth successor.

This is an important step towards the truth; I will find the dates of all these reigns, and their chronology will be fixed. If the commissioners had copied the hieroglyphs of the bas-reliefs of Medinet-Habu, whose images they relayed, the mistake I made at the end of the eighteenth dynasty would not have occurred. You will see that the eighteenth dynasty is considerably shorter if the cartouche really belongs to Sesostris, a fact which everything seems to support. There are three reigns less. Maybe I will find in Karnak some king who was excluded from the [Chronological] Table of Abydos [chronological table engraved on the Temple of Abydos], from in between Moeris and Amenophis-Memnon; I have a feeling that I have overlooked someone. I will send you, while waiting, the translation of the chronological part of a stele which I saw in Alexandria: it is extremely important regarding the chronology of the last Saites of the twenty-sixth dynasty. A priest, Psammetichus (an ordinary private person, and not the king by that name), was happily born in year three on the 1st of Paoni under the reign of Necho (II). His life lasted seventy-one years, four months and five days, and he died in year thirty-five on the 6th of Paopi of Amasis's reign.

You will be able to calculate from that, and it follows, I believe, that Psammetichus II, or for that matter Apries, ruled for longer than Manetho's extracts suggest. Moreover, I copied hieroglyphic instructions engraved on the rocks on the road to Cosseir which expressly note the duration of the reign of the Persian kings. I also have an inscription of year 13 of Artakhscheschs and then, a last one, of the reign of Ochus, twenty-six months …

My health is excellent: the climate is agreeable to me and I am doing much better than in Paris. The local people overwhelm us with friendliness.

At this very moment I have in my little room: 1. a Turkish aga, commander and chief of Kourna at the palace of Mandouei; 2. Sheikh-el-Beled of Medinet-Habu, who is in charge of the Ramesseum and the palace of Ramesses-Meiamoun; 3. the sheikh of Karnak, in front of whom everyone prostrates himself among the columns of the ancient palace of the Egyptian kings. From time to time I send them pipes and coffee, and my dragoman is in charge of their amusement while I write: all I have to do is to respond at set times *'Thaibin'* (all is going well) to the question *'Ente thaieb?'* (is it going well?), which, every ten minutes, is regularly directed at me by these good people, who I invite to dinner in turns. We are inundated with presents; we have a herd of sheep and fifty-odd chickens which at this very moment are feeding and foraging around the portico of the palace of Kourna.

The English captain who arrived yesterday told us that Ibrahim-Pacha has left Cairo to establish a line of defence between El-Arisch and Gerasa, that is on the frontier of Syria. This is excellent news for my travel plans. I don't know anything about oriental politics, and that is because I don't receive a word either from Europe, nor even from Alexandria. – Patience! But that is really difficult! If Pariset would join me at least we could talk about Europe, but he hasn't even sent me a word. Goodbye, then, my dear friend. I will write to you from Syene [Aswan] before clearing the First Cataract, if I can find a way of forwarding my letters. I am sending this one by courier to Osyouth, where we have a Coptic agent. –... Tell M. de Férussac that I have collected fossils at Beni-Hassan where there are thousands of them, and that I also found some very beautiful ones at Thebes, collected for him...

P.S. – Please communicate my letter to the count d'Hauterive with my compliments. Tell him that the *Iconography of the Pharaohs* will be superb.

5.

Caesar's Son in Nubia

The hieroglyphs copied from the Bankes obelisk from Philae (now at Kingston Lacy House, Wimborn, Dorset) had allowed Champollion to make his first major breakthrough and he suspected it would be a good area for making extensive notes.

Champollion to Champollion-Figeac – 8 December 1828,
the island of Philae

Now, my dear friend, as of five o'clock in the evening I am on the sacred island of Osiris at the farthest frontier of Egypt, and among the black Ethiopians as a hearty Roman soldier once said while on a hunt near the cataracts.

I left Thebes on 26 November and my latest letter was dated from that enchanted world. I had to refrain from giving you details regarding this ancient capital: how to speak of something like that in only a few lines, while you have no more than scratched the surface! Only on my return to this ancient soil, after having meticulously studied it, will I be able to write with a comprehensive understanding, conclusive ideas and well-ripened results. Thebes is still for me, who has crossed it for four or five entire days, no more than a mass of colonnades, obelisks and colossi: I will have to examine one by one the disparate members of the monster in order to get a precise idea. So have patience until the time that I will plant my tents in the peristyle of the palace of the Ramesses.

On the evening of the 26 we went ashore at Hermonthis, and in the morning of the 27th we rushed to the temple which stung my curiosity, as I had no exact idea of the date of its construction. No one has yet drawn even one of its royal legends: I spent the entire day there and, based on its inscriptions and sculptures, the result of this prolonged examination convinced me that the temple was constructed under the reign of the last Cleopatra [51 -30 B.C], the daughter of Ptolomaeius-Auletes, and in commemoration of her pregnancy and felicitous birth of a stout son, Ptolemy-Caesarion.

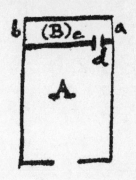

Cella of the birth temple of Caesarion

The cella of the temple is in fact divided in two parts: a large room (A, the principal chamber), and a very small one (B) serving as the sanctuary; you can only get to it through a small door towards the right corner. The entire face of the back wall of chamber B (which is called the delivery room in the hieroglyphic inscriptions) is taken up with a bas-relief showing the goddess Ritho, wife of the god Mandou, giving birth to the god Harphre. The goddess in labour is supported and attended by a number of goddesses of the highest rank; a divine midwife takes the child from the breast of the mother; a divine wet-nurse extends her hands to receive it, assisted by a nanny or nurse who will put it to sleep. The father of all gods, Amon (Amon-Ra) helps with the labour accompanied by the goddess Sovan-Ilihya, the Egyptian Lucine, goddess of child-birth. Queen Cleopatra is also inserted to assist with the divine birth, of which her own will not be or rather was no more than an emulation. Wall (c) of the goddess-in-labour depict the suckling and education of the young newly-born god; and on walls (a) and (b) the twelve hours of the day and night are figured in the shape of women with a star disk on their heads. So the astronomical table of the ceiling, copied by the Commission of Egypt, can only represent the theme of the birth of Harphre. This zodiac in other words has nothing to do with the summer solstice, nothing with the time of the foundation of the temple of Hermonthis, and poor Jomard lost all his marbles and all his astronomy over this tableau, as over all the others.

Leaving the small chamber (B) to enter the grand one, you will see a large bas-relief sculpted on the wall of the main room (A). It shows the goddess Ritho getting up from child-birth, still supported by the Egyptian

Lucine Sovan, and presented to the assembly of gods; the divine father, Amon-Ra, affectionately takes her hand to congratulate her with the happy child-birth, and the other gods share in their master's pleasure. The remainder of the room is decorated with tableaus in which the young Harphre is successively presented to Amon, to Mandou his father, the gods Phre, Phtha, Sev (Saturn), Meu (Hercules), etc., who welcome him by giving him their characteristic insignias, blessing the child by parting with all their power and their individual attributes. Ptolemy-Caesarion, with his childish face, attends all these gifts to his alter-ego, the god Harphre, whom he represents on earth. All this is priestly flattery, but completely within the parameters of the Egyptian imagination, which assimilates its kings among the gods. For the remainder, all the inscriptions inside and outside the temple of Hermonthis are in the name of Ptolemy-Caesarion and his mother Cleopatra. There can therefore be no doubt about the reason for its construction. The columns of the quasi-pronaos, which precede it ,were not carved at all. The work has remained uncompleted, and this is also perhaps related to the reason for the dedication of the temple: Augustus and his successors, who completed so many of the temples started by the Ptolemies, did not allow this one to be finished as it was none other than a monument to the birth of Caesarion [36-30 B.C], of the very son of Julius Caesar, a royal child whose rights they did not recognise at all. Other than that, a cacheff [local governor] has found it an excellent dwalling for a house, a farmyard and a pigeon loft, masking and cutting the temple up with walls of mud walls whitened with whitewash.

On the evening of the 28th we were near Esne with no intention of stopping there. I therefore directed us a little to the south where we disembarked on the eastern bank to see the temple of Contra-Lato. I arrived too late: some twelve days ago it had been demolished to reinforce the quay of Esne which is under attack from the Nile and will end up being flushed away.

On my return to the maasch, I found that it was filled with water: luckily it had been anchored at a shallow location and, as it soon touched the ground, it hadn't sunk completely. Nonetheless our provisions were soaked, we lost our salt, our rice, our flower, etc., but all this is nothing compared to the danger that would have threatened us if this leak had opened while we were sailing across the river: we would have sunk like a stone. May the great Amon be praised therefore! While we were sorting out our disaster on the morning of the 29th I went to pay a visit to the temple of Esne which, thanks to its new destination as a cotton warehouse, will escape for some more time the ravages of the barbarians. I noted, as I expected, a rather attractive architecture but detestable sculpture. Its most ancient part is the back of the pronaos, that is to say the door and the back of the cella, against which the portico is placed: this part dates back to Ptolemy-Epiphanes [Ptolemy V, 205-180 B.C]. The cornice of the façade of the pronaos carries the imperial legends of Claudius, the cornices of the lateral bases the legends of Titus and, inside the pronaos, the walls and columns are covered with the legends of Domitian, Trajan, particularly Antonius, and also Septimius-Severus, which I find here for the first time. The temple is dedicated to Chnouphis [Khnum], and I gather from the hieroglyphic inscription on one of the columns of the pronaos that, if the sanctuary of the temple still exists, it goes back to the time of Tuthmosis (Moeris). But all that is visible in Esne is modern or very modern. What then, in view of these facts, becomes of the prodigious antiquity that some have wanted to attribute to an Egyptian monument that was only very recently finished!

On the night of the 29th we were in Elethya (El-Kab). I swept through the enclosure and ruins, a lantern in my hands, but I found nothing: the remainders of two temples had disappeared. They were also recently demolished in order to repair the quay of Esne, or some building constructed by the Pasha. Was I mistaken to hurry to come to Egypte?

I went to the grand temple of Edfu (Apollonopolis magna) in the afternoon of the 30th. This one is intact, but its sculpture is very inferior. What is best and the most ancient dates back to Ptolemy-Epiphanes: then come Philometor and Evergetes II, and at last Soter II and his brother Alexander. These latter ones commissioned prodigious works here: I found Berenice here, wife of Ptolemy-Alexander, whom I knew about already from a demotic contract. The temple is dedicated to Aroeris (the Greek Apollo). I will study it in depth, as all the others, when I return to ascend the Nile.

The quarries of Silsilis (Djebel-Selseleh) aroused a keen interest in me. We went ashore on the 1st of December at one: there my eyes, which were suffering from fatigue of so many sculptures of the time of the Ptolemies and the Romans, reexamined with rapture pharaonic bas-reliefs. These quarries are very rich in engravings of the eighteenth dynasty. There are small chapels carved in the rock by Amenophis-Memnon, Horus, Ramesses the Great, Ramesses... (lacuna), his son, Ramesses-Meiamoun, Mandouei etc. They contain beautiful hieratic inscriptions; I will study all this on my return, and promise myself extremely interesting results on this site.

On the same night of the 1st of December we arrived at Ombos. I rushed to the great temple at two in the morning; its most ancient part is by Ptolemy-Epiphanes and the rest by Philometor and Evergetes. A curious fact is the epitaph of Dropion, Tryphaene or any other analogous Greek surname constantly given to Cleopatra, the wife of Philometor, on both the large hieroglyphic dedication sculpted on the anterior frieze of the pronaos and the bas-reliefs of the interior. This is a conundrum for you, 'Greeks of Egypt', to explain: I have come across this name before in the demotic contracts of Egypt. – The temple of Ombos is dedicated to two divinities: the right and most noble side to the old Sevek with his crocodile head (the Egyptian Saturn and the most awesome shape of Amon), to Hathor and to the young Khons. The left side of the temple is dedicated to another triad of lesser gods: to Aroeris (the Aroeris-Apollo of the Greek dedication) to the goddess Tsonenofre and their son Pnevtho. On the wall of the general enclosure of the temples of Ombos I found a doorway of an excellent workmanship and from the time of Moeris: this the remainder of the primitive buildings of Ombos.

It wasn't until the morning of the 4th of December that the wind would let us arrive in Syene [Aswan], the last town of southern Egypt. There I had to submit to yet more burning disappointment: the two temples of the island of Elephantine, which I went out to visit as soon as the flaming heat of the sun had extinguished itself, had also been demolished, nothing is left but their site. I had to content myself with a ruined doorway in granite, dedicated to Alexander [317-305 B.C] (son of the conqueror), to the god Elephantine Chnouphis [Khnum], and a dozen hieroglyphic proscynemata [adorational acts] engraved on an old wall, lastly, some disparate pharaonic debris which was used as building material for constructions during the Roman period. I had inspected what remained of the temple of Syene in the morning: it has the most execrable sculpture, but I found for the first time the imperial legend of [Emperor] Nerva [96-98 AD], which hasn't been found anywhere else as far as I know. This small

View of Ombos (in *l'Egypte ancienne*, 1839, by Champollion-Figeac)

ugly temple was dedicated to the gods of the countryside and the cataract, Chnouphis [Khnum], Sate (Juno) and Anoukis (Vesta).

At Syene [Aswan] we evacuated our maasch and had our luggage transported by camel to the island of Philae. At five in the afternoon I myself mounted a donkey and, supported by an Arab Hercules because of rheumatic pain in my left foot, I went to Philae while crossing all the quarries of pink granite which were graffitied with hieroglyphic inscriptions from the pharaohs. Incapable of walking and having crossed the Nile by boat in order to get ashore on this blessed island, four men helped by six others because the incline is almost perpendicular took me on their shoulders and hoisted me until very near the very small temple, where they had prepared a room for me in the old Roman buildings which looked rather like a cell but very clean and sheltered from nefarious winds. In the morning of the 6th, supported by my servants, Muhammed the Barabra and Soliman the Arab, I went out to visit the temple in great pain. On my return I went to bed and I still have to get up as my Parisian gout has judged this the right moment to precipitate towards the first cataract and stalk me during its passage; other than that [the attack] is very benign and I will be relieved of it tomorrow or the day after. While waiting, our boats for the Nubian voyage are being prepared; something new to see. I will write to you from this country if I have an opportunity to do so before my return to Egypt; everything is well otherwise. Don't worry, the gods are with us. —...

It is here, at Philae, that I finally received some letters from Europe, one from my wife of 15 August, and two from you,... of 25 August and 3 September. That's all. The other's are god only knows where, but at least it is something! And I have learned how to be content with as much.

6.

The Turning Point

Abu Simbel

Champollion to Champollion-Figeac – 1 January 1829,
Ouady-Halfa, 2nd Cataract,

Here we are, my dear friend, I arrived in good fortune at the extreme end of my expedition: I have before me the Second Cataract, a barrier of granite which the Nile knows how to conquer but which I won't be crossing. Beyond are no doubt further monuments, though they are ultimately of little of value. We would moreover have to do away with our boats, whistle for camels which are hard to find, cross deserts and risk starving to death, as twenty four mouths want to eat at least as much as ten and provisions are already extremely rare here: our biscuit from Syene [Aswan] has saved us. I therefore have to stop my descent straight [down the Nile] and tack sails in order to start in earnest with the exploration of Nubia and Egypt of which I have formed a general impression while descending. My real work starts today even though I already have six hundred drawings. So much still needs to be done that I almost terrified by it: in any case, I am assuming that I will [be able to] deal with it honourably in eight months of work. I will explore Nubia during the month of January, and mid-February I will establish myself in Thebes until the middle of August, after which I will rapidly go up the Nile while stopping at Dendera and Abydos. Everything else is already in my collection. Next we will see Cairo and Alexandria again. A few days of rest in Cairo and then back to Alexandria at the end of September. So I count on you for having the ministry of the navy arrange things in such a way that we will find a suitable vessel ready to set sail from Alexandria for Europe during the first days of October 1829. This shall be my plan!

My last letter was from Philae. I couldn't remain ill for long on the sacred island of Isis and Osiris: my gout disappeared in a few days and I could resume examining the monuments. Everything is very modern, that is to say from Greek or Roman times, with the exception of a small temple of Hathor and of a propylon attached to the first pylon of the temple of Isis, which were constructed and dedicated by poor Nectanbo I; it is also the best there is around here. The sculpture of the large temple, started by Philadelphus, continued under Evergetes I and Epiphanes, completed by Evergetes I and Philometor, lives up to that entire era of decadence: the parts of the buildings constructed and decorated under the Romans are executed in the worst possible taste and when I left the island I was truly worn out by the barbaric sculpture. I nonetheless stayed here for another few days in order to complete the mythological section, and I made up for it to myself by walking along the rocks of the first cataract, which are covered in historical inscriptions from the time of the pharaohs.

We left our maasch and our dahabiah at As-Souan (Syene) [Aswan], as those two boats were too large to cross the cataract; on the 16th of December our new armade below the cataract was ready to welcome us. It was made up of a small dahabiah (the flag ship) with a French section above a Tuscan one, of two boats of the French party, two of the Tuscan party, the kitchen boat carrying the blue flag and a boat with the armed forces, that is the two kavass (guards of the Pasha) with their silver-knobbed canes who accompany us and fulfil the tasks of the executive power. I forgot to say that the flag ship is armed with a canon which our new friend Ibrahim, the mamour of Esne, lent us on his passage through Philae: we also fired a forceful salute when we arrived at the Second Cataract, the destiny of our pilgrimage.

We set sail from Philae with a fair wind in order to commence our Nubian journey: we went by Deboud without stopping, wanting to arrive at the earliest moment at the furthest part of our journey. This small temple and the three propylons are only of a modern era. On the 17th [of December], at four at night, we were opposite the small monuments of Qartas where I found nothing of interest. On the 18th we went by Taffah and Kalabsche without anchoring. We subsequently passed the tropic of cancer and from the moment we entered that zone of scorching heat we were all shivering because of the cold and we had to put on our burnous and mantels. In the evening we slept beyond Dandour and merely waved at the temple with our hands. We did much the same the next day the, 19th, to the monuments of Ghirsche, which are of a good epoch, and also to the large temple of Dakkeh which dates back to the time of the Ptolemies. At night we disembarked at Meharaka, an Egyptian temple from the early times, turned into a Coptic church long ago. On the 20th I stayed for an hour in Ouady-Esseboua, or Valley of the Lions, which is named after the sphinxes which adorn the dromos of a monument built under the reign of Sesostris, though it is truly a provincial building, constructed from stone joined with mortar. I have taken a fragment of this mortar and of that of the pyramids etc. etc for our friend Vicat;[1] it is a collection which I think will please him. We lost the 21st and the 22nd, despite the wind and calm, to negotiating the big elbow of Amada where on my return from the Second Cataract I will have to study the temple, which is important because of its antiquity. We at last cleared it on the 23rd and arrived very early in Derr or Derri. There I found as consolation a pretty temple carved into the rock that still preserved some bas-reliefs from the time of Ramesses the Great, and I discovered the names and titles of seven sons and eight daughters of this Pharao.

The cacheff [local governor] of Derr, whom we paid a visit, told us quite frankly that, having nothing to offer us for supper, he would dine with us, which was arranged: this will give you some impression of the splendour and the resources of the capital of Nubia. We had counted on being able to buy bread; this was impossible as there is neither an oven nor a bakery. On the 24th, at sunrise, we left Derri, passed the ruined fort of Ibrim and went to bed on the eastern bank at Ghebel-Mesmes, a charming and well-cultivated area. We travelled on the 25th, partly by wind, partly by rope, and while we contemplated a rather beautiful crocodile enjoying his idleness on a sand bank near where we went to sleep we had to console ourselves, as we would not arrive at Ibsamboul [Abu Simbel] on the same day.

At last, on the 26th at nine in the morning, I went ashore at Ibsamboul [Abu Simbel] where we stayed until the 27th. Here I could revel in the most beautiful monuments of Nubia, but not without difficulty. There are two temples which are completely chiselled into the rock and covered with sculptures. The smallest one of these tombs is a temple of Hathor dedicated by queen Nofre-Ari, the wife of Ramesses the Great, decorated on the outside with a façade against which rise up to about thirty five feet, likewise carved out of the rock, six colossi representing the pharaoh and his wife with one their sons the other their daughters at their feet, including names and titles. The carving of these colossi is of an exceptional quality and I bear a deep grudge against Gau [who published a supplement to the *Description* in 1817] for having endowed their appearance, which is so svelte and elegantly curved, with the shape of fat magots and a pedestrian width in the view which he published of the second temple of Ibsamboul. This temple is covered with attractive reliefs and I had the most interesting ones copied.

All on its own the grand temple of Ibsamboul is worth the voyage to Ibsamboul: it is a miracle and even in Thebes it would stand out as something beautiful. It is daunting to imagine the work lavished on excavating it. The façade is decorated with four seated colossi which are no less than sixty one feet high. Of a most accomplished workmanship, all four represent Ramesses the Great; their faces are portraits and perfectly resemble the traits of the king encountered at Memphis, Thebes and elsewhere. It is a masterpiece worthy of utter admiration. That is what the entrance is like: the interior is entirely in keeping with it, but it is quite a task to visit it. When we arrived, the sands and the Nubians, who are supposed to sweep the former away, had closed off the entrance. We had it taken away in order to secure in the best possible way the small aperture they had made, and we took careful measures to prevent the collapse of this infernal sand, which in Egypt as much as Nubia threatens to gobble up everything. I almost entirely undressed, wearing only my Arab shirt and long underwear, and pressed myself on my stomach through the small aperture of a doorway which, unearthed, would have been at least twenty five feet high. It felt as if I was climbing through the heart of a furnace and, gliding completely into the temple, I entered an atmosphere rising to fifty-two degrees:[2] holding a candle in our hand, Rosellini, Ricci, I and one of our Arabs went through this astonishing cave. The first chamber is supported by eight pillars against which as many colossi of thirty feet high each are backed up, again depicting Ramesses the Great. A string of historical bas-reliefs of this pharao's conquests in Africa dominate the walls of this enormous room... The other chambers, of which there are sixteen, abound in religious bas-reliefs that present extremely interesting details. All of this culminates in a sanctuary at the back of which are four seated statues which are larger than life and of an exquisite workmanship.

This group, representing Ptah, Amon-Ra, Re-Harakhte and Ramesses the Great seated in their middle, has not been drawn properly by anyone. Gau's drawing is ridiculous next to the original.

After two and a half hours of admiration, having seen all the bas-reliefs, we felt we needed breathe in some fresh air and we had to go back to the mouth of the furnace while taking our precautions upon leaving. I put on two flannel shirts, a woollen burnous and my large mantel, in which I was wrapped the moment I emerged into the light; and there, seated near one of the outside colossus whose immense calve blocked the blasting northern wind, I rested for half an hour in order to let my abundant perspiration calm down. I subsequently went back to my boat, where I sweated for another hour or two. This experimental visit proved to me that one could stay down the catacombs of the temple for two and a half to three hours without restricting your respiration, except a weakening of one's legs and joints; I therefore concluded that on our return we could draw the historical bas-reliefs by working in parties of four (in order not to use up too much air) for two hours in the morning and two hours in the evening. It would be a difficult assignment; but the result would be of such interest, the bas-reliefs are so stunning, that I would do anything to have them as well as their complete legends. I compare the heat of Ibsamboul [Abu Simbel] to the one of a Turkish bath and this visit will amply stand in for it.

We left Ibsamboul on the morning of the 28th. Towards midday I ordered a stop at Ghebel-Addeh where a small temple is carved into the rock. The majority of its bas-reliefs were stuccoed by Christians, who have decorated this new surface with paintings of saints and particularly Saint George on his horse: but I who came to see its more ancient saints concluded, popping the stucco, that this temple was dedicated to Thoth by king Horus, son of Amenophis-Memnon, and I managed to have three bas-reliefs copied which are extremely interesting for mythology. We went to sleep at Faras. The 29th, an almost level calm allowed us to advance to just beyond Serre and on the 30th at noon, we at last arrived at Ouady-Halfa at half an hour from the Second Cataract, where we placed our columns of Hercules.

Towards sundown, I went for a walk towards the cataract. – Only yesterday did I seriously get down to work. I found here, on the western bank, the debris of three buildings, but no more than foundations which carry the end of hieroglyphic legends. The first, the most northernly one, is a small square building without sculpture and very uninteresting. The second on the other hand intrigued me very much; it is a temple whose walls were built from large dried bricks, while the inside was supported by sandstone pillars or columns of the same material, but, like all those from the most ancient times, these columns looked like Doric ones, shaped in very regular folds with little articulation. This first temple, dedicated to Horamon (Amon Generator) was erected under king Amenophis II son and successor of Tuthmosis III (Moeris), which I found out by having my Arab crew search with their hands around the remnants of the pillars and columns where I noticed traces of hieroglyphics. I was rather lucky to find the end of the dedication of the temple on the post of the first doorway. Attached to a brick wall of the temple I also uncovered, and had the sand removed by hand, a large stele showing an adoration scene and a list of gifts made to the temple by Ramesses I, with three lines added by the pharaoh who succeeded him, and whose proper name reads like Thothei or Athothei, Athothis, the Rathothis and Rathoris of the royal lists, and not Mandouei as I thought earlier.[3] In the end, under the guidance of Dr Ricci, we had all our crews look over the sanctuary (or rather the site it had occupied) with shovels and pickaxes and we found another great stele which I knew was there through drawings by the Doctor, and extremely important because it shows the god Mandou, one of the grand divinities of Nubia, guiding and handing over to Ortosan [Senusret I] (of the sixteenth dynasty) all the people of Nubia with their names inscribed in a sort of shield attached to the kneeling chained figures, each representing its five people. These are their names or rather those of the cantons in which they live: 1 Schamik, 2 Osaou 3 Schoat 4 Ascharkin 5 Kos; three other names are entirely erased. As for those which are there, I doubt that one will find them in any Greek geography; one would need a Strabo [famous geographer of Augustus's reign] of two thousand years before Christ.

A second temple, which is larger and also completely destroyed, lies a little more to the south; it is from the reign of Tuthmosis III (Moeris) and is also made of brick with pillars-columns of primitive Dorics and doorposts of sandstone: the great temple of the Egyptian city of Beheni lay on this site, which, judging by the fragments of pottery that are dispersed over today's deserted plain, seems to have been rather large. It was no doubt the fortress from which the Egyptians controlled the peoples between the first and the Second Cataract. This large temple was dedicated to Amon-Ra and Phre like the majority of the grand monuments of Nubia. There you have it; all that remains at Ouady-Halfa and it was more than I expected after an initial inspection of its ruins. – I end my letter here my dear friend: Lenormand will bring it to France. He will give you a complete report of the Greek inscriptions of Philae and Dakke etc. I will take care of the others when I have time and room to do so.

My last word is to wish you a happy new year and also to all our friends. I embrace you warmly with this thought.

PS – Give my news to my wife. Tell her that I will write to her from Ibsamboul [Abu Simbel] where one of our couriers is supposed to meet us.

Champollion to M. Dacier – 1 January 1829, Ouady-Halfa

Sir

Although I am separated from you by deserts and by the entire stretch of the Mediterranean, I feel the urge to join, at least in my thoughts and with all my heart, those who offer you their wishes for the new year. Coming from the depths of Nubia, mine are no less fervent or sincere; I beg you to accept them as a witness of the remembrance which I will always cherish of the kindnesses and the paternal affection with which you have deigned to honour my brother and me.

I am proud, at present, that, having followed the course of the Nile from its mouth to the Second Cataract, I have the right to announce to you that nothing needs to be changed in our *Letter on the Hieroglyphic Alphabet.* Our alphabet is correct; it applies with equal success, first, to the Egyptian monuments of the Ptolemies and, next, which is of greater interest, to the inscriptions of all the temples, palaces, tombs of the Pharaonic eras. Everything sanctions thus the encouragement which you gave to my hyroglyphic undertakings at a time when no one felt any inclination to favour them.

I am now at the extreme end of my journey to the south. The Second Cataract has stopped me, first of all through the impossibility of clearing it with my armada of seven sails, and in the second place Tuthmosis. It is not for me to emulate Cambyses [who lost an army in the desert]; I am in any case a little more attached to my companions than he probably was to his. Today, I will therefore turn my prow to Egypt in order to ascend the Nile while studying in depth the monuments of its two banks: I will collect any details worthy of some interest and, basing myself on the general impression which I have sofar formed, it will be a very rich and abundant harvest.

Towards the middle of February I will be in Thebes, as I will have to devote at least fifteen days to the magnificent temple of Ibsamboul, one of the miracles of the Nubia created by the colossal might of Ramesses-Sesostris, and one month will subsequently suffice for the monuments between the first and Second Cataract. Philae was virtually exhausted after the ten days we spent there during our descent of the Nile, and the temples of Ombos, Edfu and Esne, which the Egypt Commission has so much vaunted at the expense of Thebes, which these gentlemen did not absorb, will barely hold me up as I have already classified them and because I will find, on the most ancient monuments with their superior style, the mythological and religious details which I would only want to draw from their purest sources. I will restrict myself to a few historical inscriptions and certain details of costumes which symptomise decadence. Despite that it is useful to have them.

My portfolios are already overflowing: I am already taking pleasure in the thought of successively placing under your eyes all of ancient Egypt, religion, history, arts and crafts, customs and habits. A large part of my drawings are coloured and I am not afraid to say that they in no way resemble those of our friend Jomard, as mine reproduce the true style of the originals with scrupulous accuracy. The great Rochette was able to proclaim that the Egyptians never had but one god, one king and one man who was neither man nor king nor god. All of Thebes — and that is not a negligible quantity — is sadly one enormous protest against that elegant phrase.

I beg you, Sir, to receive my renewed assurance of my very respectful attachment to you.

PS Rosellini and Duchesne have asked me to send their respectful regards.

Champollion to Augustin Thevenet – 1 January 1829, Ouady-Halfa
My dear little friend, in order to wish you a happy New Year, I am writing you these three lines accompanied by a few more… I want to prove to you that, despite the distance, I don't forget those whom I love; that it is all

very well that I am in the depths of Nubia, have a Capuccin beard, am dressed like a desert Arab not knowing any longer what a hat is or a pair of trousers, eat pilau with my fingers, smoke three times a day and drink Nile water ceaselessly. – all this is going no deeper than my skin and I am still always down below 'the devilish Dauphinois'.[4]

... The Second Cataract has abruptly stopped my flotilla composed of six superb boats with three beds and a flag ship of four, armed with a canon which the commander of the Esne province lent me.

I would like to have gone further, but was forced to tack my sails as my caravan of twenty four mouths (not counting the famous canon) would risk dying of famine deep down desolate Nubia; but here I had planted my Herculean columns in advance. So I will ascend the Nile while creaming off on my way all that I can find in the way of hieroglyphs – on the monuments which I visited while going down in order to get an impression and assess the amount of work ahead of time... My health has kept up and I hope that that will last – I am abstemious as much by necessity as by volition and, one supports the other, I am avoiding the illnesses of this country. You must be shivering at the moment... Warm yourself well at your fire and think often of your friend...

From Champollion's diary

Ouady-Halfa, 30 December 1828: Our small flotilla has been here since noon of the 30th of December. When we arrived a salute from the canon heralded that we had reached the terminus of our descent of the Nile: the Second Cataract lay before us. As is the custom in Nubia, where the same name is given to dispersed shanties in the space of several miles, the name Ouady-Halfa was given to a rather stretched-out canton. Several buildings made out of mud on the border of the farmable land of the eastern bank of the Nile serve as the home of a cacheff and to poor Nubians who this official of their lawless government oppresses as he wishes; a few palms and sycamores, of which some are magnificent, several acres of dourra grain and beans (*loubieh*) are all the assets of this unlucky population which has nothing in common with the Arabs, neither in language or in their physiognomy. Their poverty is such that ten paras is for them quite a sum. Other than that they are pleasant people and very lively, as are all the Barbars whose svelte figures, soft and open appearances, reddish-brown teint lapsing into blackness, recalls the ancient Egyptian race of whom the Copts have preserved no traces at all.

On the 30th, when the sun was going down, I crossed over to the left bank in order to go for a walk to the cataract and to track down the remainders of temples which Doctor Ricci had pointed out to me. We went down an extremely difficult route (because it consisted of sand) to the beginning of the cataract without finding them.

Cataract. — One should not think of more than a limited section of the Nile being hampered by an infinite number of pointy rocks, some touching the water, others rising above it at different heights, and several forming a jam of islands which are sometimes covered with bushes and spiky shrubs, which lends a highly unique aspect to the cataract. The rocks across which the Nile progresses with such tribulation are of the type of stone which we call hard serpentine but not basalt, which you might think at first glance.

On the 31st, better informed than yesterday, I went on board Lenormand's boat and told it to go down the river to just below the houses of Ouady-Halfa and very near the ruins which I wanted to inspect; still on the western bank, the reis let us out. I recognised first of all the foundation of a temple, next that of another more sizeable one, lastly the ruins of a small square building of no importance.

But my first goal being to trace the stele of king Osortasen [Senusret I], of which I had a drawing that Doctor Ricci had made, I moved from right to left across the ruins, anywhere where some rubble might give rise to the hope of finding it. I put M. Lenormand to work, and M. Duchesne, and also my Arab servant Soliman who went further inland with his useless rifle on his shoulder. I followed him after seeing a modern ruin of dried brick and I reached the desert. The heat was fortunately tempered by a strong northern wind and without much exhaustion I was able to cross this plain which is unfarmed and invaded by the sands which whirl in cascades to as far as the river. Often the sandstone, forming the substratum of the soil, appears on the surface and shows a brilliant reflection of azur due to the sunlight. While nearing a few conical mounds separating the desert proper from the river Nile, which is equally desolate, I saw that they were deposits consisting of reddish and blueish sandstone. But here, as in the whole of Nubia after Ibrim, mounds and hills have such regular shapes that you would take them from very near for real pyramids or enormous structures of various types.

Weary from searching in vain for the stele of Osortasen I returned to the temples. I first looked at the second temple, about which I wrote a report. I noted that I was standing on the remainder of a temple of Horamon, whose stone parts (it is mostly of dried brick) go back to the reign of Amenophis II, son of Tuthmosis III. While clearing the sands that cover the bases of the pillars of this building, I spotted in the hollow near its brick wall the top of two sculpted bas-relief figures. I thought it was a stele and soon I was certain of it. Summoning the crew of the small boat, they swept away the sand of the bas-relief with their hands and I found a stele with the date of Ramesses I and then an addition by his successor Mernephta. I next affirmed that the large temple nearby was from the time of Tuthmosis III and dedicated to the god Thoth, the king of Nubia, according to the inscriptions of Dakke.

The other boats and the dahabiah came down to join me with all members of the expedition; they had gone to the cataract where Messrs. Lenormand and Duchesne had engraved the names of the entire French expedition in a sort of stele. Ricci visited the ruins and recalled that the stele, the object of my first quest, was in the third central chamber of the sanctuary of the small temple. I organised a party of all our sailors and, arming them this time with spades and picks from the dahabiah, we found the long-searched for stele in a second.

It is in fact a most curious historical monument; it commemorates the submission of the Nubian peoples to king Ortasen of the sixteenth dynasty. Assuring me that it was possible to bring along this monument, our crew set to work and in less than half an hour, aided by a single rope, they had dragged the block to the edge of the Nile. My after-dinner time was taken up with writing to my brother, M. Dacier, to M. the Viscount de Rochefoucauld. I did not go to bed until well into the night.

1 January 1829. – The next morning, on the 1st of January 1829, the sailors went to the small temple and transported the stele of Ramesses I to the riverbank. The two monuments were stowed on board, the former on the dahabiah and the other, the stele of Osortasen, on the first Tuscan boat, Gaetano's [boat].[5] During this operation I finished my letters and gave them to M. Lenormand to whom I said goodbye.[6]

We all left at nine in the morning, with our booms lowered from the mast as all we had to do was flow with the current. From that moment we turned towards the north, and I was overjoyed to go in that direction as each second would bring me closer to Thebes and also Paris. Humming a departure song, our Barbars seized their oars and we followed the fall of the river. I busied myself with editing my notes on the monuments of Ouady-Halfa, which soon disappeared from our view, as did the black rocks of the cataract. Our march was delayed by a rather fierce northern wind.

At sunset we went ashore Gharbi-Serre, located opposite an ancient fortified village that is collapsing. The cafas which served as our table was placed on the high bank of the river in a farm area and next to a loudly-squeaking sakieh or pot wheel which two bulls kept moving along. The fare was delicious, for a Nubian dinner; our chef had surpassed himself and two bottles of Saint-George, which the tropics had rather bludgeoned, gave the meal a distinct festive air that suited the first day of the year.

After dinner, handing out the bakshish (New Year gifts) to our domestics. All the members of the expedition took their coffee on board the dahabiah (flag ship) and we drank a bottle of Grenoblois ratafia on the success of our expedition. I went to bed at eleven.

2 January 1829. – Having left Gharbi-Serre at six thirty, we made rather good progress while the wind calmed down during the night. Soon we passed Faras and its island, and at eleven thirty we went ashore on the eastern bank in order to find the excavations of Maschakit, knowing that they were a little below the place where we had disembarked. When we went back to our boats, we had gone along the riverside till the next closest mountain range where we found what we were looking for. They were rather small items, but extremely interesting for various reasons. Clinging to its crevices, we had to clamber up the limestone rocks that drop almost vertically into the river from a fairly tall height. There I found a grotto dedicated to Anouke by the Ethiopian prince Poeri, a friend and companion of Ramesses the Great, and a few steles and inscriptions.

While I copied the inscriptions and had Messrs. L'hôte and Ricci draw the bas-reliefs, the northerly wind, which had swelled a little before we arrived at the foot of the rock, strengthened and all of a sudden a hurricane practically unleashed itself. We had fortunately completed our work and, having returned to our boats, we sailed for half an hour in the hope that the current would overcome the force of the head wind. But the *schemali* turned furious, the Nile foamed like the sea, and huge waves rose up. Our poor dahabiah lolled in such a way that I almost felt under attack from seasickness. In the end this ordeal forced us to go ashore. We halted on the eastern bank and as we reached it we saw that our small boats had also stopped a little above us, because they hadn't been able to continue their journey to Ibsamboul [Abu Simbel] where they had been told to go while we examined Maschakit.

We moored opposite the cave of Ghebel-Addeh, which is half an hour by road from Maschakit and which is separated from it by a third large hill at whose top are the modern ruins of Addeh, which would appear to have been a considerable village. There doubtless lay the Egyptian burg called Amenheri, as this local name can be found in the temple of Thoth at Ghebel-Addeh to the north of these ruins, and in the speos of Maschakit in the middle.

The *schemali* blew for the rest of the day, the sun extinguished itself without [however] abating its fury. Nighttime was as stormy as daytime but much more depressing because while the sun hovered on the horizon we had at least the pleasure of musing over an imposing spectacle: the Nile furiously battering the riverside, the solar disc obscured by bleached clouds of the sands which the wind blew up and through which you could see, cut out in sombre grey, the isolated and picturesque mountains of the eastern bank, lastly in the north the enormous rock of Ibsamboul with its river of golden sand precipitating into the Nile like a gigantic waterfall.

3 January 1829: When the wind had settled a little, we left at six in the morning, and in an hour and fifteen minutes my dahabiah had dropped anchor at the foot of the temple of Hathor in Ibsamboul. I had a very bad night and woke up with an attack of gout in my right knee when we departed. This particularly upset me because there are such fine things to be achieved in Ibsamboul! But patience. Having forgotten [to bring] my gout kit from Thebes and having used the glued-taffeta cap of my sponge for the gout of Philae, I polished off the one of Ibsamboul with the sponge of M. Lehoux.

As we disembarked here (where we found the boat with our kavass [guards], who arrived last night despite the storm), we busied ourselves with securing the hole through which you enter the grand temple with beams and boards. The Nubians hadn't filled it up since our first visit, which they are nonetheless used to doing in order to create an opportunity for bakshish when a [new] traveller arrives. They even wanted to charge [a] captain Reynier of the British navy, who visited Ibsamboul a few days before us, admission of twenty piasters.

The entrance was judged safe and usable towards noon and a first party went down into the temple in order to draw its bas-reliefs at three. We also took a number of barometric measurements and to everyone's amazement the thermometer did not go higher than twenty eight Reaumur, at most. Captain Reynier and even Ricci had measured, the one forty two degrees Reaumur and the other more than a hundred Fahrenheit and when I entered the temple during our descent of the Nile the heat had seemed to me so intense, and I sweated so much, that forty two degrees seemed very plausible to me: nonetheless, our thermometers did not rise above twenty eight [degrees] and we have to trust them. One must therefore attribute the constant sensation of a very fierce heat that one experiences in this magnificent excavation to the abrupt contrast between the state of the atmosphere outside and its condition inside, where no winds or stirring of any kind will offer solace to the sufferer as it would ordinarily out in the open.

While work progressed in the temple, I attended to my gout and put in order my notes since Ouady-Halfa. I was distracted from this by a scuffle between one of the crew of the kitchen boat and its *reis*, the sort of fool who lets himself be dominated by his crew: I sent our dragoman Boutros to find out what was happening and, based on his report, the mutineer was whipped by one of our kavass with the added threat that he would be sent away if anyone made another complaint against him.

Our young people returned as one would from leaving a Turkish bath, all sweaty, yet presenting the first sketches of superb historical bas-reliefs of the great chamber of the grand temple.

4 January 1829. – The second division, composed of Messrs. Duchesne, Bertin and L'hôte, as my gout still did not allow me to walk, entered the temple at nine thirty and left it at eleven thirty. The thermometer indicated one or two degrees less than yesterday. In the afternoon the first party went through the furnace and continued yesterday's work. I used my time to summarise notes for my hieroglyphic dictionary and to offer my condolences to the excellent professor Raddi who, ardent geologist as he is, had been horribly duped. While we were in Ouady-Halfa he explored

the entire area of the cataract, choosing beautiful and large samples of all its rock formations; driven by his enthusiasm, he had himself carried his heavy treasure over considerable distances and had filled a large basket selected for this purpose. He then told one of his sailors to transport the basket to his boat but this star-crossed Barbar, swiftly opining that his burden weighed too much, had begun to lighten it rather by dropping the largest and most stunning specimens, precisely the ones which had cost the naturalist so much sweat and which thrilled him most. Only today when he wanted to catalogue them did he realise his gigantic loss. Rebuked severely, the Barabra nonetheless persisted in the view that you could find these stones everywhere in Nubia and that it wasn't worth crying about them too much.

5 January 1829. – I still woke up with gout in my knee and a vague pain on the outside of my left foot. I therefore stayed in bed. But in order to occupy my time I had a paper tracing, the best they could do, made in the temple of the grand stele carved on the bulk elevation between the third and the fourth colossi of the row on the left near the secos. I was given the first seven first lines, of which I made a copy leaving a blank for all doubtful characters so that I could copy them myself from the original as soon as my legs would let me enter the temple. This memorial is all the more curious as it contains a decree from the god Ptha in honour of his most beloved son Ramesses the Great. The young people continued their drawings of the historical bas-reliefs.

6 January 1829. – As my gout had calmed down considerably, I made plans to enter the great temple at last and to see its miraculous catacombs. I particularly had to concern myself with noting down the hieroglyphic legends, the explanatory glosses of the historical bas-reliefs which were being drawn in full colour. I therefore left at two in the afternoon and made the painful journey which separated my dahabiah from the entrance of the great temple supported by Muhammad and the kavass Ahmed-Aga. I rested for a few moments at the foot of the grand colossus on the left in order to let my sweatiness pass: after which, undressing myself almost completely and wearing nothing except underwear, shirt and woollen socks, I descended into the furnace whose extreme heat continues to overwhelm for the first few moments, but you soon feel more at ease as

perspiration springs into action and sweat streams down your entire body. I thus started my exploration. After having verified and corrected the inscriptions of the bas-reliefs on the right, copied by Rosellini, while often using a ladder, I transcribed those on the left and started with the huge inscription of the tableau in which Ramesses is told that this enemies are attacking his lines and that his battle chariot is ready. I next checked several questionable points in the drawings of the bas-reliefs and left the temple at four fifteen. I took care to clothe myself excessively – the right word when you wrap your body in a shirt, two flannel vests, a crossed redingote, a burnous and a wide coat of wool, leaving aside the Arab waistband around my redingote and [my] good trousers of cloth underneath. I crossed the road from the temple to the boat without feeling for a moment the blasts of a very violent northern wind that was blowing at that moment either. I remained prostrate for two hours on my bunk, sweating blessedly, which I hope will relieve me for a little while from the distress caused by my gout.

7 January 1829. – I continued with the copy of Ptha's decree after the paper tracing which was brought to me from the temple. After sundown I went out to copy the legends of several steles in honour of Ramesses the Great which are carved on the rocks to the north of the temple of Hathor.

During the evening, while I was playing a game of chess, a Nubian with a magnificent figure, capped like the pharaohs in certain bas-reliefs, his hair divided in an infinite number of locks twirled like corkscrews and forming a type of bend exactly like the hairdo of the ancient Egyptians, entered our tent.

His poised looks, serene and noble, recalled those of Ramesses on the neighbouring monuments. This Barbar, dressed in a long blue gown covered by a white coat, a native of the island of Argo near Dongola, had no beard at all and seemed quite young to us. He was a rhapsodist: moreover, he held in his hand a lyre of a flawlessly ancient shape, whose sound chamber resembled the turtle carapace which Thoth-Hermes is supposed to have used for the first lyre. This fresh-faced Orpheus sat down in our midst and we invited him to give us a few demonstrations of his talent. As soon as he had tuned his instrument he played a few savage airs to a very quick beat. Then he sang, accompanying himself on the lyre, a long verse recital of the campains of Ismail-Pacha and Ibrahim-Pacha [the sons of the Pasha] in the Senaar, at Chagui and in the Kordofan. Several strophes described canonboats passing through the Second Cataract (a unique achievement), pulled by the heroes of the Nizam-Gedid. Afterwards followed the nomenclature of the chiefs, of all the Pasha's officers, as in the revue of the Iliad. Above all, he did not forget to mention  the European officers who took part in the expedition and sacrificed a strophe to the ferocious Muhammad-Bey-Defterdar who had cut off twelve hundred heads to revenge the tragic death of Ismail. He ended by improvising a long song in my honour in which he said that I had come from the country of Roum (Europe)

> Tu viens de la grande cataracte,
> De nos pays si lointains,
> Dans le grand galion,
> Sous le grand montagne,
> Toi notre grand général,
> Envoye par une puissant monarque,
> Il a abordé sous la montagne d'Ibsamboul,
> Revêtu d'une pelisse de Sammour,
> Ceint d'un châle de cachemire,
> Notre grand général,
> Mandataire d'un puissant monarque etc.

... Finally, at the moment when, on my sign, our dragoman opened his case to take out the talari for the bakshish which we wanted to give the poet, he cried out:

> O grand dragoman
> Qui tiens la clef du chef,
> Ouvre la grande malle,
> Et, par la vie et la tête de ton chef,
> Donne-moi un bakchish considerable.

The Nubian improviser withdrew very contentedly from his séance and we went to bed, sated with praise and the odours exhaled by the wig of our modern bard.

8 January 1829. – I continued with the copy of the decree of Ptha on the paper pressing taken from the grand temple. A Nubian came to sell a young gazelle which he had caught in the nearby mountainside of Ouady-Halfa; we made a deal for twenty piasters. The tiny animal is very pleasant but still a bit wild; in a few days it will be used the noise and pandemonium of the dahabiah.

9 January 1829. – I completed the copy of Ptha's decree after the tracing which, having been badly executed by Abd-el-Ouahed, despite this young Philaean Barbar's remarkable intelligence, and being covered with coloured stucco, has forced me to leave many blanks. At night, at one thirty, I entered the grand temple with the usual precautions; I did not find that the heat wasn't more stifling than usual. I think that these chambers, which one could consider as basements in their present state, maintain virtually the same temperature and that neither our stay here, nor the large number of candles and lamps which we kept alight, has much of an influence on the atmosphere in the temple. I worked there until four fifteen; exhaustion forced me to leave as quickly as I could. I copied fifteen columns of inscriptions from the great bas-relief on the right wall, I collated the six first lines of the decree of Ptha after the original which is still in a very good state. I returned to the dahabiah, packed in clothes, and, after sweating for two hours, found that I had been relieved of the lingering traces of gout which I had felt in my right knee and left foot before entering the grand temple. The copying of the right wall continued.

10 January 1829. – In the morning I went on board the boat of our kavass and ordered the reis to bring us right up to the foot of the mountains of Ibsamboul by towing us up the Nile in order to be able to study the part of the rock which the river bathes and erodes. Returning from Ouady-Halfa I had spotted several sculptured steles in that area of the mountain, though at such a height that it was physically impossible to reach it with the object of drawing [them]; the rock drops straight into the Nile without crevices that might be used for climbing. I was correct to set out

via the river with this expedition and position myself in front of the steles, because I was able to copy their exceptional inscriptions without much difficulty, aided by a large and a small telescope. These steles are memorials which recount varying tributes of Ethiopian princes and Nubian chiefs to Ramesses the Great or to one of his successors, Menephta IV. At about three, I returned to the great temple in order to write a report of the entire exterior façade, whose inscriptions I copied.

11 January 1829. – I used this day to copy in neat handwriting the texts of the historical bas-reliefs so that they could be included in the drawings to which they belonged without committing all the errors and many travesties which exist in already published transcriptions.

I also continued my report on the great temple. The northern wind was today extraordinarily violent. A courier arrived from Cairo: bringing letters for the Tuscans and nothing for me. At night, a walk across the rocks at the bank of the Nile.

12 January 1829. – The morning was taken up writing to my brother, to Violi, and continued with doing the preparatory work for the second part of the legend of the bas-reliefs of the right wall of the temple, based on the [paper] tracing.

13 January 1829. – An hour after my lunch (a Nubian bavarois), I went in the great temple where I perspired profusely but without my respiration feeling troubled, nor much pain in my joints; I collated from the original a small section of the legends of the right wall and twenty six lines of the grand stele containing the decree of Ptha. Having finished this work, I returned to the boat after more than three hours in its blazing, oppressive atmosphere; and yet I felt better when I left than when I slid into the temple. Upon my exit the brutally whistling northern wind caused an extremely painful sensation to my eyes and teeth. I immediately covered my face with my coat and got back to the dahabiah, guided by Soliman, stumbling at every step on the sandy and cascading slope that divides the temple from the riverside where our boats are moored. After my dinner and my siesta I somewhat arranged my reports on the monuments of Nubia.

14 January. – I woke up very early. Informed by Angelelli and Salvador Cherubini I climbed the sandy hills to the north of the temple of Hathor in order to study inscriptions engraved on the rock at a very considerable height above the Nile. I copied two onomastic texts, that is containing nothing but the names and titles of two chief teachers who, passing the rocks, had felt the urge to carve their legends beginning with 'made by' (fecit), like all inscriptions of that type. A few incisions, the arrangement of the rock and these inscriptions made think that the sands deposited on this small platform might be hiding a speos of some sort: we put six Nubians to work, who, despite their efforts and the brilliance of their song 'Daim-allah-Daim-allah', found absolutely nothing besides pure rock in its primordial state. I returned to have lunch in the dahabiah; after which I returned to the great temple which I entered to do my report on all its bas-reliefs which decorated the eight pillars of the grand chamber. I left after two and a half hours of work without feeling the outside air at all as no wind was blowing at the time. After my dinner I wrote to Messrs. Drovetti, Lavison and Acerbi, with the date of the 12th.

15 January. – This morning the Nubian who had sold us the gazelle wanted to part with a crocodile which he had killed with a gun shot that had hit it in the nape of its neck; we declined this acquisition because he had gutted the animal and thrown away its bones and meat. This crocodile of about six feet had a dull green colour and each of its scales was grooved with black marks forming a rosette; the bottom of its stomach was yellowish. It displayed absolutely all the shades of colour which the Egyptians use in the hieroglyphic inscription of its image. I next went to the great temple where I worked on the description of the bas-reliefs of the two lateral chambers on the southern side. I transcribed the subjects which decorated the pillars of the second chamber. The heat did not appear to me to be more intense than that of other days even though we had constantly kept candles and lamps alight in the temple, not to mention the take up of air by a dozen or so workers or servants. I only noticed that one sweats rather a lot more abundantly in the lateral chambers than in the big one and in the two others on the axis of the temple. After dinner I verified and copied the inscriptions of a few steles to the north of the temple of Hathor. In the evening, a walk on the side of the great temple; the effect of the

moonlight on the colossus is astonishing.

16 January 1829. – I woke up very early in the morning in order to finish a few letters. As soon as M. Bertin, who had gone in the temple to finish the last sheet of the wall to the right, had returned to the boat we started preparing for our departure. As all the drawings of historical tableaus had been completed and having myself gathered all the necessary information on the remainder of the decoration of the temple, our stay in Ibsamboul [Abu Simbel] had been completed. We therefore demolished the scaffolding of boards which we had put up in order to support the sands and to prevent it from interring us in the temple while we were working there. The mass promptly collapsed on the door of the temple and covered it more than six feet above the cornice. Masses of stones covering the mounds raised before the two northern colossi followed the sands and now obstruct the entrance of the temple, which can no longer be dislodged except with four or five days of work. This is irritating for the curious who will come after us, but that is hardly our fault.

At about one in the afternoon, our boats, flying their flags, distanced themselves from the riverside cheered by the Nubians, who launched in chorus into a departure song; reaching the middle of the river, I took one last look at the temple of Hathor whose presence gains infinitely by being viewed from a distance because one then grasps the entire magnitude of its six colossi of a truly extremely amazing craftmanship. I said goodbye to the enormous statues of the façade of the grand temple whose gigantic shape grows as one moves away from it. I cannot but feel sad while leaving this beautiful monument forever, as it would seem, the first temple from which I am distancing myself and to which I will never return.

Since the northern wind was very mild today, we went up the river quite quickly. Above Ibsamboul, the right bank and the left bank unfold into a similarly desolate view; a few strips of land cultivated with dourra, beans or ricinus pop up here and there along the flanks of the Nile, which collect from everywhere the yellow golden sands that cloaked the protrusions of sandstone whose blackened points prick up from afar and herald the desert in all its terror.

A very long crocodile was asleep on a small isle near where my boat passed it. Doctor Ricci took aim at the monster when it went back into the river: the bullet definitely hit its target because the crocodile made two or three convulsive movements before disappearing, but it did not resurface as it wasn't mortally wounded.

A little further, following the bend of the Nile towards the east, I was told of the arrival of a courier; a boat was sent to pick him up from the eastern bank and brought him to my side of the river. He brought a letter from my brother, couriered by M. Darcet junior, left at Assouan [Aswan] by Pariset and which Mansour, our factotum at the first cataract, sent me with letters from Msarra and Lenormand. Night having fallen, we stopped on the right bank, at Nere, a little higher than Fourgoundi, in order to dine on the riverbank and in the moonlight.

We continued our journey until one in the morning under the most stunning moonlight till now.

17 January 1829. – At sunrise, we found ourselves in view of Ibrim, the Primis of the ancient geographers, their last known location in Nubia beyond which it does not appear that the power of the Ptolemies and the emperors had much influence. Ibrim is interesting because of its savage appearance. It is quite a tall mountain, cut in a cliff by the river which gnaws at its base; still visible at its summit are the ruins of an extremely stretched-out fortress built by sultan Selim who, after having conquered the country, established a type of garrison colony made up of Albanians. This stronghold was one of the last refuges for the Mamelukes. The present Pasha laid siege to it and conquered it. Since then the fortress has been abandoned and is no more than a pile of ruins.

There are four small speos in the face of the rock of Ibrim, which are of rather great interest as they go back to the reigns of the kings Tuthmosis II and Tuthmosis III, his son Amenothis II and of Ramesses the Great; they were carved out by the governors of the country, princes, one of them an Ethiopian, and who seem to be recounting the homage rendered to the pharaohs during their visit to Ibrim. The first of these caves is the oldest one I have seen in Nubia; you can only get to these caverns by boat and enter them for the most part with scaffolding. Armed with this machinery, I paid them a meticulous visit. As the base of the rock left us enough room to arrange our table (a *cafas*), we dined there with excellent appetite. We immediately left afterwards in order to continue our journey.

At about four, before arriving at the island of Artiga, we saw on a large island a very large crocodile sleeping in the sun. We went upstream in order to let Doctor Ricci and M. L'hôte go ashore who, armed with their guns headed with caution towards the monster, but it quickly leapt into the river warned by the shrieks of the geese surrounding it and fleeing at the approach of our hunters. My Nubians affirmed that these birds act as sentinels, spies for the crocodiles.

Thus cheated for the hundredth time of the sweet hope of eating grilled crocodile we continued going up the river and our crew treated it as a matter of honour to catch up with the other boats which had gone ahead during our crocodile hunt.

Quickly a race developed between the dahabiah and the boats. As soon as they thought a move was made to overtake them, the beating oars, the cries of sailors, the epigrams hurled, some in Arabic others in Barbar, produced a racket powerful enough to disturb the peace and quiet of any faraway desert inhabitant. Yet this noise had the advantage that we advanced with speed. At night we continued travelling, as I wanted to arrive at Derri that day. The moon spreads its light and in Nubia you will certainly be able to see as well at eight in the evening as you would in Paris on the same day in the middle of the day. The sailors continued rowing with enthusiasm and the *reis* Douchi entertained them by singing several songs, whose refrain the crew repeated in choir... [One of them,] which is rather popular with Egyptian and Nubian sailors, has as many couplets as those who sing it are inspired by the towns and villages which they encounter; it is a song with endless couplets. It usually ends with a strophe on the native area of the *reis* of the boat, which they extol as handsomely as they can.

We arrived in Derri at seven thirty in the evening. Our table was set op on the river bank at the foot of magnificent palms with which it is strewn and which, soaring fifty to sixty feet, are the most beautiful I have seen on this journey so far. The moon radiated a brilliant clarity and we had a very cheerful supper, surrounded by the inhabitants of Derri who were unable to resist their curiosity, rather exceptional for this hour around here because after the coffee I went for a walk in the village and encountered no one on its streets, if you can give such a name to the road-like distance that separates the houses and their enclosures from one another. Here and there are superb sycamores which are most attractively tall and covered with bunched foliage under which you will find a divine shadow during the heat of the day. The most beautiful one stands by the home of the cacheff. A group of these large trees screens the city square on whose one side is the mosque, built from coloured bricks. Opposite stands a small building called Sebil and used for putting up *djellabis* (caravan merchants) arriving from Sennaar or the Sudan. It is a square block with arcades which make it look like an oven with two openings; it is moreover covered with white lime stucco. In passing on my nocturnal stroll, I saw by the glimmer of the fire which lit up the interior of these two stoves, several *djellabis* higgledy-piggledy on the floor, stretched out with their black slaves of both sexes which they bring to Bournou or Khordofan. It was a spectacle which I can only inadequately describe.

Having returned to the boats, and seated alone on the bank of the Nile at the foot of a palm, I was soon approached by three Derrians dressed in wide robes of white tick, with matted hair. They surrounded me, squatting on their heels and with a large white stick resting on their shoulders. They remained completely silent for a good quarter of an hour; this was out of politeness. At last the most distinguished one ventured to ask me whether I would like to buy some brandy (*araqi*): knowing that this would be date-liqueur I answered that I did not need any. Conversation having thus been engaged, I questioned the Nubian on the number of palms that this canton had; he asserted that there were 700,000 (with a pinch of salt), and that each one, productive or not, green or dry, cost 25 paras of yearly taxes to the Pasha. I knew that in Egypt this tax was 65 for small date palms and 80 for large ones, whether they bore fruit or not. I asked him for the reason of this difference, which surprised me as the date palms of Nubia seem more beautiful and larger than those of Egypt, and their dates were much better. They answered that in Nubia the majority of date palms were male and so, because the female date palms were much less numerous in proportion to the ones above the cataracts, the government had taken this difference into account: that nonetheless the 25 paras per specimen was high enough to ruin the country and continue the misery of its inhabitants, because after having received the taxes the agents of the government would, as in Egypt, fix themselves the prices of the dates.

18 January 1829. – We went extremely early in the morning to the temple hewn out of the eastern mountainside and a few steps away from the houses of the town. This temple was dedicated to Amon-Ra and Phre by Ramesses the Great. This assignment is not worth the same time as in Ibsamboul; some bas-reliefs are no more than outlines. This is because they were originally carved in a bedding of stucco pasted on the walls of rock and because, as the stucco fell down, nothing has remained on the stone except incisions scoured by a chisel.

We ate in the grand chamber of the temple at four thirty. Having finished our work, we returned to our boats and said adieu to the capital of Nubia, a large village of two hundred houses, yet more pleasant and clean than many towns in Egypt because its streets are spacious, and most of all because the houses are surrounded by small borders of palms, santh and a few sycamores; at around eight we went ashore on the left bank near the temple of Amada.

19 January 1829. – This entire day was spent drawing and copying the bas-reliefs of the temple of Amada, a charming building founded by Tuthmosis III (Moeris), continued by his son Amenothoh II and completed by Tuthmosis IV. Its sculpture is of a most beautiful style; its dedications on the architraves especially display divine perfection. The colours of the bas-reliefs have withstood time, despite the miserable plastering job with which the Copts have covered the whole to turn it into a church. For the drawing of several bas-reliefs of which I wanted to have complete copies I had to chip away with hammer blows the stucco with its bad paintings representing saints and which cover the Egyptian sculptures. Uniquely, this action was ordered by a Christian and executed by Muselmen, for the sake of idolatry.

20 January 1829. – I completed the description and the copy of the most interesting bas-reliefs of the temple of Amada. At two in the afternoon we had left the riverside and gone up the Nile in very good time. Towards five we saw a large cangia sailing before us. Aiming our telescopes, we agreed that this vessel, whose sails were new (a rare thing in Nubia), carried a party of Europeans; these conjectures were correct, but seen from up close the French flag was an English standard and we were certain that this boat carried Lord Prudhoe who, according to the cackle of Derri, we had

been told, had passed the first cataract and was on his way to Sennaar. It was in fact he himself who, spotting my flotilla, had dropped anchor at Korosko and was waiting there for our arrival, assuming correctly that we would be thrilled to spend a few hours together.

Soon my dahabiah was moored next to his. He went ahead of us to the riverbank with Major Felix, his travel companion. We went on board his boat where we talked news and antiquities until midnight. He was thrilled by our portfolios and these gentlemen gave us suggestions on several areas which we should visit meticulously in Thebes. I said goodbye to them with some wistfulness, seeing not without alarm leave for such a perilous journey a man who, while possessing an immense fortune, has the considerable courage to throw himself into a dangerous but for the sciences useful expedition to Sennaar and Abyssinia during such an advanced season.

21 January. – Very early [in the morning] we left each other, Lord Prudhoe heading south and we towards the north, perhaps never to see each other again. The sky was covered with white clouds and a suffocating heat lay heavily on the land: to this I attribute the fact that we came across a succession of six crocodiles peacefully sleeping on the riverside. The first five were very young but the last one, nestled on a small sandy isle in the middle of the river like all the patriarchs of its species, was certainly twelve to fifteen feet long. I watched it from very close by, and I was awed when this initially motionless hulk started to get ready to plunge into the river, getting on its feet, raising its head and arching its back. The bullets which we aimed at it hit its armour, rebounded and dispersed into the river at a distance of twenty yards. We reached Bereda at night for supper and to spend the night; the night was extremely cold.

22 January 1829. – Departing very early in the morning we advanced quite well, until ten thirty when all of a sudden a thunderous northern wind started blowing, changing the Nile which had hitherto been so peaceful into a small furious sea, and we were forced to moor on the left bank, a little above and opposite a number of shacks called Siale. Sitting down on the riverbank in the shade of a bouquet of santh in order to see whether all our boats were safely anchoring, I saw in the north-east towards the mountains of Meharraqa a whirlwind which, forming suddenly, rushed

across the desert throwing up in the air enormous clouds of sands.

Champollion to Champollion-Figeac – 12 January 1829, Ibsamboul [Abu Simbel]

I revisited the colossi which mark with such nobility the most magnificent grave of Nubia. They were to me as beautiful as the first time [I lay eyes on them], and I regret not having a fairy lamp to transport them into the middle of the place Louis XV in order to shatter in one clean movement all detractors of Egyptian art. Everything is on a colossal scale here, not excepting the work which we have undertaken, whose result will be able to lay some claim to public attention. Everyone who knows this place will understand what difficulties one has to overcome in order to draw a single hieroglyph inside the great temple.

It was on the 1st that I left Ouady-Halfa and the Second Cataract. We slept at Gharbi-Serre and the next morning, towards noon, I landed on the right bank of the Nile in order to study the caverns of Maschakit... I had to climb up a steep rock in order to get to a small chamber hewn into the mountainside and decorated with badly damaged sculptures. I nonetheless was able to make out that it was dedicated to the goddess Anoukis (Vesta) and other guardian gods of Nubia by an Ethiopian prince who, being governor of Nubia under Ramesses the Great, beseeches the goddess that the conqueror may forever crush the Libyans and nomads under his sandals...

It would appear therefore that, from time to time, the African nomads troubled the peaceable farmers of the Nile. It is very remarkable furthermore, that, here, on the monuments of Nubia, I have up till now only found the names of Ethiopian and Nubian princes as governors of the country under the reign of Ramesses the Great and his dynasty. It would seem that Nubia was so much integrated into Egypt that the kings completely trusted the locals and even gave them troops to command. I could cite, for example, a stele still carved in Ibsamboul and in which someone called Mai, commander of the troops of the king in Nubia and born in the area of Ouaou (one of the cantons of Nubia), emphatically sings the praise of pharaoh Athothei I (Mandouei I), the fourth successor of Ramesses the Great; it also follows from several other steles which several Ethiopian princes erected for the hero of Egypt.

On the third, at night, our work in Ibsamboul started. Our task was to explore the still virgin territory of the great temple, and that is the *mot juste*, for the little that Belzoni and Gau published of the interior bas-reliefs poorly resembles the original; everything is unreliable, design and colour. We have planned to copy in large format and colour all the bas-reliefs which decorate the grand hall of the temple, the other rooms contain nothing but religious scenes...

We have already six large tableaus (bas-reliefs) of:

1   Ramesses the Great on his chariot, his horses pulling ahead in full gallop. He is followed by three of his sons who are also mounted on war chariots; he is chasing the Assyrian army and attacks a fortress.
2   The king on foot, about to strike down an enemy chief and piercing another with a lance...
3   The king is seated amidst his army chiefs; they have come to inform him that the enemy (the Bacterians?) is attacking the front of his army... Further away you see an enemy raid of war chariots which are without order fighting the methodically arranged line of Egyptian chariots. This section of the scene is full of movement and action: it is comparable to the most gripping battles painted on Greek vases, which these scenes involuntarily bring to mind.
4   A rousing tableau depicting the triumph of the king and his solemn parade (in Thebes no doubt) standing on a superb chariot pulled by trotting and richly bedecked horses. Before the chariot, two lines of African prisoners, one black the other Barbar, form perfectly arranged groups full of effect and movement.
5 and 6. Two large scenes showing the king offering homage of the prisoners of various nations to the gods of Thebes and those of Ibsamboul...

This will give you some sense of the magnificence of the dress and chariots of the pharaohs and you will be able to grasp the astonishing power of these beautiful bas-reliefs which were painted with such great care...

Here you have our memorable campaign of Ibsamboul: it has been the most difficult and glorious one which we could have undertaken during our entire voyage. Both the French and Tuscans have rivalled each other in rising to the challenge and in devotion, and I hope that towards the fifteenth we will set sail and return to Egypt chanting victory. Adieu, my dear friend, I embrace you as well as all our friends. I suffered from three days of gout when I arrived here; but the steam baths which I took in the temple have cured me, for a long time I hope...

PS – My compliments to M. Arago, whom I have only after our return, from the Second Cataract started to forgive his opposition to our voyage...

From an article written by Lenormant, who left the expedition at the Second Cataract.

In order to get an idea which is fairly accurate of the innumerable details of this tomb, it was necessary to light a huge number of candles which one joins together like torches on top of long poles and which one aims at the sections one is studying. As the air does not circulate in this dark room one would be at risk from asphyxiation by fumes if one were to light torches or fires of straw. One therefore has to forego the vista that this long enfilade of chambers which lower and narrow themselves towards the sacred sanctuary would make. Instead of this impression of the whole, one stumbles as one touches these silent galleries: there are twenty chambers, to the right, to the left, in all directions, and you find yet another one amazingly. Everywhere the forms of the eternal myth unfold and refresh themselves, like streams in an endless sea. Everywhere its expression is both monotonous and grandiose; and when at last you stop before the four seated statues placed at the end of the sanctuary, when one has dared to defy the immobile and fixed gaze of this mute senate without trembling, one wonders whether this grotto does not contain any other secrets...

Champollion to Doctor Pariset, 16 January 1829, Ibsamboul
[Abu Simbel] (received 26 January 1829, Thebes)
So it has been decided, my dear Imouth, that you will visit and revisit Thebes without me! If I were to believe the gossip in Nubia, as there is between the two cataracts as much of this as between the Pont d'Austerlitz and the Pont d'Iena, you arrived in Thebes having gone as far as Syene [Aswan], but, instead of crossing the cataract of Assouan

[Aswan] to come and join me, you have, they say, headed your prow towards Thebes where you are supposed to have stopped for a few days. I myself won't be there until the 15th of February. I thus abandon, with great difficulty trust me, the hope of seeing you and the pleasure which I was picturing of strolling through the oldest of royal cities with you, of sharing with you my impressions, taking pleasure in yours, and to both give in before these splendours to the thralls of enthusiasm, the real source of motivation for those [of us] who have eyes and hearts.

I also deplore that you will not have admired Ibsamboul: it is irony of the great Sesostris! He changed a mountain into a palace, whose doorway is flanked by four superb seated colossi that measure no less than sixty two feet. The grand chamber, supported by eight colossi of twenty five feet, is decorated with immense bas-reliefs showing the battles, conquests and triumphs of our hero. All these scenes are painted and I have large coloured copies of them. You will at least see those.

Please, wherever you may be, write to me a line from Thebes and tell me about your plans and work. Doubtless you will not have received the letter which I wrote to you in December from Philae. When I think of the fact that I won't be able to talk Egypt with you in Egypt itself, I rail against and deprecate the circumstances which are forcing you north while all my business is to the south. Write to me quickly or else I will send all the crocodiles of Nubia after you. Adieu, always entirely yours.

Pariset was about to leave for Nubia in order to meet Champollion when he received orders to leave for Asia Minor to study the specific type adopted by the plague and cholera there. From Tripoli in Syria he wrote the following letter as he called his friend:

Pariset to Champollion

'Maiamoun', cherished by Amon
After September you will leave for Paris. We, my friend, will stay for five or six months in order to study the men of the Delta. You are admiring the miracles of ancient Egypt, – we scrutinise the infinite abominations of modern Egypt. Oh! How far one is removed from the other! – The more I think about it the more I am astonished by the antiquity of Egypt, its wisdom, genius, knowledge, power. And the more I see, the more I am convinced that modern-day Egypt should be placed at the centre of the

type of nations that one should mistrust and flee from. And all this under a brilliant sky and on a land that is abundantly fertile beyond belief. Man fails nature everywhere. One might say there is esprit only when nature has none! – September! September! Come, – and lead us near my dear Champollion!

Champollion to Champollion-Figeac – 10 February 1829, El-Melissah (*between Syene [Aswan] and Ombos*)

We are plagued by bad luck, my dearest friend. Since our departure from Syene [Aswan], to which we said goodbye on the 8th of this month, here we are on the 10th, and far away from having covered the distance which separates us from Ombos from which you would ordinarily get to Osouan in nine hours; but a brutal northern wind has been blowing without interruption for three days and is making us do pirouettes on the waves of the Nile, which has swelled like a small sea. We moored with great difficulty at Melissah where a sandstone quarry of no interest is located; other than that, perfect health, content and preparing ourselves for devouring Thebes and digesting it, if it isn't more than we can chew. We were, moreover, much cheered up by the courier who arrived yesterday in the middle of our maritime trials, and who at last brought me your letters of 26 September, 12 and 25 October, and of 15 November. Well, adding the two earlier ones, these are the only letters that have reached me. I am delighted, I and everyone here, by all the good things you say about our poor France, it is rather time that she is allowed to breath in again and it is good for us to hear that things are going well. We have such spectacles before our eyes that our heart tingles with pleasure thinking that the same is happening in France. So, vivat!

Do thank our venerable M. Dacier for the elegant lines which he was kind enough to write on 26 September. I hope that he will have received my letter from Ouady-Halfa and will excuse the lateness of my wishes for New Year's Day, which will already have gone by when they reach him. But Nubia and particularly the Second Cataract is far removed from Paris and only one's heart covers such distances quickly.

The loss which our friend Dubois has suffered has moved me deeply. I know how exceptional a person his sister-in-law was and I share his grief with my whole heart. I will write to him from Thebes after having researched Egypt and Nubia in depth. You can tell him in advance that our

Egyptians will from now on strike a much more attractive figure in the
history of art than before; I will be bringing back a series of drawings of
great things, capable of converting even the stubborn. – Will we at last see
an Egyptian obelisk on one of the squares of Paris? That would be great!
I hear that people haven't shrunk away from [another] similar proposal. I
believe it to be highly feasible and M. Drovetti will give his positive
support. I will communicate to M. Drovetti the letter which M. de Mirbel[7]
wrote to me, and I imagine that something like that could be arranged
with his majesty the Pasha of Egypt, who never turns down something
gainful. I will write to M. de Mirbel as soon as I hear from M. Drovetti
who obviously is capable of and will have to negotiate this deal. While we
are waiting, send M. de Mirbel my regards and my special respects to
Madame.

My latest letter was from Ibsamboul; I should therefore resume my
itinerary from this beautiful monument which we have now worn out, as
we almost did to ourselves due to the difficulty of examining it.

We left it on the 16th of January and early on the 17th we moored at
the foot of the rock of Ibrim, the Primis of the Greek geographers, in
order to visit a number of caverns which you can see towards the basis
of this enormous mass of sandstone.

There are four of these speos (the name which I have given to rock
caves other than tombs), from different eras, but all belonging to
pharaonic times...

The most recent one of these speos is a monument of the same type
from the time of Ramesses the Great. It was also hewn by a governor of
Nubia in the honour of the gods of Ibrim, falcon-headed Hermes and the
goddess Sate, and to the glory of the Pharao, whose statue is seated in
the middle of the local deities at the end of the speos. The southern
territories were at that time governed by an Ethiopian prince of whom I
have found monuments in Ibsamboul and in Ghirsche. This man is shown
in the speos of Ibrim as respectfully swearing fealty to Ramesses the Great
and at the head of his government, which consists of two hierogrammates,
next a grammate of troops, the overseer of the royal estates, and other
scribes without any particular description.

One should note, to the credit of Egyptian courteousness, that the
wife of the Ethiopian prince Satmei is shown immediately after her
husband and before the other officials. This shows, as do thousands of

similar facts, how much Egyptian civilisation differed from the rest of the east and came close to ours; you can judge the measure of civilisation of a people after the more or less acceptable position of women in its social organisation.

On the night of the 17th of January we arrived at Derri or Deir, the present capital of Nubia, where we had supper on arrival... Having started a conversation with a local Barbar who, seeing that I was alone on the deserted riverside, had politely come to join me offering date liqueur, I asked him whether he knew the name of the sultan who had built the temple of Derri; he responded at once that he was too young to know but that the old men of the region seemed to agree that this Birbe was built around three hundred years before Islam, but that all these old men were uncertain as to one point, namely whether it was the French, the English or the Russians who had constructed this great work. Nubian history in action. Jomard would be jolly pleased with the chronological system of the Derri Barbars: they leave any amount of desirable margin for his solstices and equinoxes.

The Derri monument meanwhile, though it is modern in comparison to the date given by my knowledgeable Nubian, is a work of Ramesses the Great... In it I found a list, ranked by age, of the sons and daughters of Sesostris which will help me to complete the one from Ibsamboul [Abu Simbel]. We reproduced a few fragments of historical bas-reliefs; they are almost all defaced or destroyed. It was here that I was able to draw my conclusions regarding an interesting detail; I refer to the lion which always seems to accompany our heroic Egyptian in the scenes at Ibsamboul and Derri. I wanted to know whether this animal was placed there symbolically in order to assert the power and valour of Sesostris, or rather whether this king, like the captain-pasha Hassan and the pasha of Egypt, really had a tame lion who was his constant companion on military campaigns. Derri has decided the question. Above a lion throwing himself on the Barbars slain by Sesostris, I actually read the following inscription: 'the lion servant of his majesty tearing his enemies to pieces'.

Other than that, this temple is a cave carved into the sandstone rock on a very grand scale: it was dedicated by Sesostris to Amon-Ra, the supreme god, and to Phre, the sun force hailed under the name of Ramesses, who was the guardian of the hero and his entire dynasty.

This fact explains why you will find king Ramesses presenting offerings or praise to a god with the same name, Ramesses, on the monuments of Ibsamboul, Ghirsche, Derri, Seboua etc. You would be rudely mistaken if you were to assume that this sovereign had started a cult to himself. Ramesses is just one of the thousands of names of the god Phre, Ra or Re (the sun) and these bas-reliefs are proof of no more than clerical flattery towards the living king; by addressing the god of the temple with the name which the king also adopted, and sometimes even by giving him the traits of his face, when the god Ramesses is not depicted with his hawk's head. I noticed that the sculptures generally give the principal temple deities the characteristics of the face of the founder king and queen. This you will even see at Philae in the section of the grand temple of Isis built by Ptolemy-Philadelphus: all the Isis of the sanctuary are portraits of queen Arsinoe, who clearly has a face that is Greek. But this is much more striking in the ancient monuments (the pharaonic ones) where the faces of sovereigns are real portraits.

On the evening of the 18th we reached Amada where we stayed until the afternoon of the 20th. There, as we were in the middle of the desert, I had the pleasure of being able to study a temple from the right era at leisure and without being distracted by the curious. This monument, deeply covered in sand, consists first of a type of pronaos, a chamber supported by twelve square columns covered in sculpture and by four columns which I might best describe as proto-Doric, or Doric prototypes, because they evidently belong to that group of Greek columns; and interestingly enough to note down, I have only found them in the most ancient Egyptian monuments, that is the tombs of Beni-Hassan, at Amada, at Karnak and at Bet-Oualli, which has the most modern ones as they date back to the reign of Sesostris or rather the one of his father...

On the 21st we were in Ouady-Esseboua (Valley of Lions), whose name derives from an avenue of sphinxes positioned along the dromos to this temple which is a semi-speos [cave], a building half made of freestone and half hewn from the rock. Hands down it is the worst job from the time of Ramesses the Great; the stones of its masonry are badly cut, its gaps were plugged with cement on which they continued the decorative, quite averagely-executed sculpture. This temple was dedicated by Sesostris to the god Phre and to Ptha, lord of justice...

The entire day of the 22nd was lost because of a very fierce northern wind which forced us to moor and stay put on the riverbank until sundown. We used the calm in order to reach Meharrakah whose temple we saw while going down the Nile; it has no sculpture at all and no interest for me who only searches for, as our Arabs say, hadjar-maktoub, written stones.

The sun of the 23rd rose over us in Dakke, the ancient Pscelcis. I hastened to the temple and the first hieroglyphic inscription catching my eyes told me that this was a sacred site dedicated to Thoth, lord of Pselk; thus I added another hieroglyphic town name to my map of Nubia and I would now be able to publish a map of Nubia with its ancient names in sacred characters.

The monument of Dakke is doubly of interest. From a mythological point it yields infinitely priceless material on the nature and attributes of the divine being the Egyptians called Thoth (Hermes's older brother); a series of bas-reliefs showed me, after a manner, all transfigurations of this god. I watched him first (no surprise here) linked with Har-hat (the great Hermes Trismegistus), his primordial form, of which he, Thoth, is no more than the last transformation, his incarnation on earth, following Amon-Ra and Muth incarnated into Osiris and Isis. Thoth ascends to the celestial-Hermes (Har-hat), divine knowledge, the spirit of god, while passing through the forms: 1 of Pahitnoefi (he whose heart is golden); 2 of Arihosnofri or Arihosnoufi (he who creates harmonious songs); 3 of Meui (thought or reason). Under each of these names Thoth has a distinct figure and paraphernalia, and the images of the various transformations of Hermes no 2 cover the walls of the temple of Dakke. I forget to mention that here I found Thoth (the Egyptian Mercury) armed with the caduceus, the customary sceptre of the gods with two intertwined snakes and a scorpion.

On the historical front, I concluded that the most ancient section of the temple (its penultimate chamber) was constructed and carved by the most celebrated of Ethiopian kings, Ergamenes (Erkamen), who according to the account of Diodorus of Sicily relieved Ethiopia from its theocratic government in a terrifying way, true, by cutting the throats of all the priests in the land. He clearly didn't do as much in Nubia as he erected a temple, and this monument proves that Nubia ceased to be subjected to Egypt from the fall of its twenty-fifth dynasty, the Saites who were dethroned by Cambyses, and that this country passed under the yoke of the Ethiopians until the time of Ptolemy-Evergetes's conquests who joined it again with Egypt. He also continued with building the temple of Dakke, which had been started under Ergamenes, as did his son Philopater, and his grandson Evergetes II. It was Augustus who commissioned, but did not complete, the interior sculpture of the temple.

Near the pylon of Dakke I found the remnants of a building of which a few large blocks of stone still preserve part of its dedication: it was a temple of Thoth built by pharaoh Tuthmosis IV. Yet another fact which, like many similar ones, proves that the Ptolemies, and the Ethiopian Ergamenes too, did nothing but reconstruct temples in places where they already existed in pharaonic times, and to the same deities that had always been honoured. This is a very important point to make for refuting that the last monuments of the Egyptians contained any new forms of divinities. The religious system of this people was so much one, so much linked to all its divisions, and in such an absolute and precise way fixed since times immemorial, that the Greek and Roman domination brought no innovation: the Ptolemaens and the Caesars only restored, both in Egypt and Nubia, what the Persians had destroyed, and rebuilt temples where they had been and under the same aegis.

Dakke is the most southern point I have come across work done under the Ptolemaens and the emperors. I am convinced that Greek or Roman domination extended, at most, up to Ibrim: from Dakke to Thebes I also found an almost continuous series built during that era. Pharaonic monuments are rare but those from the time of the Ptolemaens and the Caesars are numerous and practically all unfinished. I drew from this [the conclusion] that the destruction of the pharaonic temples which originally existed in Nubia between Thebes and Dakke must be attributed to the Persians who had to follow the valley of the Nile until Seboua, where in order to get to Ethiopia (and to return from it) they would have taken a desert route, which is infinitely shorter than going via the river, which is in any case impractical for an army because of the numerous cataracts; this desert route is still the one which the majority of caravans, armies and single travellers use. This [short-cut used by the] Persian military operation saved the monument at Amada, which would have been easy to demolish as it isn't very large. From Dakke to Thebes you will therefore see nothing but second editions of temples.

The exceptions are the monument of Ghirsche and the one at Beit-Qually, which the Persians couldn't flatten because it would have been necessary to pull down the mountains in which they are hewn by chisel. These caves, especially the former, were nonetheless devastated in as far as nature herself applied itself to this task...

The 26th was partly spent on the small temple of Dandour. Here we return to modern times: it is an unfinished project from the time of Augustus, but even though it is not very significant in size it rather interested me as it is entirely devoted to the incarnation of Osiris in his human form on earth. Our evening of the 25th had been illuminated by a thunderous echo we discovered by accident opposite Dandour, where we went ashore. With a booming sound it repeated up to eleven syllables extremely clearly. Our Italian comrades enjoyed making it repeat verses from Torquato Tasso mixed with gunfire aimed anywhere, to which the echo responded with canon shots and peals of thunder.

It was the turn of the temple of Kalabschi on the 27th. Here I found a new generation of gods that completes the circle of forms of Amon, the point of departure and ending of all divine essences. Amon-Ra, the supreme and primordial being, who is his own father, is called husband of his mother (the goddess Muth), who is the feminine side of his own nature, which is both male and female: all the other gods are no more than aspects of the these two principal constituents but seen from separate perspectives. They are no more than abstractions from the Great Being. These secondary, tertiary, etc. forms produce an uninterrupted chain which descends from the heavens and materialises in earthly incarnations and the human shape. The last of these incarnations is Horus and this final coil of the divine chain is shaped by the name of Horamon, the omega of the gods, of which Amon-Horus (the great Amon, life force and generator) is the alpha.

The starting point for Egyptian mythology is the Triad made up of the three parts, of Amon-Ra, that is Amon (the male and the father), Muth (the female and the mother) and Khons (the child son). This Triad, manifesting itself on earth, resolves itself in Osiris, Isis and Horus, though the equation is not complete because Osiris and Isis are siblings. At Kalabschi I found at last the final Triad, the one in which its three members mirror exactly the three members of the initial Triad: Horus actually has the epitaph of husband of his mother and the son which he has with his mother Isis, who is called Malouli (the Mandoulis in Greek proscynemes), is the principal deity of Kalabschi, and fifty bas-reliefs give us his genealogy. Thus part of the final triad are Horus, his mother Isis and their son Malouli, who return precisely in the Ur-Triad, Amon, his mother Muth and their son Khons. Furthermore, Malouli was venerated at Kalabschi in a form that is the same as the one of Khons, with the same costume and paraphernalia: except that the young god has, on top, of this the title Lord of Talmis, i.e. Kalabschi, which the Greek geographers in effect call Talmis, a name which is also found in the Greek inscriptions of the temple.

I have furthermore drawn the conclusion that there were three versions of the temple of Malouli: one under the pharaohs and from the reign of Amenophis II, the successor of Moeris; one from the time of the Ptolemies; and the last one, the actual temple, which was never completed under Augustus, Caligula and Trajan. The legend of the god Malouli in a bas-relief fragment from the first temple, used for the construction of the third, differs in no respect from the earlier legends. So, the local cults of the towns and burgs of Nubia and Egypt were never modified. Nothing was subject to innovation and the old gods still ruled on the day that the temples were closed by Christians. These gods moreover, in some way divided up Egypt and Nubia, forming a type of feudal partitioning. Each town had its patron: Chnouphis [Khnum] and Sate governed at Elephantine, at Syene [Aswan] and at Beghe, and their jurisdiction stretched out across the whole of Nubia; Phre at Ibsamboul [Abu Simbel], Derri and Amada; Ptha at Ghirsche; Anouke a Maschakit; Thoth, the overseer of Chnouphis over the whole of Nubia, with principal fiefdoms at Ghebel-Addeh and at Dakke; Osiris was lord of Dandour; Isis queen at Philae; Hathor at Ibsamboul and finally Malouli at Kalabschi. But Amon-Ra was sovereign everywhere and inhabited as a rule the right of the sanctuaries.

Egypt was the same and, anchored to the soil by the entire weight of its religious beliefs, you understand why this divisional cult couldn't change. Moreover, this cult, which was exclusive so to say to each area, caused no friction between neighbouring towns as each one would allow in its temple, based on a highly calculated spirit of courtesy, the worship of deities honoured in adjacent cantons (like syntrones). Thus I found that in Kalabschi the gods of Ghirsche and Dakke in the south, and those of Deboud in the north, take up a distinguished position; at Deboud the gods of Dakke and Philae; at Philae those of Deboud and Dakke to the south, those of Beghe, Elephantine and Syene [Aswan] to the north: at Syene, lastly, the deities of Philae and those of Ombos.

It was also in Kalabschi that I saw the colour violet being used on painted bas-reliefs for the first time. I ended up discovering that this colour came from the mordant or tincture applied to the surfaces of tableaux which were to be covered with goldleaf. Thus the sanctuary of Kalabschi and the chamber that preceded it were gilded as was the sanctuary of Dakke.

Near Kalabschi is the fascinating monument of Beit-Oually which engaged us on the 27th, 28th, 29th, and 30th of January until noon. There my eyes recuperated from the barbaric sculptures in the temple of Kalabschi — gaudy because no one knew any longer how to make something beautiful — while they surveyed the splendid historical bas-reliefs which decorate this speos in style and of which we have complete copies. These tableaus deal with the campaigns against the Arabs and the African people, the Kouschi (the Ethiopians) and the Schari who are probably today's Bischari; campaigns of Sesostris at the time of his youth, when his father was alive as Diodorus of Sicily expressly states, who in fact has him subjugate the Arabs and almost all of Libya.

King Ramesses, the father of Sesostris, is seated on his throne in a naos, and his son, dressed like a prince, presents a group of Asiatic Arab prisoners to him. Further on the pharaoh is portrayed as conqueror, striking down a man of that nation himself while at the same time the prince (Sesostris) leads military chiefs and a flock of prisoners before him. The king is pursuing the Arabs on his chariot and his son axing the gates of a town under siege. The king treats the conquered Arabs with contempt, of whom a long row is brought to him as captives by his son...

The right wall shows the details of the campaign against the Ethiopians, the Bischari and the black people. In the first scene, which is extremely wide, you see the barbarians being routed completely, fleeing to their forests, mountains or marshes. The second scene, which covers the remainder of the wall, depicts the king seated inside a naos and receiving his eldest son (Sesostris) with a sign of his hand, who brings before him: an Ethiopian prince called Amenemoph, son of Poeri, supported by two of his children, one of whom hands him a cup as if to give him the strength to go up to the throne of the father of his vanquisher; Egyptian military chiefs; tables covered with gold chains, panther furs, sacks containing gold powder, ebony trunks, elephant teeth, ostrich plumes, neat piles of bows and arrows, costly furniture, and all sorts of booty taken from or imposed on the enemy as a result of the victory; filing behind these treasures march a number of Bischaris prisoners, men and women, one of them carrying two children on her shoulder and in a sort sling; next people guiding to the king living animals of the species which are most typical of Africa, the lion, panthers, ostrich, monkeys, the giraffe, brilliantly drawn, etc etc. I hope that in this we may recognise Sesostris's campaign against the Ethiopians, whom according to Diodorus he forced to pay an annual tribute in gold, ebony and elephant teeth (bk I para. LV).

All other sculptures of the cave are religious. The monument was dedicated to the great god Amon-Ra and his secondary form Chnouphis [Khum]. In his legends the first of these gods states several times that he has handed over all seas and existing lands to his cherished son 'The lord of the world, sun guardian of justice, Ramesses II.' Inside the sanctuary this pharaoh is shown being suckled by the goddesses Anouke and Isis. 'I am your mother, the Elephantine lady', says the first 'I welcome you on my knees and offer you my breast so that you will be fed, Ramesses.' 'And I, your mother Isis,' says the latter 'I, lady of Nubia, grant you the periods of panygerics [jubileums] (those of thirty years) which you imbibe with my milk and which will result in a pure life.' I had these two scenes copied as well as several others, among them two bas-reliefs showing the pharaoh as the conqueror of the people of the south and the people of the north...

On the first of February we saw a cangia advance towards us which was flying the Austrian flag: this was a novelty for us and we were wondering where it might be going. Meanwhile the boat also advanced towards us and I recognised M. Acerbi, the Austrian consul in Egypt, who hailed and greeted us with his hand. We halted our boats and spent a few hours chatting about our work with this fine man, a polemicist and distinguished man of letters who had treated us in such a pleasant and generous way during our stay in Alexandria. We left each other, he for the Second Cataract, we to return to Egypt, with a promise to meet again in Thebes, the Paris of Egypt and meeting place for travellers, whatever the metropolis of Cairo and sad Alexandria may think...

As our work had finished we returned to our boats, eager to leave and to profit from the remainder of the day in order to reach Philae and so to return to Egypt and say goodbye to wretched Nubia whose dryness had completely exhausted my travel companions. Moreover, by again setting foot in Egypt we could look forward to having bread that was a little more palatable than the meagre unleavened biscuits with which we were daily regaled by our chief baker who easily scaled the heights of our Arab chef who had been presented to us in Cairo as a cordon bleu *maitre*.

It was at nine in the evening when we again set foot on Egyptian soil while going ashore the island of Philae, thanking its deities Osiris, Isis and Horus that we hadn't been devoured by hunger between the two cataracts...

I sacrificed almost an entire day to a small neighbouring island of Philae, the isle of Beghe, where the Commission of Egypt indicates the existence of a tiny Egyptian building. I did indeed find several columns of a minuscule of appalling workmanship from the time of Philometor. Yet a few inscriptions told me that I was on the island of Snem, the name of a place I had come across often in the legends of the gods and the goddess Hathor between Ombos and Dakke. This was one of the most holy places of Egypt and a sacred island, a goal for pilgrims long before its associate Philae, which was called Manlak in Egyptian. From this derives the Coptic Pilach, the Arab Bilaq and the Greek Philae, though it isn't even remotely related to the *fil* (elephant) of Jomard.

The temple of Snem (Beghe) was consecrated to Chnouphis [Khum] and the goddess Hathor, and the actual monument is again the second edition of a rather more ancient and extended temple built under pharaoh Amenophis II, the successor of Moeris. I found the remains of this temple and the remnants of a colossal statue of the same pharaoh which decorated one of the pylons of the ancient building...

Before leaving Philae, I went to the cataract on a pleasure trip with Messrs. Duchesne, L'hôte, Lehoux and Bertin to which we brought a good leg of lamb and a salad, which we ate in the shadow of a santh (a very prickly mimosa), the only tree in the place, facing the breakers of the Nile whose swooshing reminded me of our Alpine torrents...

I returned at last to Syene (Osouan) [Aswan] which I had left in December. While waiting for our luggage to arrive on camelback from Philae and for our new Egyptian flotilla to be put together (as we had left our Nubian boats at the cataract, which they couldn't clear), I revisited the ruins of the temple of Syene dedicated to Chnouphis and to Sate under emperor Nerva. It is a monument to the extreme degeneration of art in Egypt; nonetheless it interested me... because the symbolic name of this town, representing an architect's or mason's plumb line, is no doubt an allusion to the ancient position of Syene [Aswan] under the tropic of cancer and to the famous wells in which the sun fell down perpendicularly on the solstice of summer; Greek writers constantly repeat this story, which may actually have derived from the truth, though it would be dating back to an immensely remote age.

While going down the Nile towards the cataract by boat I went by all the granite rocks near Syene [Aswan]. On them I found homage of an Ethiopian prince to Amenophis and to queen Taia, his wife; a votive offering to Chnouphis [Khum], the local deity, for the prosperity of Ramesses the Great, his daughters Isenofre, Bathianthi and their brothers Scha-hem-kame and Merenphta;... lastly several proscynemes by ordinary individuals or public functionaries to the divinities of Syene and the cataract, Chnouphis, Sate and Anouke.

I visited the island of Elephantine for the second time, which as a whole is barely the size of a decent-sized park for the upstanding citizens of Paris though some modern chronologists have wanted to turn it into a kingdom in order to rid themselves of the old Egyptian dynasty of the Elephantines. The two temples were recently demolished in order to build barracks and warehouses for Syene; and so the small temple dedicated to Chnouphis [Khum] by pharaoh Amenophis III has disappeared. I found nothing except two stiles in granite which belonged to another temple dedicated to Chnouphis, Sate and Anouke, consecrated by Alexander the son of Alexander the Great...

The 15th, still at Ombos, dreadful wind!

Do refresh people's memory of me, those who haven't forgotten me; among them will doubtless be the publicans of the Pantheon. Tell M. de Saint Prix that I found rather unusual and unprecedented methods of legal procedure in Egypt, from the first Egyptian legislator Menevis through to Barthole and Cujas.[8]

Thousands of greetings to Carlotto and to all the Tuesday regulars[9] of the higher religions, including *papa* Giulio who will have his rhinoceros or hippopotamus whips and M. de Férussac his stones and several shells.

I am already thrilled by the prospect of perhaps finding a new courier in Thebes. I will be there at the end of the month. – Goodbye then my friend. – I find your letters a bit short. Do remember that I am thousands of miles away from you and that even the smallest trifle contains reviving miracle salts. The nights are so long! Always smoking or playing a card game of bouillote – you get tired of it, and it would be so nice to rifle again through the parcels from Paris! You will think I am demanding, but I am entitled to it after the modest letter of twenty seven pages which I have written to you and which I am ending as quickly as I can, fearing that you will think that the biggest talkers in the world come from the Second Cataract. Goodbye, then, I embrace you and all our friends. Yours with all my heart and soul.

[PS –] As the couriers which we send to Cairo go by foot and the wind does not prevent them from walking, I am having the one who brought me your letters leave tonight, or tomorrow before daybreak. – Thousand greetings to M. Letronne. Tell him that the lintel on which the inscription of Ombos was engraved was gilded and that the letters left a brilliant red colour which is still highly visible. I wasn't able to confirm his Serapis at Tafah, the stone which was supposed to show it was no longer there.

7.

The Mysteries of Thebes

Farewell

Champollion to Champollion-Figeac – 12 March 1829, Thebes
The opportunity arose, my dearest friend, to send you some news. From the morning of the 8th I have been here and in very good health, as is the entire cavalcade, as we have to my relief brought to an end, and with great success, the expedition to Nubia and upper Thebes. We are still living in our boats in order to explore more easily the palace of Luxor, at whose feet we are moored. I saw its beautiful obelisks again. Why all that silliness of carrying the one from Alexandria back when you can have one of these for the modest expense of at most 400.000 francs? The minister who would put one of these stunning monoliths up on one of the squares of Paris will immortalise himself with little effort.

In a few days we will establish ourselves at Kourna in a rather comfortable house and from there we will go at ease along the Theban plain. I will write to you a little more in a few days; content yourself with these few lines. Everything is going well, – I embrace you with my entire heart.

Champollion to Champollion-Figeac – 25 March 1829, Biban-el-Molouk
You will no doubt, my dear friend, have received the lines I wrote in haste on the 11th of March or thereabouts, which the Austrian consul Acerbi[1] promised to dispatch from Alexandria via the first ship leaving for Europe as he left the royal city... I am keen to use our boats for our work in Luxor because this magnificent palace, which has been profaned more than any other monument in Egypt, *fellah* shacks obstructing, masking and disfiguring its beautiful porticoes, not mentioning the wretched house of

some Bimbachi perching on a platform that has been aggressively pick-axed in order to channel the sweepings of the Turk, and which lead to the superb sanctuary sculpted under the reign of the son of Alexander the Great, this magnificent palace, as I said, has no amenities that are clean enough to set up our camp. So we had to hold on to our maasch, the dahabiah and small boats, until our work at Luxor ends.

We left the left bank on the 23rd and, after having sent the bulk of our luggage to a house in Kourna which a very decent and excellent man called Piccinini, the agent of M. d'Anastazy in Thebes, let to us, we went on our way to the valley of Biban-el-Molouk [Valley of the King.] where the graves lie of the kings of the eighteenth and nineteenth dynasty. This valley, which is steep, stony, encircled by rather high mountains and completely devoid of any vegetation, must be insufferably hot in the months of May, June and July; our assignment was to quarry this rich and inexhaustible mine during a season when its temperature, though already very high, was meanwhile still bearable. Hence our caravan made up of donkey and savants settled in on the same day and we occupied the best and most splendid lodgings you will find in Egypt. King Ramesses (the fourth of the nineteenth dynasty) offered us his hospitality, as we all lived in his magnificent tomb, the second which you encounter to the right upon entering the valley of Biban-el-Molouk. This well-preserved tomb receives enough air and light for us to be phenomenally housed. We occupied the three first rooms which measure sixty five paces; its walls of fifteen to twenty feet high and its ceilings are all covered with painted sculptures whose colours have almost all preserved their brilliance. It is a truly a princely dwelling…; the floor is entirely covered with mats and reed. The map will give you an idea of what it is like.

The two kavass (our body guards) and the servants sleep in their two tents pitched up at the entrance of the tomb. This is our base camp in the Valley of the Kings, genuinely at death's door as there is neither a wisp of herbs nor a living creature, with the exception of the jackals and hyenas which gorged the donkey that carried my Barbar servant Muhammad the night before last. It happened at a hundred feet from our palace, while the donkey-driver was spending his night of Rammadan in the comfort of our kitchen, which has been set up in the total ruin of royal tomb. I thought that all these details would amuse the family…

The announcement of an archaeological Commission for the Peloponnese, given to Dubois,[2] gave me enormous pleasure; I know that this has been one of his greatest wishes for a long time. I hope that he will already have left: I would therefore like to know whether he is in Paris or in Athens in order to be able to write to him. I want to know whether he is already under the colonnades, − or in the Altis of Olympia at the head of four hundred pick-axers, which would be even better. − As for pickaxes, I will tell you that I started doing excavations at Karnak and Kourna. I am already the owner of 18 mummies of all shapes and sizes, but I will only bring the most remarkable ones with me, particularly the Graeco-Roman mummies which sometimes have both Greek and Demotic and hieratic legends. I have several of this type and a few of intact mummified babies which are rare, up to now.

All the bronzes that I found in Karnak, and even the ones taken from houses in Thebes, from about fifteen to twenty feet below the actual ground level, are in a total state of oxidation which prevents any conclusion being put forward about them. I appointed the former chief-searcher of M. Drovetti, called Temsahh (the crocodile),[3] who seems to be an astute man who does not cease to predict great things, as the head of excavations on the eastern bank. I am not counting on very much because you would have to dig in style and my means aren't sufficient. It would be wonderful if I had received the supplementary funds I have been asking for. Time flies and I will probably receive a definite answer the moment I will have to leave Thebes, the only place where one can find great and beautiful things with absolute certainty... If I bring back something good, it will be sheer chance on the one hand and pure generosity on the other, mine, because I am not under any obligation to bring back a collection of antiquities for the Louvre, − the funds requested for that purpose were very deliberately refused. Nonetheless, I will try to spice up my searches a little during the months of June, July and August, the time when I will be either in Karnak or in Kourna. I have forty men behind me, and I will see whether the results roughly compensate the expenses, and whether my budget can support them. I also have thirty six men who search in Kourna, at shared cost with Rosellini. Clearly I won't be able to consider moving any large pieces hitherto missing from the royal museum, as transport alone to Alexandria would exhaust my finances.

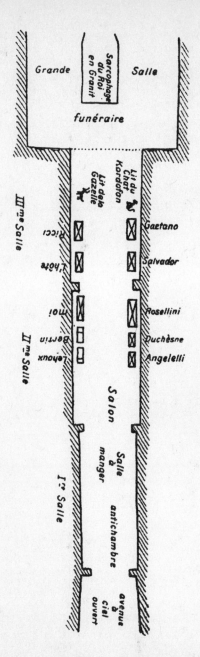

The lay-out of Champollion's stay in the tomb of Ramesses IV

So I return to the idea that, if the government wants an obelisk in Paris, it is a matter of national pride to have one of the ones in Luxor (the one to the right upon entry), a monolith of supreme beauty and of a height of seventy feet, a monument of Sesostris, of an exquisite workmanship, and in a state of astonishing preservation. Insist on this and find a minister who wants to immortalise his name by embellishing Paris with such a miracle: 300,000 will do the trick. I hope people will seriously think about it. If it is to be done, an architect or practical engineer (but no academic!) with pockets full of money should be dispatched, and the obelisk will come down. Labour costs nothing here. My excavators – infernal labour – get 20 paras (3 sols and 3 liards) and I am paying them generously; they are flourishing with this treatment.

So poor Dr Young is incorrigible? Why flog a mummified horse? Thank M. Arago for the arrows he shot so valiantly in honour of the Franco-Pharaonic alphabet.[4] The Brit can do whatever he wants, – it will remain ours: and all of old England will learn from young France how to spell hieroglyphs using an entirely different method from 'the Lancaster one'.[5] Other than that, may the Doctor continue to agitate about the alphabet while I, having been for six months among the monuments of Egypt, I am startled by what I am reading fluently rather than what my imagination is able to come up with. I have results (and this should remain between the two of us) which are extremely embarrassing for a regiment of theories, and which we shall have to keep under wraps; my presence here was in no way a mistake, many things which I suspected only vaguely have taking shape here and assumed an unassailable certainty.

After all this I will resume the thread of my itinerary and the description of the monuments since Ombos, where my last not very detailed letter was dated.

Leaving Ombos on the 17th of February we arrived as a result of the uselessness of the *reis* of our large boat and the limpness of our rowers only on the evening of the 18th at Ghebel-Selseleh (Silsilis), the enormous quarries where I had promised myself an ample harvest. This expectation was fully realised and the five days we spent there were well used...

Erected by the overseers of the buildings or by the princes who came from Upper Egypt in order to celebrate the panegyrics of the years 30, 34, 37, 40 and 44 of his reign, several steles contain exciting details about the family of the conqueror. One of these steles tells us that Ramesses had two wives. The first one Nofre-Ari, was the wife of his youth, the one who appears with their children on the monuments of Ibsamboul and Nubia. The second (and last one, up to now) was called Isenofre. She was the mother of princess Bathianti, who appears to have been his favourite daughter, the Benjamin of Sesostris's old age, and of prince Schahemkeme, the one who lords over the panegyrics [jubileum feasts] during the last years of reign of his father as three of the grand steles in Silsilis prove. It was probably this son who succeeded him, relinquishing his princely name and taking the one of Thmeiothph (possessor-of-the-truth, or rather he-who-is-possessed-by-truth); he is the Sesoosis II of Diodorus and the Pheron of Herodotus. Like his father he was an active patron of buildings, of which there are but few traces left. In the speos of Silsilis you will find a small chapel in his honour which was consecrated by the overseer of lands named Ombite, and called Pnahasi; a stele (date defaced) dedicated by the same Pnahasi and stating that building blocks were extracted from the quarries of Silsilis for the construction of a palace which this king had built in Thebes, of which there isn't a vestige left, as far as I know...

In the morning of the 24th of February we examined the portico and colonnades of Edfu (Apollonopolis magna). This building, which is imposing because of its silhouette, nonetheless shows the fingerprint of the decadence of Egyptian art under the Ptolemies to whose reign it belongs completely. No more antique simplicity; you will see affectation and a profusion of often awkward ornaments marking the transition of the noble gravitas of the pharaonic monuments to the tiresome riot of such bad taste on the temple of Esne which was built during the time of the emperors...

This grand and magnificent building was dedicated to a Triad composed of the god Har-Hat, the personification of science and light whose image in the material world is the sun; the Greeks equated him with their Apollo; the goddess Hathor, the Egyptian Venus; their son Har-Sont-Tho (Horus, pillar-of-the-world) who corresponds to Amor (Eros) of the Greek and Roman mythologies.

The qualifications, titles and forms of these divinities, which we marked with care, threw a beam of light on several important sections of the Egyptian theogony. It would be too long to set this out in similar detail.

I also had a series of fourteen bas-reliefs of the interior of the pronaos reproduced which show the rise of the god Har-Hat, symbolised by the sun, his going to sleep and his symbolic forms during each of the twelve hours of the day, with the names of the hours. This collection is of great interest to the understanding of how little the Egyptian myths were really related to astronomy.

The second building of Edfu, called the Typhonium, is like other small temples going by the name of Mammisi (cradle of childbirth) which were always built next to the grand temples where one of the Triad was venerated. It was the twin of the celestial dwelling where the goddess had given birth to the third person in the Triad who is always portrayed in the form of a child. The Mammisi of Edfu shows in effect the youth and education of the young Har-Sont-Tho, son of Har-Hat and Hathor, to whom eulogy associated Evergetes II, also shown as a child and sharing the caresses which the gods of all denominations lavish on the newly-born of Har-Hat...

Having ended our work at Edfu and tired of the coarse hieroglyphs and pitiful Egyptian sculpture from the time of the Ptolemies, we soothed our eyes in the tombs of Elethyia (El-Kab), where we arrived on Saturday the 28th of February. We were welcomed by rain(!) which came down in torrents, with thunder and lightning, during the night of the 1st to the 2nd March. So we can say as Herodotus said of king Psammenite: 'in our time it rained in Upper Egypt'.

I eagerly traversed the inner walls of the old city of Elethyia, which still stands, as does a second enclosure which circled around the temples and sacred buildings. There wasn't a column that was still standing upright; a few months ago the Barbarians demolished what was left of the two interior temples and the entire temple situated outside the city. I had to content myself with sifting through the stones which the pillagers had forgotten and on which there were some sculptures left.

I hoped to find a few fragments of legends that would allow me to establish the time of construction of these buildings and the divinities to which they were devoted. I was very lucky to come across enough to convince myself completely that these temples of Elethyia, once dedicated to Sevek (Saturn) and to Sowan (Lucine), belong to different pharaonic eras; those within the town were built and embellished under the reign of queen Amense, under the one of her son Tuthmosis (Moeris) and under the pharaohs Amenophis-Memnon and Ramesses the Great. The kings Amyrtee and Achoris, two of the last princes of the Egyptian race, repaired these antique buildings and added new buildings. I found little in Elethyia which recalled the Greek or Roman era. The temple outside the city belongs to the reign of Moeris.

Generally the tombs or hypogeans hewn into the Arab mountain chain which neighbours the city go back to an even earlier age. The first one we visited is the one of which the Commission of Egypt published the painted bas-reliefs concerning farming, fishing and navigation. This tomb was carved for the family of a hierogrammate called Paphe who was attached to the college of priests of Elethyia (Sowan-Kah)… This tomb is extremely old. A second grave, of a grand priest of the goddess Ilythia or Elethyia (Sowan), the eponymous goddess of the city, carries the date of the reign of Ramesses-Meiamoun, the first king of the nineteenth dynasty; it depicts a lot of family details and several agricultural scenes in a very poor state. I noticed among other things the thrashing or beating of corn sheaves by oxen, and above this scene you will read in almost entirely phonetic hieroglyphs the song which the overseer of the thrashing is supposed to sing, clearly in old Egypt as in the one of today everything is done by singing and each type of work has its own song.

Here is the one of thrashing grain, a type of short speech addressed to the bulls and which I next found with very minor variation in much more ancient tombs:

Hi-tenou neten (sop snaw)	Thrashing for you (bis)
Ne-eheou	O bulls
Hi-tenou neten (sop snaw)	Thrashing for you (bis)
Hen-oipe-neten	Bushels for you
Hen-oipe-ennetennev	Bushels for your masters.

The poetry is not terribly brilliant: the melody probably carried the song…

On the third of March, in the morning, we were very graciously received by Ibrahim-Bey, the mamour or governor of the province. With his help we were given permission to study the grand temple of Esne which is buried under cotton and which, serving as the general warehouse for this province, is stuccoed with Nile silt on its entire exterior. Equally the openings between the first line of columns inside the pronaos are closed with mud walls which meant that we often had to work with a candle in our hands or with ladders in order to see the bas-reliefs more closely.

Despite all these obstacles, I gathered all that is important to know from a historical and mythological point of view about this great temple. Based on little more than conjecture, a speculative manner of interpreting the zodiac on its ceiling, this monument has been considered the most ancient monument of Egypt. The study I made of it, on the contrary, has convinced me beyond any doubt that it is one of the most recent ones in Egypt: the bas-reliefs which embellish it and most of the hieroglyphs are in such a pedestrian and tortuous style that you can see immediately the supreme flourishing of art's degradation. The bulk of this pronaos was erected under the emperor Claudius whose dedication is on the frieze of the pronaos in large hieroglyphs. The cornice of the façade and the first row of columns were carved under Vespasian and Titus. The back part of the pronaos carries the legends of the emperors Antonius, Marcus-Aurelius and Commodus. Several columns inside the were decorated under Trajan, Hadrian and Antoninus, but with the exception of several bas-reliefs from the time of Domitian, all those on the right and left wall of the pronaos carry images and legends of Septimius Severus and his son Antonius Caracalla. There are also three or four bas-reliefs which interested me highly because they portray Geta, the son of Septimius Severus, whose brother Caracalla cruelly assassinated while proscribing his name throughout the empire at the same time. It would seem that this prohibition by the tyrant was executed to the letter deep down into the Theban hinterland because the cartouches/proper names of Geta have all been hammered and obliterated, though not to the extent that I wasn't still able to read very clearly the name of this unfortunate prince: emperor Caesar-Geta, director…

So the antiquity of the pronaos of Esne has now been analysed beyond dispute: its construction does not go back further than Claudius and its carvings do not go further back than Caracalla and that includes the famous zodiac about which so much has been said.

What is to left of the naos, i.e. the back wall of the pronaos, dates back to Ptolemy-Epiphanes and this is earlier than what was thought. The search we executed behind the pronaos convinced us that the proper temple was razed to its foundations.

Let fans of the antiquity of the monuments of Egypt in the meantime console themselves: Latopolis or rather Esne (as this name may be read in hieroglyphs on all the columns and bas-reliefs of the temple), was not at all a village during the golden age of the pharaohs; it was an important city adorned with beautiful monuments, I uncovered proof of this on the columns of the pronaos...

A short distance separated us from Thebes and our hearts was beating fast because we would see its mighty ruins again; our stomachs

Ancient Egyptian song for thrashing grain

joined in this longing, too, because there was a rumour of a boat with fresh provisions having arrived for me at Luxor... Yet during the night an extremely turbulent northern wind detained us between Hermonthis and Thebes, to which we were let go only on the next morning, the 8th of March, very early in that morning.

Our small armada went ashore at the foot of the ancient quay whose foundation has been worn away by the Nile and which won't defend the palace of Luxor, whose furthest columns almost touch the edges of the river, for much longer. This quay is clearly from two eras. The oldest Egyptian quay is made from large dried bricks linked by tremendously durable cement, and its ruins form colossal blocks of a height of fifteen to eighteen feet and a width of twenty-five to thirty, which is similar to the rocks inclining towards the river from whose midst they jutted forward. The sandstone quay is from a very much later period; I noticed a number of stones which still show fragments of sculpture in the old style and have come from demolished buildings.

Our work at Luxor ended (just about) before we went to set up camp at Biban-el-Molouk, and I am now in a position where I can give you all necessary details regarding the construction of all the sections that make up this magnificent building.

The founder of the Luxor palace, or rather the palaces of Luxor, was pharaoh Amenophis-Memnon (Amenothis III) of the eighteenth dynasty. It was this prince who built a series of buildings which stretch from the south to the north, from the Nile to right up to the fourteen gigantic columns of a height of forty five feet whose foundations also belong to this reign. You will read dedications in the name of Amenophis in large hieroglyphs of a very shallow relief and brilliant workmanship on all the architraves and other columns which grace its courts and interior chambers, all of them intact, totalling a hundred and five. I will give you the translation of one of these so as to give you an idea of all the others which aren't very different, give or take a few more royal titles:

Life! The mighty and moderate Horus, ruling through justice, organiser of his country, he who balances the world, because he, great because of his power, smote the barbarians; the king lord of justice, loved by the sun, son of the sun, Amenophis, moderator of the pure land (Egypt), had these constructions built and consecrated to his father Amon, the lord god of the three zones of the universe in Oph of the south; he made them in lasting and good stone in order to erect a durable building, this is what the son of the sun, Amenophis, favourite of Amon-Ra has done.

These inscriptions therefore remove any kind of doubt about the exact era of the construction and decoration of this part of Luxor. 'My' devotional dedications are not verbless, like the Greek inscriptions analysed by M. Letronne which were so much derided for that reason; regarding this point you can tell him that I will bring him Egyptian votive inscriptions from the temples of Philae, Ombos and Dendera, in which the verb 'construct' always appears.

Generally he bas-reliefs which decorate the palace of Amenophis are concerned with religious rites performed by this prince in honour of the great divinities of this part of Thebes, being: Amon-Ra, the supreme god of Egypt who was almost exclusively worshipped at Thebes, his eponymous city; Amon-Ra Generator, mystically entitled 'the husband of his mother' and shown in a priapic shape; this is the Egyptian Pan featuring in the Greek writers; the goddess Thamoun or Tamon, i.e. female Amon, one of the forms of Neith as a companion to Amon Generator;

the goddess Muth, the great divine mother, the companion of Amon-Ra; the young gods Khons and Harka who complete the two great Triads worshipped in Thebes:

Father	Mother	Son
Amon-Ra	Muth	Khons
Amon Generator	Thamoun	Harka

The pharaoh is shown making offerings, sometimes extremely lavish ones, to these various divinities or accompanying their bari or sacred arches as they are carried in procession by the priests.

Yet in two rooms of the palace I found a series of bas-reliefs which are even more interesting and concern the person himself of the founder, and had them reproduced. Here a word on their basic plot.

Thoth announces to Tmauhemva, wife of pharaoh Tuthmosis IV that Amon Generator has granted him a son. – The same queen, whose pregnancy is expressly visible, guided by Chnouphis [Khum] and Hathor (Venus) towards the chamber of child-birth (the mammisi); the same princess placed on a bed and giving birth to king Amenophis; women supporting the recumbent, divine spirits ranged underneath her bed and raising the sign of life towards the new-born. The queen suckling the young prince. – The Nile god painted in blue (the season of low water level) and the Nile god painted in red (the flooding season), introducing the small Amenophis as well as the small god Harka and other divine children to the great gods of Thebes. – The royal child in the arms of Amon-Ra who caresses him. – The young child being invested by Amon-Ra; the guardian goddesses of Upper and Lower Egypt giving him the crowns which symbolise sovereignty over the two countries, and Thoth choosing his grand name, that is his royal first name sun-lord-of-justice-and-truth, which distinguishes him from all the other Amenophis on monuments.

One of the last chambers of the palace, which has a more religious character than all the others, and which must have served as a royal chapel or sanctuary, is exclusively decorated with Amenophis worshipping the two Triads of Thebes, and in this chamber, whose roof still exist, you will find a second sanctuary boxed in the first...

This is the only modern part of the old palace of Amenophis; the following is not worth mentioning except as something unusual. If you read the characters on the lintel of an architrave which was restored and carved under one of the Ptolemies in the room which precedes the sanctuary, the resulting dedication is bizarre, as if the adjoining old stones of the architrave containing the older dedication didn't matter. Look:

> First stone (new): 'Restoration of the building by king Ptolemy, living, loved by Ptha...'
> Second stone (old): '... world, the sun lord of justice, sun of the son, Amenophis had these buildings erected in honour of his father Amon etc.'

On the old stone, which the Lagide [family name of the Ptolemies] replaced, you would have read the legend: 'Mighty Aroeris etc, lord of the world etc.' They weren't at all concerned whether the new legend did or did not match the old one...

The entire northern part of the Luxor complex is from another era and forms a discrete palace though it is linked by a splendid colonnade to the Amenopheum or palace of Amenophis. We have to thank Ramesses the Great (Sesostris) for these buildings, and rather than embellishing the palace of Amenophis, his ancestor, he wanted to erect a separate edifice, which inference follows from the following dedication carved in large hieroglyphs above the cornice of the pylon and repeated on the architraves of all colonnades that haven't yet buried been today's shacks:

> Life! Aroeris, child of Amon, master of the upper region and lower region, twice expedient, the Horus of full force, friend of the world, the king (sun guardian of the truth), seconded by Phre, the preferred son of the king of the gods, who, seated on the throne of his father, rules over the earth, has had these edifices erected in the honour of his father Amon-Ra, king of gods. He built this Ramesseum in the city of Amon, in the Oph of the south. This is what the son of the sun, (the favourite of Amon, Rhames), vivifyer forever, has done.

It is therefore a separate building, distinct from the Amenopheum, and this explains elegantly why these two great buildings are not lined up in the same way, a gross shortcoming which all voyagers have commented upon, assuming wrongly that these constructions were of the same date and formed a single whole, which they don't.

It is before the north pylon of the Ramesseum of Luxor that the two celebrated obelisks of pink granite, of such skilled purity and beautiful conservation, rise up. These two enormous real jewels of more than seventy feet high were erected in this place by Ramesses the Great, who wanted to decorate his Ramesseum with them as the hieroglyphic inscription on the left obelisk, northern side, middle column, expressly states...

I have two exact copies of these two stunning monoliths. I took them with extreme care, correcting the erroneous observations of the Commission and complementing them with excavations which we made right up to the base of the obelisks. Sadly it is impossible to have the end of the eastern face of the right obelisk and the western face of the left obelisk; we would have had to demolish several houses made of earth and move out several destitute families of *fellahs.*[6]

I won't dwell for too long on the contents of the legends of these two obelisks. You already know that far from containing great religious mysteries, refined philosophical speculations, secrets of the occult sciences, or at least astronomical lessons, as has been believed for so long, they simply are rather sumptuous signatures of the buildings in front which monuments of this type stand...

The obelisks, the four columns, the pylon and the vast peristyle or court surrounded by columns which touch, is all that remains of the Ramesseum on the right river, and you will read dedications to Ramesses the Great everywhere, with the exception of only two places in this exceptional building. It would appear that towards the eighth century BC the ancient decoration of the grand gate situated between the two bulkheads of the pylon was for some reason in a very bad state, and that their entire masses were fitted anew. The bas-reliefs of Ramesses the Great were replaced by new ones which are still there, and which represent the chief of the twenty-fifth dynasty, the Ethiopian conqueror Sabaco or Sabacon who for many years governed Egypt with great mildness, making the usual offerings to the guardian gods of the palace and city of Thebes.

These bas-reliefs, on which you'll see the name of the king which is written as Schabak and which you can read very clearly even though they were defaced by hammering at a very remote time, these bas-reliefs, I said, are also highly unusual for their style. With vigorously pronounced muscles its figures are highly articulated and revealing without anticipating the heaviness of the sculptures of the Ptolemies or the Romans... These are the only sculptures of his reign which I found in Egypt.

I will end my monumental note for today. I will talk in my next letter about the tombs of the Theban kings which we are at this moment excavating.

2 April 1829

I am finishing my letter today as the courier will leave this very morning for Cairo. No news since the 25th; still in good health and spirit.

This evening, I am going to throw a dinner party for our young people in one of the prettiest chambers of the tomb of Ousirei (Sethos I) [Seti I]; it will be the birthday party of Mlle Zoraïde,[7] a day which I have declared to her namesake, and promised to celebrate with a panegyric. It ought to have been celebrated on the 1st of March but we were in amidst the horrors of the cataract, barely having any bread to eat; it was therefore postponed until today. The dinner won't emulate the brilliance of the setting, but we are doing our utmost not to let it undershoot it by too much. I am preparing it as a surprise for our young ones. One dish would top it off: this is a slice of young crocodile in a spicy sauce. Fate willed that a freshly killed one was brought to me yesterday. I am relying heavily on this dish to make an impact. – We will drink to your health, all of you inhabitants of Paris, so that you will be present at our feast. Adieu my dear friend, I embrace you with heart and soul.

PS – Our dish of crocodile went off overnight, – the meat has become green and putrid. What a pity! We'll have to console ourselves though we are probably escaping indigestion or at least bloated stomachs.

During the birthday dinner of his daughter in the tomb, Champollion toasted Giovanni Belzoni, who had found its entrance on 16 July 1817. – At the time, having received a long letter (30 November 1817) from Sir Henry Salt, M. Dacier had advised Champollion to join the 'giant of Padua', as he called Belzoni, as quickly as possible. Having discovered the entrance to five royal catacombs, Belzoni, like Salt, wanted someone near him who

Giovanni Belzoni, expert on hydraulics, circus strongman, and first modern excavator of Egypt

could decipher hieroglyphs: 'Next to this giant you will yourself take giant steps and you will find the answer to the enigma more quickly' Dacier had said, very pleased that Henry Salt showed more confidence in Champollion than in his compatriot Thomas Young. But, preoccupied with developing a revolutionary system (he thought) of 'mutual teaching', Champollion decided not to go. By coincidence, at the same time when

Champollion had read his famous *Letter to M. Dacier* on 27 September 1822, containing Champollion's discovery of Ramesses name ('le mot d'enigme') several large barges loaded with gigantic facsimiles of the tomb were filing down the Seine. Almost as soon as Belzoni arrived in Paris and even though he was in constant touch with William Bankes, for whom he had organised sizeable excavations, particularly on the island of Philae, he expressed his boundless enthusiasm for Champollion.

The 'Giant' or 'Titan of Padua', as he was called in Paris, was very popular there, both because of his enormous size and because of the exhibition of the royal tomb. People found the fresh beauty of half a dozen funerary chambers from the famous catacomb, displayed in their natural grandeur with rigorous accuracy, a source of inexhaustible admiration. Alessandro Ricci, among other artists and an architect, had worked for twenty seven months on faithful copies of its ancient master-pieces. When Champollion entered Belzoni's subterranean world, 'whose fairytale effect was heightened by successful lighting' he was mesmerised. He helped Belzoni against Jomard who from the start had spread the rumour, particularly at the court, that Belzoni would be inaccurate, even though the *Description de l'Egypte* contained no information on this catacomb as it was discovered afterwards. In December 1822 a cata-logue appeared which was written anonymously by Champollion as his name could not be mentioned because of William Bankes, to whom Belzoni had to send this publication. The objects of the exhibition perished in a fire – people say in Padua – a few years after the premature death of Belzoni in 1823.

Champollion to Champollion-Figeac – 18 May 1829,
Biban-el-Molouk [Valley of the Kings]

The courier we dispatched to Cairo at the beginning of April has not yet returned. This extraordinary delay is worrying us and we are thinking of sending a second courier after him, who will leave this evening in order to find the latecomer dead or alive. If he reaches Cairo he will present this letter to the consulate, which will forward it to you. This is why it is going to be short, saving all details on the tombs of the kings which I want to present to you for the next courier, who will leave as soon as I will have finished my work at Biban-el-Molouk.

I cannot believe that I have stayed here for so long, but the walls of these tombs and in particular its ceilings are covered with such interesting subjects that I have had to listen to the voice of conscience as one would seek in vain for scenes of this genre elsewhere and decide to reproduce these images and inscriptions. Reserving the elegant hand of our draughtsmen for the completion of historical tableaus which concern the history of Egyptian art directly, I did this work myself. Moreover, I can only rely on myself for these diabolical scenes which illustrate all the powers of hell and the customs and conventions of the other world in utterly monstrous and complex forms. Its psychology is most refined. I will talk to you about it and a good many other things in the letter which I will write to you next from the Valley of the Kings.

I gather from your latest that people would like me to address letters to M. such and such [hitherto Champollion had announced his discoveries in this way]; I think it is extremely pointless to put down names of people who don't understand an iota of the matter. Besides, my letters contain compressed results, — they are simplified notes, a kind of announcements and not polished letters as they would have to be for the great and the good. I think you will agree with me about this, and if you had taken the precaution to put your name to the letters, as they are addressed to you, no one would have slipped their name in at the top. You were wrong. — as for M. de la Bouillerie [minister of the Royal Household], who has put so much energy into supporting my undertaking, you are right in keeping him informed so that he receives one of the earliest communications of my results. One must see him from time to time for that reason and show him that he has not been forgotten and that we are counting on him for the publication of the harvest of the expedition, which won't put him off at all as he was the first one to believe in me. If this seems agreeable, take care not to commit yourself to anything because if the work sells, which it is likely to do, it is right that we should have a robust interest in it. It would suffice, I think, to have a subscription for a hundred to a hundred and fifty copies. Beyond that anything is premature. Let's not count our chickens before they have hatched.

The prolongation of my stay among the tombs of the kings is being put to good use by my young people who are updating my portfolios of Nubia and Lower-Thebes by making copies of the work done by the Tuscan artists. The series is already impressive and of the greatest importance.

Amid so much work our health is keeping up brilliantly, except for Salvador's who had an illness from which he has now quite recovered. I also have to say that the great Amon-Ra is favouring us: the tomb in which we live is a benediction for this season. – The temperature is quite stable at around 20 to 21 degrees, though two steps away from our front door the thermometer marks 35 to 36 in the shade and 47 to 48 in the sun. Moreover, the previous month has gone by, as it would, without the *Khamsin* rearing itself. You doubtless know that this is a burning and devastating wind which throws up masses of dust and withers everything it finds in its way. I will leave Egypt without having any idea of this wind, the true Typhon of the poor Thebes area.

I won't write to Rosine [Champollion's wife] this time, the courier has to leave straightaway: so let her know about my letter. Also write to Figeac that I am doing well.[8] Has Dubois reached his destination. Where is he? What is he doing? Is our army advancing as quickly as it disembarked? Lost in the desert and down in the tombs, we have had no news at all for two months and counting about what is going on in the rest of the world. This is hard, very hard: because despite our stoicism and though the transience of people is written around us in dazzling characters, though we meditate from time to time at the top of the arid mountain from where the entire width of the great skeleton of Thebes unfolds, we are still attached to our poor earth, to its fallen inhabitants, and most of all to those who are shivering beyond the Mediterranean. I cannot tell you how much we were moved by a number of November, December and January newspapers, and what joy we felt about the good things that are happening in France. France…! Let's not talk about it any further, my heart swells and I still have to roam across the ruins of Thebes for a few months. After that, only pleasure and only joy. Adieu, I embrace you, and all those who are our on our side, with heart and soul.

PS – According to Theban whispers, Pariset has made a detour towards the pest, which, they say, has manifested itself in Syria. There is none in Egypt.

26 May 1829, Thebes (*Biban-el-Molouk, Valley of the Kings*)
The topographical details given by Strabo [geographer from Augustus's reign] leave no room except for searching the valley of Biban-el-Molouk,

the site of the ancient kings. The name of this valley which one might be tempted to derive entirely from the Arab by translating it 'gates of the kings', but this is both a corruption and translation of the ancient Egyptian name Bib-an-Ouroou (tombs of the kings), as M. Sylvestre de Sacy [a scholar of Oriental languages] has argued very well, will remove any doubt on this subject. It was the royal necropolis and they chose a site ideally suited for this melancholy destination, an arid valley encased by extremely high rocks sliced in peaks or by completely eroded mountains, almost all of which have deep slits caused either by the extreme heat or by internal crumbling and whose saddles are strewn with black stripes as if they have been partly burnt. There is no vegetation peering through either its slopes or the bottom of the valley, which looks like the bedding of one of our great Alpine torrents which has not seen water for centuries. With the exception of a few serpents and lizards no animals haunt this valley of death: I am not taking the flies, foxes, wolves and hyenas into account because these four hungry species have only been attracted by our stay among the tombs and the smells of our kitchen.

Upon entering the part of this valley which is set back furthest, through a narrow entrance which is clearly man-made and which still shows faint remainders of Egyptian sculpture, you will soon see, at the foot of the mountains or on their slopes, square doorways which are usually blocked and which you have to approach in order to see their decoration: these openings, which are all alike, give access to the royal tombs. Each is the opening to its own tomb, for at the time none of them were connected to each other; they were all isolated. Only treasure hunters, ancient and modern, have forced communication between them.

Arriving in Biban-el-Molouk, I impatiently assured myself that the sixteen tombs (I am only talking here about the tombs whose sculpture has been preserved and the names of kings for whom they were hewn) were really as I previously argued for several reasons those of kings belonging to the Theban dynasties, that is princes whose family came from Thebes. The quick inspection I had given them before going down to the Second Cataract as well as the visit of several months on my return have wholly convinced me that these tombs contained the bodies of the kings of the eighteenth, nineteenth and twentieth dynasties, which are in effect all three Diospolitan or Theban dynasties. Thus I found first of all the tombs of: Ramesses I; Menephta I (Ousire); Ramesses the Great;

Menephtha III; Rhameri, all kings of the eighteenth dynasty, and the one of the oldest of them, Amenophis Memnon, interred separately in the isolated valley to the west. Next the tomb of Ramesses-Meiamoun, who is very clearly the chief of the nineteenth dynasty and one of the great Egyptian conquerors, called Sesostris by the ancient authors, who were not able to distinguish the two famous Ramesses by their military exploits, and the tombs of six pharaohs all of them called Ramesses, descendants of Meiamoun which form the nineteenth and the beginning of the twentieth dynasty.

No order whatsoever, neither dynasty or succession, was followed when choosing the location of the various royal tombs: each one of them had theirs hewn at a point where they thought they would come across a vein in the stone which would be suitable for sculpture and the immensity of the projected excavation. It is difficult not to be surprised when after going through a rather plain doorway you enter huge galleries or corridors, covered with perfectly polished sculpture which on the whole preserves the brilliance of their most vivid of colours and leading to rooms supported by pillars which are even more laden with decorations, until you arrive finally at the main room, the one which the Egyptians called the Golden Room, more vast than any of the others and in the middle of which reposes the mummy of the king in an enormous sarcophagus of granite. The maps of these tombs which the Commission of Egypt published give a precise idea of the extent of their excavation and the colossal work which was involved in order to accomplish them by pickaxe and chisel. Almost the entire valley is lumbered with hills formed by small stacks of stone which come from the terrifying amount of work done at the centre of these mountains.

Doubtless you will hardly be expecting to find here a detailed description of the each of these tombs; a few months have barely been enough to edit a fairly detailed note on the innumerable bas-reliefs which they harbour and in order to copy their most interesting inscriptions. I will, however, give you a general idea of these monuments by a quick and very succinct description of one of them, the one of pharaoh Ramesses, the son and successor of Meiamoun, who is called Amenephthes in the lists of Manetho and appears to be the Menophres after which an Egyptian epoch is called. The decoration of royal tombs was systematical and what you find in one reappears in virtually all the others, with a few minor exceptions as I will tell you later on.

The post of the entrance doorway is embellished with a bas-relief (the same for all the first doorways of the royal tombs) which is ultimately nothing but the preamble or rather the summary of all pharaonic decorations. It shows a pale yellow disc at the middle of which is the sun with a ram's head, i.e. the sun going down, entering the underworld and being worshipped by the kneeling king. To the right of the disk, i.e. the east, is the goddess Nephthys and to the left (west) is the goddess Isis, who occupy the two extremities of the god's procession along the upper hemisphere. Next to the sun and within the disk, a large scarab is sculpted which is here as elsewhere the symbol of regeneration or successive rebirths. The king is on his knees on a celestial mountain which is also touched by the feet of the two goddesses.

The general tenor of this arrangement is to refer to the king as being dead. During his life, analogous to the sun on its course from the east to the west, the king has to be the vivifyer, the illuminator of Egypt, and the source of all the physical and moral goods that its inhabitants require. Naturally, therefore, in death the pharaoh was similarly compared with a setting sun which descends towards the shadowy underworld that it has to traverse in order to rise again in the east and give light and life to the upper world (in which we live), in the same way that the king had to renew himself either in order to continue his transmigrations or in order to inhabit the celestial world and be accepted into the fold of Amon, the universal father.

This explanation is not a figment of my imagination; the time for conjecturing about old Egypt is no more. All of the above is a conclusion based on the [collective] weight of the legends which cover the royal tombs.

This identity or comparison of the king with the sun in its two states during both parts of the day is the key or rather the motif and object from which all other bas-reliefs are no more than successive extensions, as you will see.

Part of the scene described is always a legend, whose translation follows here:

> See what Osiris, lord of Amenti (the western region, inhabited by the dead), says:'I will grant you a place in the sacred mountain

> of the west like all the other great gods (the preceding kings),
> you Osirian-king, lord of the world, Ramesses, etc. still living.'

This last expression proves, if it were needed, that the pharaonic graves, enormous undertakings which took up a stupendous amount of time, were started while the [kings] were alive, and that, conform the well-known spirit of this unusual nation, one of the first concerns of any Egyptian king was to preoccupy himself continually with the execution of the monumental tomb which would be his last resting place.

This is what the first bas-relief, which is always to the left when entering these tombs, shows even better. This scene was clearly intended to reassure the living king about the doubtful omen which the premature crafting of a tomb would seem to herald while he was full of life and health. It shows the pharaoh dressed in royal clothes presenting himself to the hawk-headed god Phre, i.e. the sun at the high point of its arc (at noon), who addresses his agent on earth with these consoling words:

> See what Phre, great god, lord of the skies, says: 'We will grant
> you a long series of days in order to rule over the world and
> exercise the royal paraphernalia of Horus on the earth.'

On the ceiling of the first corridor of the tomb you will also read magnificent promises to the king regarding his life on earth and details of privileges which have been accorded to him in the celestial worlds; these legends were placed here in order to soften the descent to the sarcophagus chamber whose incline is of course never gradual enough.

Immediately after the quite delicate type of oratorical persuasion of this tableau, the issue is broached more frankly in a symbolic scene in which the ram-headed sun disk leaves the east and advances towards the frontier of the west, indicated by a crocodile, the emblem of the shadows which the god and the king each must enter in their own way. Immediately after a very long text follows which contains the names of seventy five appearances of the sun in the under world as well as invocations of these divinities of the third order, each of whom presides over one of seventy five subdivisions of the underworld called Kelle, the abode which 'envelops, encircles and zones in'.

These general, summary tableaus are followed by ones that develop their details. The walls of ensuing hallways and chambers (almost all the walls nearest to the east) are covered with a long series of scenes showing the advance of the sun through the upper world (the king during his life) while on the opposite walls the sun is dwelling in the underworld (the king after death).

The numerous scenes about the progression of the king above the horizon and in the world of light are divided in twelve series, each one introduced by a rich gate with swinging door which is sculptured and guarded by an enormous snake. These are the gates of the twelve hours of the day and these reptiles all have poignant names, such as Tek-ho, serpent with a blazing face, Sate-mpefbal, serpent whose eye lances the flame, tapentho, the horn of the world etc. etc. Alongside these disturbing creatures you will constantly read the legend: 'he lives above this great door and will open it for the great sun god'.

Near the door of the first gate, sunrise, the twenty four hours of the astronomical day are portrayed as humans, each with a star on their head and walking towards the bottom of the tomb as if to mark the direction of the god's progress and as if to indicate the one you should follow to take in these scenes, which yield even more striking results because for each of the twelve hours of the day the god's barge is depicted as navigating the celestial river of primordial fluid or ether, the substance of all physical things according to ancient Egyptian philosophy, with the individual gods who successively assist him and a representation moreover of the celestial places he passes through and the mythical scenes that are peculiar to each of the hours of the day.

Thus, at the first hour his *bari* or barge starts moving and receives homage from the spirits of the east. Among the scenes of the second hour you will see the great serpent Apophis, the brother and enemy of the sun, lorded over by the god Atum. In the third hour, the sun god reaches the celestial region in which it is decided which bodies souls will inhabit for their new transmigration. You will see Atum, seated in judgement, weighing human souls with his scales while they come forward in succession. When one of them is condemned you see him being taken back to earth in a *bari* which progresses to a gate guarded by Anubis and being guided while being severely hit with rods by hound-headed figures, emblems of celestial justice; the culprit stands underneath an enormous sow above which 'greed' or 'gluttony' is engraved in large characters, without doubt the capital sin of the delinquent, some contemporary glutton.

During the fifth hour, the god visits the Elysian fields of Egyptian mythology which are inhabited by blissful souls recuperating from the vicissitudes of their earthly transmigrations. They wear ostrich feathers on their heads, the sign of their virtuous and just conduct. You will see them presenting offerings to the gods, or even pick fruit from the celestial trees of this paradise under the direction of the lord of blissfulness. Further on, others hold sickles in their hands; these are the souls who are cultivating the fields of truth. Their legend says: 'They pour libations of water and make offerings of grain from the fields of glory; they hold a sickle and harvest the field which are their desert; the sun god says to them: "take your sickles, harvest your grain, take it to your dwellings, relish it and present them to the gods as a pure offering."' Elsewhere, finally, you see them bathing, swimming, leaping, and frolicking in a great basin filled with celestial and primordial water, all of which under the watch of the god, Celestial Nile. In the following hours, the gods prepare to fight the great enemy of the sun, the serpent Apophis. They arm themselves with spears and grab their nets because the monster inhabits the waters of the river on which the sun vessel is sailing. They pull strings, Apophis is caught, shackles are fastened, they pull the enormous reptile out of the river with a cable which the goddess Selk attaches to his neck and which twelve gods pull, aided by a rather complicated mechanism operated by the god Sev (Saturn), attended to by genies at four crucial points. But all this stuff would be useless against the struggling Apophis without the enormous hand (of Amon) at the end which grasps the cable and ends the mettle of the dragon. At last, at the eleventh our, the captive serpent is strangled and shortly afterwards the sun god arrives at the horizon where he will disappear. It is the goddess Netphe (Rhea) who, sparring for Thetys of the Greeks, rises up from the depths of the celestial waters; and mounted on the head of her son Osiris, whose body ends in a volute like a siren, the goddess then receives the huge Celestial Nile, the old Ocean of the Egyptian myths, in her arms.

The progress of the sun through the shadowy underworld during the twelve hours of the night, i.e. the opposite of the preceding scenes, is sculpted on the walls of the royal tombs facing the ones which I briefly summarised. Here, virtually without exception painted black from top to toe, the god proceeds through the seventy five circles or regions over which preside as many divine figures of all shapes and armed with swords. These circles are inhabited by condemned souls undergoing various torments. This is really very much the original of Dante's Hell as the variety of torture is quite impressive and I am not surprised that some travellers, horrified by these scenes of carnage, believed to have found evidence of habitual human sacrifice in ancient Egypt, though the legends remove any kind of uncertainty in this regard: they are the affairs of the other world and they don't impinge on the uses and customs of the present.

In the majority of the regions of inferno visited by the sun god, the condemned souls are punished in an original way. These immoral and obdurately criminal spirits are virtually always portrayed as humans, though sometimes in the symbolic form of a crane or of a hawk with a human head, and are completely painted in black to indicate both their perverse nature and their domicile among the dark shadows. Some are tightly strung to posts while the guardians of the region censure them for the sins they committed on earth while brandishing their swords. Others are suspended upside down. With their hands tied to their chests and their decapitated heads they march in long lines. Some of them drag their errant hearts behind them on the ground with hands tied behind their backs. Living souls are boiled in great kettles, either in their human form or otherwise in the shape of a bird, or only their heads and their hearts. I also saw hearts being thrown into a cauldron with the emblem of happiness and celestial calm (the fan), to which they had forfeited all their rights... Within each region and near the victims you will always read their sentence and the torture they are undergoing. 'These enemy souls', it says 'no longer see our god as he lances the rays of his disc; they no longer inhabit the earth and no longer hear the voice of the great god as he passes through their zones.' While in contrast you'll read on the opposite walls next to the pictures of the blissful souls: 'They have found grace in the eyes of the great god; they inhabit the dwellings of glory, there where one lives a celestial life; the bodies which they left behind will rest forever in their tombs while they enjoy the presence of the supreme god.'

This double series of scenes thus reveals the Egyptian psychological system at its two most important and most moral points: rewards and punishment. Everything the ancient [writers] have said about the Egyptian doctrine of the immortal soul and the positive goal of human life is true. It is truly a great and fortuitous idea to symbolise the double destiny of the soul by the progress of the sun through the heavens and underworld, the most awesome of celestial phenomena, and to complement this imposing and magnificent spectacle with painting.

This psychological gallery occupies the walls of the two grand corridors and the two first chambers of the tomb of Ramesses V, which I have used as the model for my description of the royal tombs because it is the most complete one of all of them. The same subject is repeated on the ceilings, though arranged with a straightforward astronomical slant and following a more ordinary plan as it concerns science, and occupies the entire length of those of the second hallway and the two first chambers that follow...

You are right if you think I collected with meticulous care this priceless residue of antique astronomy, which had to be linked to astrology in a country where religion was the immutable basis of social order. In such a political arrangement all learning will show two distinct sides: observed facts, which on their own constitute our present sciences, and a metaphysical side which links knowledge to religious beliefs. This is a bond which is necessary, indispensable even, in Egypt where in order to stay strong and to remain so forever religion wanted to embrace the entire universe and its study with its boundless domain, which like all human ideas has its good and its bad points.

In the tomb of Ramesses V the chambers or hallways which follow the ones I have described are decorated with symbolic scenes detailing various states of the sun from either a physical perspective or, mostly, from their purely mythical bearings: but these scenes are not a connected whole, which is the reason why in other tombs they are entirely omitted or do not have the same location. The chamber preceding the one of the sarcophagus, generally devoted to the four genies of Amenti, contains in the most complete tombs the king's appearance before a court of forty two divine judges who have to decide the fate of his soul, a tribunal of only one instance which granted or refused the king the honour of being buried. One entire wall of this room in the tomb of Ramesses V displays the images of the forty two assessors of Osiris mixed with the warranties he is deemed to submit or have had submitted in his name to these stern judges who, each one of them, look as if they are charged with the investigation of a particular crime or sin and to smite it in the soul subjected to their jurisdiction. This great text, which is divided in forty two verses or columns as a result, is strictly speaking only a negative confession as you will be able to see from the following examples:

> First name of the king
> O lord (such)! The king, sun moderator of justice, seconded by Amon, has not committed any evils
> O lord! The son of the sun, Ramesses, has not cursed the gods
> O lord! The king etc. has not been drunk
> O lord! The son etc. has not been slothful
> O lord! The king etc. has not taken goods donated to the gods
> O lord! The son etc. has not told any lies
> O lord! The king etc. has not been licentious (literally, has not fornicated with woman or man)
> O lord! The son etc. has not defiled himself with impure acts
> O lord! The king etc. has not shaken his head when hearing the truth
> O lord! The son etc. has not unnecessarily lengthened his words
> O lord! The king etc. has not had to eat his heart (ie. repent for something evil)

Finally, next to this curious text in the tomb of Ramesses Meiamoun you will see even stranger images, images of the capital sins. There are only three that can still be made out; they are luxury, sloth, and gluttony depicted in a human shape with the head of a goat, tortoise or crocodile.

The grand chamber in the tomb of Ramesses V, the last one enshrining the sarcophagus, surpasses all others in pomp and splendour. The ceiling, hewn into a semi-circle with a supple arch, has retained all its painting; its freshness is such that you have to be accustomed to the miracles of conservation in the monuments of Egypt in order to convince yourself that these fragile colours have resisted more than thirty centuries. Repeated here, but in large and with more details in certain sections, are the progress of the sun through the two worlds during the astronomical day and the composition which crowns the ceilings of the first rooms of the tomb and which is the leitmotif of all royal funerary embellishment.

The walls of this vast chamber are covered from bedrock to ceiling with sculptured scenes which are painted as elsewhere in the tomb and packed with thousands of hieroglyphs forming explanatory legends. The sun continues to be the subject of these bas-reliefs, of which a large number deals under an emblematic guise with the cosmogony and natural philosophy of the Egyptians. Only a long study could extract the whole meaning of these compositions, all of whom I copied myself while at the same time transcribing all the texts. Its mysticism is most refined but underneath these symbolic appearances there are no doubt ancient wisdoms which we consider rather new.

In this description of a single royal tomb, which is as succinct as possible, I have omitted to discuss the bas-reliefs which cover the pillars supporting the various rooms; they are adorations of the Egyptian divinities, mainly those who preside over the destiny of souls, Ptha-Socharis, Atum, the goddess Meresochar, Osiris and Anubis.

All other tombs of the Theban kings in the valley of Biban-el-Molouk and in the western valley are in their entirety or in part decorated with the scenes I have just described, and in proportion to this these tombs are to a greater or lesser extent enormous and, particularly, finished.

The tombs which are truly perfect and complete are only few in number: the one of Amenophis III (Memnon), whose adornment is almost completely destroyed, the one of Ramesses Meiamoun, the one of Ramesses V, probably also the one of Ramesses the Great, lastly the one of queen Thaoser. All the others are incomplete. Some end with the first chamber which was changed into a grand sepulchral chamber. Others go as far as the second one in a complete tomb. Yet others even terminate in a small hastily hewn, crudely painted room in which the roughly outlined sarcophagus of the king rests. This proves clearly what I said at the start, that these kings commissioned their tombs as they assumed the throne; and if death crept up on them before it was finished the works were stopped and the tomb remained incomplete. By the same token you can measure the length of the reign of each one buried at Biban-el-Molouk by the completion or measure of progress of the cavity destined to be their sepulchre. One should note that the reigns of Amenophis III, Ramesses the Great and Ramesses V correspond, in the canon of Manetho, to those who ruled for more than thirty years each.

All I have to do now is mention a number of peculiarities which some of these royal catacombs throw up.

Some of the preserved walls of the tomb of Amenophis III (Memnon) are covered with plain painting, though this is executed with enormous care and finesse. The grand chamber comprises yet another section of the progress of the sun through the two hemispheres; yet this scene is painted on the walls in the shape of an enormous unscrolled papyri, with its figures drawn with simple strokes as on a manuscript, and the legends in linear hieroglyphs are almost hieratic characters. The royal museum has a few rites which are expressed in this transitional writing.

The tomb of this illustrious pharaoh was discovered in the western valley by one of the members of the Commission. Probably all the kings of the first part of the eighteenth dynasty lie in the same valley and one must look here for the sepulchres of Amenophis I and II and the four Tuthmosis. You couldn't uncover them except by organising enormous digs at the foot of the large peaked rocks at whose centre the tombs were carved. The same valley perhaps harbours also the final resting place of the Theban kings from the oldest times; this I think I am allowed to conclude from the existence of a second royal in a very ancient style which was discovered in the part of the valley that is set furthest into the background and which is of a Theban pharaoh called Skhai who is certainly not part of the last four dynasties, the seventeenth, eighteenth, nineteenth or twentieth.

In the valley proper of Biban-el-Molouk we admired, as have all travellers who have preceded us, the stunning vividness of the painting and the polish of the sculptures of the tomb of Menephtha I, who in his legends assumes the various surnames of Noubei, Athothei and Amonei, and inside his tomb the one of Ousirei, which I at first believed to be his proper name and which has been generally adopted since. But this beautiful catacomb [of Sethos I] is deteriorating by the day. Its pillars are riven and are coming loose; the ceilings is falling to pieces and the paint is scaling off. I have had the richest scenes of this tomb drawn and coloured on location in order to give Europe a precise idea of such splendour. I initially thought, based on the incomplete copies of this bas-relief published in Britain, that these four people of a very distinctive race and guided by Horus holding his pastoral staff belonged to nations which had been subjugated while pharaoh Menephthunder held the sceptre;

scrutiny of its legends told me that this tableau has a much more general meaning, however. It relates to the third hour of the day when the sun is starting to be felt through the intensity of its rays and warms up all the inhabited regions of our world. According to its proper legend it is supposed to depict the inhabitants of Egypt and those of foreign lands. So we have before our eyes the image of the various races known to the Egyptians, and you grasp at the same time the great geographical or ethnographical distances established at the time.

There are twelve men guided by Horus, the pastor of people, but they belong to four very different groups. The three first ones (nearest to the god) have a dusky red colour, well-proportioned figures, a suave physiognomy, slightly aquiline noses, long plaited hair, are dressed in white and their legend indicates their name as Rot-en-Nerome, the race of men, men par excellence, i.e. they are Egyptians.

The three next ones are very different: their skin colour approaching yellow, or rather sheepskin, a very aquiline nose, black full beards ending in a point, short clothing in various colours. They are called Namou.

There can be little doubt about the race of the three who come after: they are black people. They have the generic name of Nahasi.

Lastly, the three at the end have a skin colour which we would call flesh-coloured, or white of a most delicate shade, straight or lightly vaulted noses, blue eyes, blond or red beards, tall and very thin, dressed in cowskin which has retained its fur, real savages with tattoos on several parts of their body; they are called Tamhou.

I hurried to look for similar scenes in the other royal tombs and actually finding several of them was entirely convinced by their variations that they were supposed to depict the inhabitants of the four corners of the earth: the inhabitants of Egypt, who on their own were deemed a continent of the world in accordance with the extremely modest mindset of ancient peoples; the Asians; the proper inhabitants of Africa, the black people; lastly (I am ashamed to say this as our race comes last and is the most ferocious one in the series), the Europeans who, it has to be said, did not strike a particularly wholesome attitude in the world during those distant times. Among them should be included the blond white-skinned people who not only lived in Europe but also in Asia, from where they came.

This interpretation is even more credible because in the other tombs the same generic names show up and constantly in the same order. You will in addition find Egyptians and Africans depicted in the same way, which would be difficult to imagine otherwise; but the Namou (Asians) and the Tamhou (the European races) display important and curious variations.

Instead of the Arab or Jew, who are so plainly clothed in Menephtha's tomb, Asia is represented in other tombs (those of Ramesses-Meiamoun and Menephtha II) as three individuals who, though they still have the colour of sheepskin, aquiline noses, black eyes and dense beards, have wardrobes that are singularly splendiferous. In one they are clearly Assyrians: their rich costumes are in even their slightest details perfectly identical to those of people engraved on Assyrian cylinders; in the other they are Medes, or an ancient people from some part of Persia whose physiognomy and dress may be found thread for thread on monuments known as persepolitans. Asia was thus indifferently represented by one of its people. The same applied to our good old ancestors the Tamhou. Their clothing is sometimes different, their heads are more or less hairy and covered with miscellaneous ornaments, their wild clothes are marginally different in cut, but their white colour, their eyes and beards preserve all the characteristics of a separate race. I had these exciting ethnographic series copied and coloured. When arriving in Biban-el-Molouk I certainly did not expect to find sculptures here which could serve as vignettes of the history of ancient people in Europe, if someone were ever to have the courage to undertake such a thing. To see them though has something flattering and soothing as it makes you realise the distance we have since covered.

The tomb of Ramesses I, father and predecessor of Menephtha, called Ousirei, was buried under the debris and rubble which had fallen from the mountain; we had it dug out. It consists of two long corridors without sculpture terminating in a painted chamber of an astonishing preservation and containing the granite sarcophagus of the king, simply covered with paintings. This simplicity puts to shame the magnificence of the son whose sumptuous tomb is only a few steps further away.

I felt a burning desire to find the tomb of the most celebrated Ramesses at Biban-el-Molouk, the one of Sesostris. It is actually there; the third to the right in the main valley. But the grave of this great man seems to have been opened up, either by destruction caused by man or by the ravages of accidental torrents which have filled it right up to the ceilings with very little room to spare. It was by digging a kind of trench through the middle of these piles of stones that pack this interesting catacomb that, despite the extreme heat, we crawled across the first chamber. This grave was, in as far as one can tell, hewn on a stupendous scale and decorated with sculptures of the highest quality, judging by the small portions which still exist. An excavation which is organised on a grand scale would no doubt produce the discovery of the sarcophagus of this illustrious conqueror; there is no point hoping that the royal mummy may be found because this tomb was no doubt pillaged and sacked during a very distant epoch, either by the Persians or by treasure hunters who were as keen to destroy as the impetuous foreigners were to extract revenge.[9]

At the bottom of a junction of the valley and in the neighbourhood of this imposing tomb lies the son of Sesostris, who is called Menephtha II in his royal legends; it is a very beautiful grave, but not finished. Hewn into the width of the wall of an isolated chamber, I found in it a small chapel consecrated to the spirit of his father, Ramesses the Great.

The last tomb at the bottom of the main valley, of Menephtha III, is noteworthy because of its state of incompletion. The first bas-reliefs are finished and executed with an admirable refinement and care; the embellishment of the remainder of the catacomb, which is made up of three long corridors and two chambers, has only been traced in red after which you reach the fragments of the granite sarcophagus of the pharaoh in a very small closet whose walls have barely been trimmed and are covered with a few poor pictures, drawn and daubed in haste.

His successor, whose monumental name is Rhamerri, probably didn't worry too much about the state of his grave. Instead of having a tomb hewn for himself, like his ancestors, he found it more convenient to seize the one next to his father's, and the examination of this palimpsest grave that I was able to conduct lead me to a conclusion which is very important for the completion of the series of reigns forming the eighteenth dynasty.

As time has caused the decay of the stucco which the usurper Rhamerri applied to the older sculptures in certain parts of the tomb he wanted to seize, I made out the name of a queen called Thaoser. Time, also dealing justly with the crust with which the entrance bas-reliefs had been masked, has revealed scenes which depict this queen making the same offerings to the gods and receiving from the gods the same promises and the same assurances which the pharaohs do in their tombs, assuming the same position as they do. So it was clear that I was in a catacomb hewn to receive the body of a queen and, I should add, a queen who was exercising sovereign power, as her husband only appears behind her in this series of bas-reliefs while the queen presents herself in the first and most important ones, though he carried the title king. Menephtha-Siphtha was the name of this sous king.

After earlier on finding bas-reliefs of this king in Ghebel-Selseleh, where he had continued the decoration of the great speos of that quarry after king Horus, queen Thaoser had to be king Horus's daughter who, succeeding her father as the only inheritor of an age to rule, exercised power for a long time and can be found in Manetho's list of kings under the name of queen Achencherses. I made a mistake in Turin when I took the wife of Horus, queen Tmauhmot, for this prince's daughter, who is mentioned in the text of a group description. I wouldn't have made this mistake if the legend of Horus's queen would still have had its initial titles which disappeared after a fracture. Siphtha only had the title king because of his position as consort of the reigning queen, which likewise occurred in the case of the two husbands of queen Amense, Tuthmosis III's mother (Moeris).

The following fact slightly diminishes the odium of the usurpation of queen Thaoser and her husband Siphtha's tomb by their fifth or sixth successor, who wouldn't have felt for them the respect due to one's ancestors as he descended directly from Ramesses I, who, according to the lists, was at most the brother of queen Thaoser-Achencherses and continued the direct masculine line from king Horus. Yet this was no justification for the action of the new occupant, first, to substitute the image of the queen everywhere with his own by adding or suppressing things through dressing her up with a helmet or clothing and insignia that would only have been appropriate for kings and not queens; and in the second place, to cover all the cartouches encircling the name of the queen and Siphtha with stucco in order to have his own legend painted into it. This exercise must nonetheless have taken place in haste because after having transformed queen Thaoser into king Rhamerri no care was taken to correct the text of the pronouncements which the gods are deemed to make on the bas-reliefs, which are still addressed to the queen and which inappropriate for a king either in form or contents.

Without contest, the grandest and most spectacular of all existing tombs in the valley is the one of Rhamerri's successor, Ramesses Meiamoun. Today, time or smoke has tarnished the colours which cover the majority of its sculptures; nonetheless it makes an impression with eight small chambers which are laterally pierced into the mass of walls of the first and second corridor — boudoirs which are embellished with most curious sculpture of which we had accurate copies made. One of these small boudoirs contains among other things the depiction of kitchen work; another that of very rich and sumptuous furniture; a third a complete arsenal of all the types of arms and military insignia of the Egyptian legions; here the royal barges and cangias are shown with all their ornamentation; one of them, lastly, contains the symbolic table of the Egyptian year which is represented by six images of the Nile and six images of Egypt as a person; these alternate for each month and carry the produce which is typical of the part of the year the image presents. In one of these pretty closets I had to copy the two famous harp players with all their colours because no one has yet published them correctly.

That's enough about Biban-el-Molouk. I hasten to go back to Thebes and I am sure you won't mind following me there. I will nevertheless add that several of these royal tombs bear witness on their walls of having been abandoned a good many centuries ago and of having been visited, as in our days, by many airheads who, again as those in our time, believe they can immortalise themselves by scrawling their names on the paintings and bas-reliefs which they are disfiguring. You will find first of all Egyptians of all eras carving their names, the earliest ones in hieratic and the most modern ones in Demotic script; many Greeks of a very remote time judging by the shape of the letters; ancient Romans of the Republic; Greek and Roman names from the time of the first emperors; a flock of unknowns from the early Empire who nestle between the stars who preceded them or would follow them; moreover the names of Copts accompanied by very humble prayers; lastly the names of European travellers whom love of science, war, commerce, luck, our disenchantment, steered in the direction of these solitary graves. For you I gathered the inscriptions which are most notable because of either their contents or their paleographic interest.

In one of these handwritten notes to his brother, Champollion wrote

At Beni-Hassan-el-Qadim, in the tomb of the person called Rotei (the tomb composed of a single rectangular chamber decorated at the back by two lines of three columns, whose doorway faces west and the valley of Egypt) you will see on the southern wall an evenly hewn cavity like an armoire and here, in the depths of this cavity, I found in almost faded charcoal this quite simple inscription: '1800 3rd Régiment de Dragons'. I felt I had to retrace these lines with a brush in black ink, adding above them: J.C.F. Rst 1828 [J.-F. Champollion restituit].

18 June 1829, Thebes [The Ramesseum]

Since my return amidst the ruins of the eldest of royal cities, my days have been devoted to the study of what remains of one of its most beautiful buildings for which I had developed a special affection when I first set eyes on it. The thorough understanding which I have now gathered justifies this beyond what I had dared to hope for. The monument I want to discuss here is the one whose real name has yet to be determined and which gives rise to extremely ferocious controversy: the building first called Memnonium and then the Tomb of Osymandyas. The latter label stems from the Commission. Some travellers persist in using the former, which is certainly extremely ill-suited and highly inaccurate. Referring to this building I in the meantime only make use of its Egyptian name which is sculpted in hundreds of places and repeated in the legends of friezes, architraves and bas-reliefs which decorate this palace. It carries the name of Ramesseum because Thebes owes it to the munificence of pharaoh Ramesses the Great.

Your imagination would tremble and you'd feel a deeply spontaneous emotion when visiting these mutilated galleries and beautiful colonnades, because you realise that they are the work and were often the home of the most celebrated and illustrious of princes which ancient Egypt embraces in its long annals, each time I go through them I pay to Sesostris the respect which has surrounded him for all of antiquity.

There isn't an intact section of the Ramesseum left; but what has escaped the barbarism of the Persians and the ravages of time is enough for one to put the building back together and to have a very clear idea of it. Leaving aside its architectural worth, which is not my preserve, though I should give it its due reward by saying that the Ramesseum is perhaps the noblest and purest of the Theban monuments, I will limit myself to running quickly through the principal subjects of the bas-reliefs which decorate it and the point of the inscriptions which accompany them.

As they have largely collapsed, the sculptures which covered the exterior faces of the two masses of the first sandstone pylon have completely disappeared. There are still enormous blocks of white limestone; these are the foundations of the gate. They, like the lengths of the two masses between which this gate rose up, are decorated with royal legends of Ramesses the Great and tableaus showing the pharaoh making offerings to the great deities of Thebes, Amon-Ra, Amon-generator, the goddess Muth, the young Chons, Ptha and Mandou. In some of the scenes the king in return receives tribute from the gods, and I will give an analysis of the main one of them because it was here that I read the real name of the palace for the first time.

The god Atum (one of the forms of Phre) introduces Ramesses the Great with a helmet and royal dress to the god Mandou. This god takes his hand saying: 'Come, go to the divine home in order to pay attention to your father, the lord of the gods, who will grant you a long succession of days in order to govern the world and rule on the throne of Horus'. Further on Amon-Ra is in effect shown seated while addressing the following words to the Pharao. This is what Amon-Ra, king of the gods, and who resides in the Ramesseum of Thebes, says: 'My beloved son of my seed, lord of the world, Ramesses! my heart rejoices while thinking of your good works; you dedicated this building to me; I present you with the gift of a pure life on the throne of Sev (Saturn; the temporal world).'...

The colonnades which closed off the first courtyard laterally no longer exist. The enormous space once comprised between these galleries and two pylons is glutted with the colossal remnants of the grandest and most magnificent colossi that the Egyptians have perhaps ever erected. It is one of Ramesses the Great; the inscriptions leave no doubt about this. The royal legends of this illustrious pharaoh can be read in large and beautiful hieroglyphs towards the height of his arms and are repeated several times on the four sides of the base. This colossus, though it is seated, measures no less than fifty three feet in height. You have to admire both the might of the people who put this miracle colossus up and the one of the barbarians who have pillaged it with so much attention and zeal...

I will entirely forego the interesting bas-reliefs that cover the left side of the wall at the back of the peristyle; I hasten to enter the hypostyle hall of which about thirty columns are still intact and which will charm by their majestic elegance even the eyes of those who rail against anything that isn't Roman or Greek architecture. As for the purpose of this beautiful hall, the arrangement of its columns and the shape of its capitals, I will let the dedication of the hall itself, which is sculpted in name of the founder on the left architraves in extremely splendid hieroglyphs, do the talking:

> The mighty Haroeris, friend of truth, lord of the upper and lower countries, defender of Egypt, castigator of foreign lands, the splendiferous Horus possessor of palms and the mightiest of conquerors, the king lord of the world (sun guardian of justice seconded by Phre), the son of the sun, lord of the diadems, the favourite of Amon, Ramesses, had these edifices executed in honour of his father the great Amon-Ra, king of the gods; he had the grand hall of the assembly constructed in fine white sandstone, supported by grand capitaled columns imitating open flowers, flanked by smaller capitaled columns imitating a truncated lotus bud; a hall which he dedicates to the lord of the gods *in order to celebrate his gracious panegyric*; this is what the king, while alive, has done. [italics added]

Thus the hypostyle halls which give Egyptian palaces such a distinct character were really used, as has been assumed before, to hold either large political or religious gatherings, i.e. the thing which is called panegyric or general meetings. I was already convinced of this before discovering this interesting dedication after seeing on the obelisks of Rome the hieroglyphic image which expresses the idea of panegyric, on which this character is carved in large, noticing that they actually picture a hypostyle hall arranged with benches at the bottom of the columns...

The section of the walls of the hypostyle hall which has escaped the ravages of mankind show the richest and most developed scenes. On the back wall, to the right and to the left of the central doorway are still two enormous tableaus which are worth noting because of the large proportion of its figures and the finish of their realisation. In the first the lion-headed Pascht, spouse of Ptha, lady of the celestial palace, raises her left hand towards Ramesses's head which is covered with a helmet, saying to him:'I have prepared the diadem of the sun, may this helmet remain on your horn (head) where I placed it.' At the same time she presents the king to the supreme god, Amon-Ra who, seated on his throne, extends the sign of a pure life towards the face of the king.

The second scene shows the royal investiture of [Ramesses] with Egypt's two greatest divinities vesting royal powers in him. Assisted by Muth, the great divine mother, Amon-Ra gives to Ramesses the battle sickle, the original of the sharpened sickle of the Greek myths, a terrifying weapon called schopsch by the Egyptians, and hands him at the same time the emblems of power and moderation, the whip and the pedum, while pronouncing the following formula:

> This is what Amon-Ra, who resides in the Ramesseum, says: 'Accept this battle sickle in order to restrain foreign nations and slash the heads of the impure: take the whip and the pedum in order to govern the land of Keme (Egypt).'

The base of these two tableaux are of a different type of interest: it depicts the male children of Ramesses the Great, on foot and in strict order of primogeniture. The princes are dressed in the costume of their rank. A total of twenty three, they carry the insignia of their dignity, the pedum and a fan made of a long ostrich feather which is attached to an elegant handle; a huge family, true, but this shouldn't surprise you if you consider that Ramesses had at least two legitimate wives, queens Nofre-Ari and Isenofre, as far as we know, and that it is very likely moreover that children with concubines or mistresses assumed the same rank as legitimate children, a custom that spreads throughout ancient Oriental history. Whatever the truth in this, the title which they all share 'son of the king and his seed' is carved first above the head of each of these princes, and for some of them (the three first ones and hence the eldest) a reference to the high offices which have been bestowed on them at the time when the bas-reliefs were carved. The first one was thus qualified: left fan bearer of the king, junior royal secretary (chief teacher), commander in chief of the soldiers (army), first-born and the favourite of his siblings,

Amenhischopsch. The second one, called Ramesses like his father, was a left fan bearer of the king and royal secretary, commander in chief of the soldiers of the master of the world (the troops of the royal guard), and the third, left fan-bearer of the king like his brothers (a title usually given to princes on other monuments), was also secretary general, commander of the cavalry, that is the chariots of war of the Egyptian army. I will dispense here with writing down the names of the twenty other princes; I will only say that the names of some of them clearly allude to victories of the king at the time of their birth such as Neb-en-Shari (master of the land of Schari), Nebenthonib (master of the entire world), Sanaschtenamoun (conqueror through Amon) or to the new titles assumed into the protocol of Ramesses the Great, as for example Pataveamoun (Amon is my father) and Setpanri (approved by the king), a title which is also included in the king's first name.

At the same time I noted in this series of princes a very interesting fact. After the death of Ramesses the Great, the child who ascended the throne after him was distinguished in a highly specific way: his thirteenth son, called Menephtha, succeeded him. It is clear that because of this they changed *post factum* the dress of the prince, adorning his face with the uraeus and changing his short sabou into a long royal tunic; moreover, next to the first legend containing the name Menephtha which he retained as he ascended the throne, they chiselled the first cartouche of his royal legend, his cartouche first name sun-spirit-beloved-by-the-gods, which you will actually find on all monuments of his reign.

While leaving the hypostyle hall through the central doorway you enter the room which still contains part of its columns and whose decoration adopts a very specific character. In the section of the palace we are now going through, standard devotions are addressed to the divinities of Egypt as is appropriate in courts and peristyles open to the public and in the hypostyle hall where the grand assemblies were held. But really, here start the private part of the palace and living quarters of the king, the place where specifically the king of the gods to whom the building was dedicated was also deemed to live.

This is clear from the bas-reliefs carved on the right and left walls of the door; these scenes show four large sacred barges or bari with a small naos over which apparently a voile is thrown as if to hide from view the person who is covered. These baris are carried on their shoulders by either twenty four or eighteen priests depending on the importance of the master of the bari. The insignias which are draped over the prow and poop of the two first barges are the symbolic heads of the goddess Muth and the god Chons, the spouse and son of Amon-Ra; the third and fourth carry the heads of the king and queen capped with the marks of their dignity. These scenes, as the hieroglyphic legends tell us, depict the two gods and the royal couple coming to pay their respects to the father of the gods Amon-Ra, who is establishing his residence in the palace of Ramesses the Great. The words which each of the visitors say leave no doubt about this: 'I have come', says Muth, 'to present my regards to the king of gods, Amon-Ra, moderator of Egypt so that he may grant long years to the son he loves, the king Ramesses.'

> 'We come to you', says the god Chons, 'in order to serve your majesty, o Amon-Ra, king of the gods who takes possession of the dwelling of your son Ramesses. Grant a stable and pure life to the son who loves you, the lord of the world.'
> Ramesses only says: 'I have come to my father Amon-Ra with the gods whom he is allowing into his presence today.'

But queen Nofre-Ari, here called Ahmosis (raised by the moon), expresses more positive vows: 'This is what the divine spouse, the royal mother, the mighty lady of the world, Ahmosis-Nofre-Ari, says: "I have come to pay my respects to my father Amon. O king of gods, my heart is joyous because of your affections (i.e. the love you feel for me); I am transported while thinking of your favours; O you who is establishing the seat of your might in the home of your son the lord of the world, Ramesses, grant him a stable and pure life; may his years be counted in panegyrics!"'...

Finally, the far-end wall of this chamber is embellished with several scenes depicting the realisation of these vows and recalling the favours which Amon-Ra bestowed on the Egyptian hero: there is only one left, to the right of the doorway. The king is shown seated on a throne at the foot of the one of Amon-Ra-Atum and in the shade of the enormous foliage of a Persea, the celestial tree of life. The great god and the goddess Saf of writing, i.e. of the sciences, draw the cartouche first name of Ramesses the Great on the heartshaped fruits of the tree, while on another side of the tree Thoth is engraving the cartouche proper name of the king, to whom Amon-Ra-Atum addresses the following words:

> Advance, I am carving out your name for a long sequence of days so that it will endure on the divine tree.

The doorway which, from this chamber, leads to a second one which is also decorated with columns, of which four still exist, is specifically worth our attention both for its construction material and the sculptures which decorate it.

The bas-reliefs covering its stringcourse and posts are so deeply set back that it is clear that they were carefully rubbed down to diminish its width. I blame time and the savagery which was doubtless inflicted on several points of its surface, because, when I had the base of the doorposts cleared, I read a dedicatory inscription to Ramesses of the usual type for doors, yet in it is also said that this door was covered in pure gold. I therefore studied its surfaces in greater detail and as I studied more closely the sort of white fine stucco still sticking to the sculpture in some places I realised that this stucco had been rendered on a piece of fabric stretched over the tableaus and that the contours and individual parts of the figures had been retraced in the stucco before the gold had been applied. As this process seemed unusual to me, I thought it might be useful to make a note of it.

But two of the scenes which decorate this doorway are even more intriguing. The stringcourse and the top of the doorpost are covered with a dozen of small bas-reliefs showing Ramesses the Great worshipping members of the Theban Triad. These divinities all turn their back on the entrance of the door in question because they only relate to the first chamber and not to the second one, to which this doorway serves as entrance; but at the bottom of the doorposts, immediately above the dedication, two gods are chiselled out with their heads turned towards the entrance of the door and looking at this second chamber which thus falls within their sphere. These two divinities are, to the left, Thoth with the head of an ibis, the god of the sciences and arts, the inventor of letters, and to the right Saf, the spouse of Thoth, who has the notable title of lady-of-letters and president-of-the-library (literally word for word 'room of the books'). Moreover the god is followed by an associate divinity who, judging by his legend and the enormous eye he carries on his head, personifies the sense of sight, whereas the associate divinity of the goddess is the sense of hearing characterised by a large ear which is similarly drawn above his head and by the word sotem sculpted in his legend; plus he holds in his hand all the instruments of writing, as if ready to write down everything he hears. Could the entrance to a library be advertised any better than by such bas-reliefs?...

Here end the fragments of the palace of Sesostris; there isn't a trace left of its final buildings which must have extended towards the mountainside.[10] The Ramesseum is Thebes most dilapidated building, yet it is also doubtless the one which makes the deepest and most durable impression on the minds of travellers through its elegant majesty.

18 June 1829 [Thebes, Queen Hatshepsut]

Leaving the Ramesseum, the noble and elegant palace of Sesostris, and having studied with all the attention they deserved the numerous ancient buildings piled up on the man-made hill which is today called Medinet-Habu, I had to, in the interest of my work methods, turn to a number of intermediate or neighbouring elevations which either because of their middling size or their state of almost complete degradation attract much less attention from travellers.

I first went to the valley of El-Asasif, situated to the north of the Ramesseum, which ends abruptly at the foot of enormous limestone rocks belonging to the Libyan mountain chain; there lay the remnants of a building which is accurately described by Messrs. Jollois and Devilliers under the name of 'Ruins Located to the north of the Tomb of Osymandyas'.

As my particular goal was to determine the still unknown date of these buildings and to find out what its one-time purpose was, I assigned myself the task to inspect the sculptures and particularly the hieroglyphic legends inscribed on the single blocks and wall sections scattered over a rather considerable stretch of land.

I was first of all struck by the fine workmanship of several bas-reliefs, remnants which the first Christians had half hammered away, and a gate of pink granite, which still stands in the middle of these beautiful white sandstone ruins, convinced me that this entire building belonged to the best era of Egptian art. This gate or small propylon is completely covered with hieroglyphic legends. Two images of pharaohs on foot are carved dressed up in their insignia with extreme delicateness in a very deep bas-relief on its doorposts. All these dedications are double and were executed at the same time in name of the two princes. The one who is always to the right or rather ranks first is called Amenenthe, the other only follows after; his name is Tuthmosis, or Moeris for the Greeks.

If I was surprised to find Moeris, robed in all his royal paraphernalia, give precedence here and everywhere else in the building to this Amenenthe, who you will look for in vain in the royal lists, I was even more astonished to find that this bearded Pharao, dressed in the typical attire, is referred to with names and verbs that are feminine, as if they are dealing with a queen. I will give you the following example of the dedication on the propylons.

'Aroeris, supporter of the religious, lord king, etc. Sun devoted to the truth! (She) has built in honour of (her) father, Amon-Ra, lord of the thrones of the world; she erected this propylon (may Amon protect the edifice) in granite; this is what she has done (to be) vivified for ever.' The other post has an analogous dedication but is in the name of Tuthmosis III or Moeris.

Going through the remainder of the ruins I found this same oddity everywhere. Not only did I find the first name of Amenenthe[II] preceded by the title sovereign-lord-of-the-world, but also her proper name following the title daughter-of-the-sun. In all the bas-reliefs which show the gods addressing this ruler Amenenthe, she is treated as a queen, as in the following formula:

> This is what Amon-Ra, lord of the thrones of the world, says to his beloved daughter, Sun devoted to the truth: 'The home you constructed is like the celestial one.'

Some new facts intrigued me even more. I noticed particularly in the legends of the granite propylon that the cartouche/first names and proper names of Amenenthe were chiselled in ancient times and replaced by those of Tuthmosis III, which are layered on top of them. Elsewhere the legends of Amenenthe were also layered underneath replacements of Tuthmosis II. Several others showed the first name of an as yet unknown Tuthmosis, including in his proper name cartouche the name of a woman

Ammense, the whole also carved out over the earlier legends of Amenenthe. I then recalled having seen this new king Tuthmosis being treated as a queen in the small building of Tuthmosis III in Medinet-Habu.

By bringing these facts and varying circumstances of several observations of the same type together, the first results of my research in the great palace and propylon of Karnak, I was able to complete my knowledge of the people of the eighteenth dynasty. It follows from the combined testimony provided by these diverse monuments that (any deeper analysis is not required here):

Tuthmosis directly succeeded the great Amenothis I...; his son Tuthmosis II ascended the throne after him and died without children; his sister Ammense, a daughter of Tuthmosis I, succeeded him and ruled for twenty one years as the sovereign; the first husband of this queen was called Tuthmosis, who included the name of queen Ammense in his proper name; this Tuthmosis was the father of Tuthmosis III or Moeris and ruled in the name of Ammense; upon the death of this Tuthmosis, queen Amense married for the second time Amenenthe, who also ruled in the name of Ammense and was the regent during the first years of Tuth-Moeris; Tuthmosis III, the Moeris of the Greeks, exercised joint power with the regent Amenenthe who took him under his wings for a few years.

The understanding of this succession of people explains quite naturally the peculiarities found by the meticulous examination of the building in the El-Asasif valley. You understand why regent Amenenthe only shows up on bas-reliefs to receive the graceful words which the gods address to queen Ammense, for whom he is only the representative; this explains the style of Amenenthe's dedications where he himself speaks in name of the queen and which are similar to the ones in which you read the name of Ammense's first husband, Tuthmosis, who acted out the same passive role and was, like Amenenthe, no more than a sort of figurehead for the power she exercised.

The recarving of the majority of the legends by the regent Amenenthe show that his regency had been irritating and burdensome to his pupil Tuthmosis III. He seems to have wanted to expunge his tutor from any lasting memory. During the reign of this Tuthmosis almost all the legends of Amenenthe were thus razed and replaced by carvings of either the legends of Tuthmosis III, whose power he [Amenenthe] had no doubt usurped, or by those of Tuthmosis, Ammense's first husband and the father of the now ruling king. I noticed the systematic destruction of these legend in a train of bas-reliefs which are elsewhere in Thebes. Was this desecration of the memory of Amenenthe the result of the personal hatred of Tuthmosis III, or of grovelling flattery of the priestly class? It is impossible to determine this, but the fact appeared to us rather interesting.

All inscriptions of the monument of El-Asasif establish unanimously that this building was erected under the reign of Amenenthe in the name of Ammense and her young son Tuthmosis III. It isn't therefore later than 1736 BC, which is the approximate date of Tuthmosis III's first years when he had sole power. So these sculptures are more than 3,500 years old...

This temple of Amon-Ra at the end of one of the valleys of Thebes's necropolis was at various times restored or added to by the successors of Amenenthe and Tuthmosis III. I actually found stones coming from various parts of the temple which were used in recent times for the construction of a wall which today supports the right base of the granite propylon and which contain fragments mentioning embellishments or restorations of the building under the reigns of Horus, Ramesses the Great and his son Menephtha II, all from the eighteenth dynasty like the founders of the temple.

Finally, the last chamber of the temple, serving as a sanctuary, is covered with depressing and gross sculpture; yet the shock which I felt upon seeing these miserable bas-reliefs, compared to the refinement and elegance of the tableaus sculpted in the previous two chambers, soon disappeared when I read large hieroglyphic inscriptions saying that this beautiful restoration had been completed under the reign and in name of Ptolemy Evergetes II and his first wife Cleopatra. Yet another piece of evidence among thousands of others against the opinion of those who continue to suppose doggedly that Egyptian art perfected itself after the settlement of the Greeks in Egypt.

I will say it once more: Egyptian art owes to itself alone all that it has brought forth in greatness, pureness, and beauty; whatever the scholars may say who seem to have turned it into a religion to believe unshakeably in the spontaneous genesis of the arts in Greece, it is as clear to me as it is for anyone who has really studied Egypt or has a genuine knowledge of the Egyptian monuments in Europe that art started in Greece only as an ancillary imitation of the Egyptian arts, which were much more advanced at the time when the first Egyptian colonies came in contact with the savage inhabitants of Attica or the Peloponnese than is popularly believed. Ancient Egypt taught the arts to Greece who give gave them their most sublime expression, but without Egypt Greece would probably not have become the cradle of the classical fine arts. This captures my entire creed on this great matter. I am writing these lines looking at the bas-reliefs which the Egyptians crafted with the most elegant polish 1700 years before the Christian era. What were the Greeks up to then...?

20 June 1829, Thebes [the Memnomium/Amenopheum
and its two colossus]

I sacrificed the entire day yesterday and today's morning to the study of the melancholy remains of one of the most important memorials of ancient Thebes. Comparable in size to the immense palace of Karnak, whose obelisks you can see from here on the other side of the river, this building has almost entirely disappeared; only some rubble is left, barely rising above the ground level which has vaulted because of the successive flooding deposits that probably also sheath all masses of granite, composites and other durable materials used for the decoration of this palace. As the most substantial part of the building was made from sandstone, hooligans have gradually cut it up and converted it into chalk for building their miserable shacks; but what the visitor finds on his way still gives a pretty good idea of the splendour of this ancient building.

You should picture a space of about 1800 feet in length which has been levelled by the silting of consecutive floodings and is covered with long herbs, though its surface is creviced in many places and you can still see the architraves, parts of colossi, column trunks and fragments of enormous bas-reliefs, which the river mud hasn't yet enveloped or taken away from the view of the travellers forever. Here stood more than eighteen colossi of at least twenty feet in height. All these monoliths of various materials are damaged and you'll find their gigantic members scattered here and there, some at ground level, others at the bottom of excavations made by modern diggers. I gathered from these mutilated remains the names of a large number of Asiatic people whose captured chiefs are depicted surrounding the base of these colossi of their vanquisher, the third pharaoh Amenophis, the one who the Greeks liked to confuse with the Memnon of their epic myths. These inscriptions show

The colossus of Memnon and its companion

that we have reached the site of the celebrated Theban building which the Greeks called the Memnonium. This is what Messrs. Jollois and Devilliers sought to prove in a different manner through their excellent description of these ruins.

At the heart of this horrifying devastation of objects of primary importance which I can still discuss, its best-preserved relics establish even more convincingly, if that were necessary, that these ruins are really those of the Theban Memnonium, or rather the palace which the Egyptians called Amenopheum after the founder's name, and which I find mentioned in a flock of hieroglyphic inscriptions of neighbouring graves where once the mummies resided of several important officials who were charged with guarding or maintaining this magnificent building.

It is towards the extremity of the ruins and near the river that the two famous colossi of about sixty feet in height rise up dominating the plane of Thebes, of which one, the one to the north, enjoys such wide-spread fame under the name of the colossus of Memnon. Made of a single block of composite limestone which was transported from the quarries of Upper Thebes and placed on an immense base of the same material, both of them show a seated pharaoh in a relaxed pose with his hands extended towards his knees. I have tried in vain to find the reason for the odd mistake which the eminent and astute [Vivant] Denon made, who wanted to see in them the statues of two Egyptian princesses. The hieroglyphic inscriptions on the two sockles are still intact enough for those which cover the backrest of the southern colossus's throne and the sides of the two bases to leave no doubt as to the rank and nature of the person whose traits these brilliant monoliths reproduce and whose memory they perpetuate. The text on the backrest says literally: 'Mighty Aroeris, moderator of moderators, etc., the sun king, lord of the truth (or of justice), son of the sun, lord of the diadems, Amenothis, moderator of the pure region, favourite Amon-Ra, etc. splendiferous Horus, he who enlarged the dwelling [blank] for ever, erected these constructions to honour his father Amon; he dedicates this colossal statue of lasting stone, etc.'...

These are the titles and names of the third Amenophis of the eighteenth dynasty, who occupied the throne of the pharaohs at about 1680 before Christ. Thus the lines claiming that the colossus isn't at all the image of the Greek Memnon but really that of a local called Ph-Amenoph, which Pausanius puts in the mouth of some contemporary Thebans, are completely vindicated.

It would appear that these two colossi embellished the exterior façade of the main pylon of the Amenopheum and you will still be able to judge, by the additional figures which make up the decoration of the backside of the throne of either colossus, the grace, the extreme refinement, and the lengths to which they went when putting them together despite their state of destruction in places where savagery and fanaticism have savaged these ancient memorials. They are the figures of standing women, sculpted into the mass of the monolith itself, and they are no less than fifty feet high. The magnificence of their hairdo and the rich detailing of their costumes are in perfect proportion to the rank of the people whose memory they commemorate. The hieroglyphic inscriptions which are engraved on these statues, and which form the quasi back feet of the throne of each statue of Amenophis, tell us that the left figure represents an Egyptian queen, the king's mother who is called Tma-Hem-Va or rather Maut-Hem-Va, and the figure to the right, the queen-spouse of the same king, Taia, whose name we have already found on a lot of monuments. I also know the name of the wife of Tuthmosis IV, Tmau-Hem-Va, the mother of Amenophis-Memnon, from the bas-reliefs of the palace of Luxor which are mentioned in the quick report I jotted down of this important building...

The consecration of the palace is recalled in a highly theatrical fashion. King Amenophis starts first, speaking from the first to line and continues until the thirteenth one: 'King Amenothis said: "Come Amon-Ra, lord of the thrones of the world, you who resides in the regions of Opht (Thebes)! regard the dwelling which we built for you in this pure area, it is beautiful: come down from the height of heavens to take possession!"

Then follows the praise of the god mixed in with a description of the consecrated building and a testimony of the ornamentation and decorations in limestone, pink granite, black stone, gold, ivory and precious stones, which the king lavished on it, including two great obelisks of which there isn't a trace left today.

The seven following lines are the response of Amon-Ra to the pharao's blandishments. 'Here is what Amon-Ra says, husband of his mother, etc.: "Come nearer my son, sun lord of the truth, seed of the sun, child of the sun, Amenothis! I have heard your words and I see the buildings which you commissioned; I who am your father congratulate you on your great work, etc.'

Lastly towards the middle of the twentieth line starts another and last harangue; it is one where the gods in the presence of Amon-Ra, their master, promise him to lavish Amenothis, his beloved son, with favours and to make his reign joyful and prolonging it for a period of many years in order to compensate him for the beautiful building he has erected to act as their dwelling, a building which they profess to have taken possession of and duly visited.

So the fact that the Memnonium of the Greeks and the Egyptian Amenopheum were one and the same can no longer be in any doubt. Huge excavations undertaken by a Greek called Iani, the former agent of M. Salt, have uncovered numerous column bases, a large number of lion-headed statues in black granite; furthermore two magnificent colossal sphinxes, in pink granite and of a superlative finish, with a human head which also represent king Amenophis III. The traits of the face of this king, which here as elsewhere have something Ethiopian, are entirely like the ones which the sculptors and painters gave this pharaoh in the tableaus on the steles of the Memnonium, the bas-reliefs of the palace of Luxor and in the paintings of this prince's tomb in the western valley of Biban-el-Molouk [Valley of the Kings], a new and millionth proof that the statues and bas-reliefs of the Egyptians are true portraits of the ancient kings that are subtitled in their legends.

At a short distance from the Ramesseum the reddish limestone fragments of two colossi still stand upright: in all probability these were another two statues decorating the lateral gate on the north of the Amenopheum, which gives a good idea of the enormous width of this palace of which such splendid vestiges still remain. I didn't bother at all with the Greek and Latin inscriptions which are crawled on the legs of the great northern colossus, the celebrated statue of Memnon; all that is far too modern for me. I say this, but no one should think that I deny the reality of the melodious words which so many Romans unanimously say they heard pipe up from the colossus when struck by the first rays of sunlight. I will only say that, having sat several times on the enormous knees of Memnon at sunrise, there was not a musical note from his mouth that distracted my attention from the melancholic scene which I was surveying, the plane of Thebes, where the scattered members of this Nestor of the royal cities have found their resting place.

June 1829, Thebes (western bank)…

I visited and thoroughly studied all aspects of a small, perfectly preserved temple which is situated behind the Amenopheum in a valley formed by rocks of the Libyan mountainside and a large mound which detaches itself alongside the plane. This monument was described by the Commission of Egypt under the name of 'Small Temple of Isis'.

In this lonely and barren areas, the traveller's attention is attracted by an irregular enclosure built in dried bricks which you will see from quite far away because it nestles on a fairly elevated spot. You enter it through a small propylon of sandstone which is part of the enclosure and covered with sculptures in a terrible plodding style on the outside. The scenes which decorate the post of this gate show Ptolemy Soter II making offerings to Hathor (Venus) and the great Triad of Thebes, Amon-Ra, Muth and Chons on the right and to the left to the goddess Thme or Thmei (truth or justice, Themis) and a triad formed by the falcon-headed Mandou, his spouse Ritho and their son Harphre. These three divinities, who are the ones who are mostly worshipped in Hermonthis, are on the section of the doorpost which faces the capital of this nome.

If you are [now] somewhat familiar with the decorative scheme of the Egyptian monuments these brief details will be enough for you to say with certainty: 1) to which deities the temple behind the propylon was consecrated; 2) which deities had the pleasure of presiding over it, and here all the evidence points to the fact that particularly the principle of beauty expressed by the principle of truth, justice, were worshipped here, or, in mythological terms, that this building was dedicated to Hathor as characterised by Thmei. These are, therefore, the two goddesses who are first worshipped by Soter II; and as the building was part of Thebes and was a neighbour of the *nome* of Hermonthis,[12] the Theban and Hermonthite Triads were also worshipped in line with the good sense of the policy which I have set out earlier...

Its naos is divided in three contiguous chambers; these are three real sanctuaries. The one in the middle, the principal one, which is entirely carved, contains adorational tableaus to all the gods worshipped in the temple, though mainly to Hathor and Thmei, who appear in almost all of the scenes. Also, only the two goddesses are referred to in the dedications made in name of Philopater on the frieze to the right and left...

The shrine to the left is dedicated to the goddess Thmei, the Dike and Alethea of the Egyptian myths; furthermore all the tableaus which embellish this chapel are concerned with the important functions of this divinity in the Amenti, the western regions, or hell to Egyptians.

The two gods of this fateful place where the soul is judged, Osiris and Isis, receive homage from Ptolemy and Arsinoe, two Philopaters, and on the left wall a great scene of the 'psychostase' is sculpted. This enormous bas-relief depicts the hypostyle chamber (Oskh) or court of Amenti, with its signature decorations. Chief-justice Osiris occupies the front of the room; at the foot of his throne soars a lotus, the emblem of the material world, and above it the images of his four children, the presiding spirit over the four wind directions.

The forty two judges, the assessors of Osiris, are arranged in two lines crowned with ostrich plumes, the symbol of justice. Poised on a sockle is the Egyptian Cerberus, a monster made up of three different animals, a crocodile, lion and hippopotamus, who opens its large orifice and terrifies the guilty souls; his name, Teouomen-ement means the devourer of the east, or hell. Towards the doorway of the court appears the double Thmei, that is, depicted twice, because of her double function as goddess of justice and of the truth. The first form, called Thmei, guide-of-Amenti (truth), presents the soul of an Egyptian in his corporal state to the second form of the goddess (justice) whose legend is: 'Thmei who resides in Amenti, where she weighs hearts with her balance: no evil-doer will escape her.' Near the one who is to undergo the ordeal one reads the following words: 'Arrival of a soul in Amenti.' Further on are the scales of hell: Horus, the son of Isis with the head of a falcon, and Anubis, the son of Osiris with a jackal-head, place in the scales, the one a heart of the supplicant the other an ostrich feather: in the middle of the fatal instrument stands the ibicephalic Thoth: 'Twice-great Thoth, the lord of Schmoun (Hermopolis magna), lord of divine words, secretary of justice to the other gods, mighty in the courts of justice and truth.' This divine clerk takes notes the proof to which the soul of the deceased Egyptian is subjected and presents his report to the sovereign judge.

Clearly only the fact that this third sanctuary was consecrated to Thmei was the motivation for depicting the 'psychostase'. It was too hastily concluded on the basis of this curious scene, which is reproduced in the second part of all funerary rites, that this temple was a tomb which might well have served as the resting place of very distinguished members of the priestly class. Nothing of the kind was the case. It is true that the surroundings of the compound which encloses the monument are scattered with graves and Egyptian catacombs from all periods. But the temple of Hathor and Thmei isn't the only sacred building which was erected amid tombs: in that case you would also have to classify the palace of Sesostris or the Ramesseum, the temple of Amon at El-Asasif, the palace of

Judgement scene (in *l'Égypte ancienne*, 1839, by Champollion-Figeac)

Kourna, as funerary temples, which is impossible to maintain in the face of all evidence and squarely contradicted by the Egyptian inscriptions which cover their walls.

4 July 1829, Thebes [Kourna]

My very dear friend, I am at last and a little late perhaps responding to your three letters of 30 January, 22 March, and 10 April. But you should think of me as a man who has just been given back his life: up until the fist days of June I was living in tombs where no one is particularly concerned with what goes on on earth. Nonetheless, underneath their sombre vaults, my heart was alive and often crossed Egypt and the Mediterranean in order to dip again into its fond memories of the banks of the Seine. Such family baths refreshed my mood and strengthened my heart. This was really necessary in order to accomplish the research plan which I had laid out for myself with respect to the royal tombs of Biban-el-Molouk.

As of the 8 of June I have been living in our castle of Kourna, the small mud shack of one storey that is grand compared to the dens and burrows where our Arabic fellow-citizens hang out. We are basking daily in a temperature of 31 to 38 degrees, but you get used to everything and we have already discovered that you can breathe well enough at a temperature of 28 degrees. Other than that, I am normally only at the castle at night; as soon as day breaks I wake up, saddle my donkey and launch myself on to the plain with small steps and deeply inhale the freshness of the morning and go either to the Ramesseum, or the palace of Medinet-Habu, where I work all day long. I have almost nothing left to do among these two magnificent monuments; I have sucked them dry and wrapped them up. Fifteen to twenty days will be enough to study what remains of the Amenopheum, the real Memnonium, the small palace of Menephtha-Ousirei at Kourna, three or four small temples and the tombs in the mountainside which I have not yet seen.

On the 1st of August we will move to the eastern bank where Karnak and its immensity awaits us. Luxor is in our portfolio: one month will be enough to take down the few historical bas-reliefs which are still in the great palace of the kings, and in order to note what is most salient about the religious scenes which abound in this gigantic compound. I therefore count on setting off on the route for Paris seriously on 1 September, the day on which we will say our goodbye to Thebes, our ancient mother. While ascending, we will see Dendera again and visit Abydos. Then our mission will be over; we will go back to Cairo and from there to Alexandria, where we will for sure arrive during the final days of September. So, if you have done your bit regarding the navy, a nice ship will be waiting for us in the New Harbour, ready to take us on board during the first days of October and to drop us off at the end of the same month on the blessed shores of the Provence: because I mean to go straight to Paris.[13] I will thus be in Paris towards the end of December, as long as the vessel is in Alexandria when ordered, and taking into account the damned quarantine as well as several small detours which I am envisaging in the Mediterranean without much delaying my journey. This then is my final plan: you may rely on it and add to it your variations and conclusions. Mine are very simple and from my point of view I don't see any obstacles which could delay its achievement.

I remain rather unmoved by the fact that that scholarly English engineer thought up the brilliant idea of a three-hundred-thousand-franc ramp to make his government, and ours at the same time, go after the poor obelisks of Alexandria. Having seen the ones in Thebes I pity them. If we must have an obelisk in Paris, then let it be one of the ones in

Luxor. Ancient Thebes will be relieved and at ease while preserving the ones of Karnak, the most beautiful and admirable of them all. But I will never give my support (which one will in any case be able to do extremely well without) to a project which splices one of these magnificent monoliths in three. This would be sacrilege: all or nothing. Without spending three hundred thousand francs on preliminary works, one could ship one of the two Luxor obelisks over the Nile by alighting them on a [correctly] proportioned barge (and I nominate the one on the right for good reasons known to me even though its pyramidion is broken and it appears to be several feet shorter than its neighbour). The water of the flooding will carry it to the sea and right up to the vessel transporting it to Europe. This is feasible. If we want it, it will happen, and it wouldn't be a bad idea to focus the gaze of the nation on a monument of this magnitude so that it will go off the follies and baroque rubbish to which we give the sumptuous name of 'public monuments' – parlour trinkets which exactly reflect the size of our public figures and no more, conceptions worthy of our architects who meticulous imitate all the poverty of the early-Empire. You might call it, greatness will always be great, and nothing else. Only mass imposes and makes a profound impression on the spirit and soul. One single column from Karnak is more monument on its own than the four facades of the court of the Louvre, and a colossus like the one of the Ramesseum placed on the empty sockle of the Pont Neuf would say more than three regiments of equestrian statues of the size of Lemot's... [14]

Before leaving Thebes, I will send you several pages on Medinet-Habu where I have harvested an unbelievable number of names of ancient African and Asian people, and on the palace of Kourna, which I will be attacking tomorrow. While going up the Nile I will edit a summary of Karnak, Dendera and Abydos which I will despatch to you before arriving in quarantine and you will have a digest of my work on this holy land and the results that it yielded.

As for 'holy land', you may know that the archbishop of Jerusalem has decided to award me and Rosellini the Cross of the Knight of the Holy Grave. Our diplomas are in Alexandria where we may accept them, making a trifling contribution of 100 Louis. I think that His Grace is selling his wares too dearly and, whatever my zeal for joining the battle line and clutching the knight's lance to fight the infidel and let saintly Sion triumph, I will have to decline this honour and content myself with the one of having been worthy of it. Selling three inches of ribbon for 100 Louis! Good lord, silk must be rather precious *in partibus infidelium* [heathen lands]. His letter justifies this custom with reference to the extreme needs of the Holy Land. On the banks of the turbulent Cedron [ravine between the Mount of Olives and the Holy City] they ought to know that the scholars of Europe aren't like Croesus and that the wheel of fortune nowadays is predisposed to the industrialist — chemists and mathematicians included. May they send their ribbon to these people; only they can afford these astronomical charges!

Thousands of greetings to Letronne: I hope that my profession of faith in the Ramesseum appears reasonable to him. I look forward to his messages on Thebes. May his letter which contains them arrive soon, before we will definitely leave this capital in at most two months. Don't forget to present my respects to M. de Sacy when the opportunity arises; I would be flattered if my findings justify the interest which he has shown in my work.

I have had no response at all to two letters which I sent to M. the Duke de Blacas, one from Thebes, while going down the Nile, the other on my return from the cataracts and in which I give him a quick account of my conquests in Nubia. If he is in Paris you must go and see him and show him my digests as a scoop; he will excuse me for not sending them to him direct, the time fails me for a task which cannot be done in a minute. Did M. the Duke receive my letters? I would be in despair if they hadn't reached him and that he thinks that my silence means that I have forgotten all his kindnesses to me: such oversight is beyond my character — even less so my heart.

It is unnecessary to caution you that this present missive needs no reply. You won't have it until September at the earliest, and your response will arrive in Egypt when I will already have left. I will write to my wife about the apartment we should take; if she is unable to take care of this do it yourself as you have my proxy and choose one near you.[15] A large office and a small bedroom very nearby. Most of all a warm apartment, I will need it to get through the brutal winter which will await me on my return all right; I am already shivering.

Pariset is in Syria chasing the pest and cholera morbus. He will push on as far as Halep, but he is getting my hopes up that I will have the pleasure of embracing him in Cairo towards the end of September. Adieu my dear friend, my regards and love to the Colbert arcade, to the abbey of St Germain-des-Prés, the Pantheon and to all the good numbers of Parisian streets. I embrace you with heart and soul, and yours ever. [16]

Champollion was at the end of his tether, without wanting to admit it to himself or his brother. The long stay in the Valley of the Kings from 23 March to 8 June and, most of all, the numerous and extremely complex research which he had do in absolute seclusion in order to arrive at the exact principles of the chronology as well as those of the religion of the ancient Egyptians had severely affected his health. On several occasions he was found unconscious, lying on the ground in the subterranean chambers where he wanted to be alone. This annoyed Salvador Cherubini's greatly, to whom he often said apparently: 'I need absolute silence in order to hear the voice of history — the influence of local atmosphere is enormous!'

The stay at 'castle Kourna' was more agreeable as there were plenty of distractions. Champollion loved animals, on which he seems to have exercised a kind of instinctive charm.[17] Every day the inhabitants of the four villages of the antique site of Thebes — Karnak, Luxor, Kourna and Medinet-Habu — would bring Champollion new species animals, as if the real goal of the expedition was to found a zoo in Kourna. The care which was lavished on 'Pierre', the gazelle, and their cat, which had become well fed during their stay in the Valley, had made the locals think that they were interested in more animals to domesticate. Thus Gaetano Rosellini bought a few panther cubs that playfully gnawed his feet when he was asleep. Moreover, the continuous requests from Professor Raddi, who had returned from the Libyan desert with a beautiful collection of butterflies and rare insects, had galvanised everyone, the Bedouins included, into collecting whatever animal or beasts happened to cross their path.[18] As he did not know any Arabic, He would imitate the voice of animals he wanted to purchase, which often lead to startling surprises.

Relations with the population of the villages were all the more cordial because Champollion had given the sheikhs advice aimed against any new oppressive measures from the Pasha. The same applied to the Bedouins of the great tribe of the Ababdes whose 'classical language, unaltered since Abraham' he had admired from the age of eighteen after what one of his teachers had told him about it when he was his pupil. Accompanied by Rosellini and all members of the Franco-Tuscan expedition, he visited them and they were all surprised by the beauty, patriarchal life and hospitality of these gentle desert inhabitants. Once formidable enemies of the government in Egypt, the Pasha had granted them privileges to compensate them for their continuous harassment under the Mamelukes. The entire edge of the desert was leased to them where they gathered their harvests in peace as naturalised Egyptians. But they feared the Pasha's son, Ibrahim-Pacha, who would change everything, they said, after the death of the Muhammad-Ali. Champollion promised to mention this to the Pasha, which he did.

During their stay in Kourna, the members of the expedition worked from seven in the morning until noon, and from two till four 'exactly'; subsequently they would saddle their donkeys and two Arabic servants would be waiting to take them wherever they wanted. 'In my gluttonous zeal, I wanted to swallow and gobble up everything... The whole of Thebes was already in the bag', said L'hôte exhilarated by the five hundred sketches and aquarels which had himself already completed before the end of July. At night he would write long letters and articles for Parisian publications. Nonetheless he complained ceaselessly and one day he addressed Champollion in his mind and wrote down the following: 'You may be sure that, though I came to Egypt a little bit because of you, it isn't because of you that I am staying, but rather that it is for me and my research, my education and curiosity.' He heatedly complained about the fact that the seemingly endless hieroglyphs were so difficult. 'They give all of us indigestion! Haven't we had enough of them! Haven't we been overfed! A year of work, a year without interruption, – not a day of rest, not a minute's truce' 'I love Customs [& Excise, his employer in France], and long live Customs, which will embrace me as a result of the recommendation procured by my voyage as well as my *Notes on eastern Commerce*.'

Towards the end of July, Lehoux, Bertin and Duchesne were so overexcited by the ideas of L'hôte that they resolved to leave Thebes the very next day under some pretext. But when the 30th arrived only Duchesne left: Bertin and Lehoux gave in to Cherubini, who was devoted to Champollion, and they stayed until the end of the expedition. Champollion was not aware of the difficulties caused by L'hôte. The main reason for the discontent was that Drovetti had told them that

Champollion would procure the title of 'Governmental Commissioner' for them, which would have given a completely different impression from the very ordinary reference of artists attached to the expedition. When L'hôte returned to France, Charles Lenormant reproached him severely about his conduct. His U-turn was complete and Champollion could not have wished for a more devoted and modest supporter than L'hôte.

Charles Lenormant said about Champollion's way of working. 'We are [now] in a good position to form an idea of the measure of insight, constancy and sureness of intellect required by this undertaking...; but what rather fewer of us have been able to appreciate in the way that I do is what application such a result requires, the power of intuition which only the genius has, and at the same time a candour during the search for the truth, a noble simplicity to admit error when recognised, a patient resignation to ignore what is not yet knowable... May this testimony of sincere admiration and devoted friendship release me in part from the debt which his many signs of trust and interest have raised.'

By now the ranks of Champollion's French expedition had halved. Bibent, Lenormant and Duchesne had left for various reasons, leaving Cherubini, L'hôte Lehoux and Bertin. Rosellini was not in a much better position. His best aide, Doctor Ricci, had been hurt in his arm by a scorpion (which was later followed by paralysis and dementia) and Professor Raddi was suffering from dysentery. Furthermore, Raddi's assistant Gallastri had had to return to Italy where he died a little later. Instead of looking after himself and taking a rest, Raddi all of a sudden decided to leave for the Delta in order to cross it on foot, despite the fact that Pariset's theory predicted a high risk of the plague recurring following the high flooding of that year. He too died shortly after leaving the expedition.

At Karnak, the remaining expedition members were comfortably lodged in the small temple dedicated by Evergetes II to Osiris and the goddess Apet (Oph), next to the pretty temple consecrated by Ramesses III to the god Khonsou. There are no diary entries or detailed letters for Karnak: only the summary description at the beginning of this book — a summary written in haste after the quick exploration of the 23rd of November 1828. Karnak raised questions to which Champollion did not always have an answer.

Extremely early in the morning, the members of the expedition left Karnak on 4 September 1829 in order to have a last look at all the monuments of the left bank. They admired a last sunset over the heights of the temple propylons of Kourna and then, at nine in the evening, Champollion gave the order for departure while the entire population, children included, rushed out to say their noisy farewell. A number of Bedouins had also come and stood in silent attendance. The expedition left from underneath the same sycamore where its members had disembarked on 19 November 1828 and it was a sleepless night for Champollion who was preoccupied with the idea that he would never again see Thebes and its fairytale splendour. On the morning of 5 September, work was resumed at Dendera, but not for long. Champollion was completely exhausted.

8.

Plotting the Future

Champollion to Champollion-Figeac – 11 September 1829, on the Nile near Antinoe

The location and date of this letter will clearly tell you that my voyage of research is over and that I am returning as quickly as possible towards Alexandria in order to get back to Europe and to find there both solace for my heart and repose for my body, for the latter of which I have no great need. Since Dendera, which I left at 7 in the morning, I have in effect been living like a monk. Resting the entire day in the pretty cangia of our friend Muhammad-Bey of Akhmin, who was delighted to lend it to us, I have been leading an entirely contemplative life and my most serious occupation has been to see from which side the wind is blowing and whether our rowers are doing their bit conscientiously. The northern wind has been vexing us for a long time, this despite the current of the river which has swollen beyond measure and is above its maximum level. The flooding of this year is brilliant for those who, like us, travel as visitors and have no interest in the countryside other than to have a view. It isn't the same for the poor, miserable *fellahs* or farmers. The flooding is too strong; it has already destroyed several harvests and the farmers will have to eat the grain which the Pasha has set aside for the next sowing. We saw entire villages being drenched by a river which had spared only a few diminutive shacks built of sun-dried lime. The waters extended in many places from one mountain to the next, and wherever more elevated lands were not submerged we saw wretched *fellahs*, women, men and children, hastily carrying baskets full of earth aiming to fight an immense river with dykes of three or four inches in height and so to save their houses and the few provisions they have left. It is a depressing tableau which deeply affects the heart. This is not a country that believes in partnership and the government does not demand a penny less despite the numerous disasters.

As you can imagine, it was with considerable regret that I said goodbye to the splendours of Thebes where I lived for six months. Our last lodgings were at Karnak in the temple of Oph (Rhea) next to the grand temple on the south in middle of the avenues of sphinxes and at the gate of the great palace of kings.

... You will find more details about my conquests in Karnak in the summary – which I will send you from the Lazaret – on this accumulation of palaces and temples, this astonishing reunion of buildings of all ages of the Egyptian monarchy, brilliant constructions before which even the iron mouth of M. Quatremère would close itself.

Having left Thebes on the 4th of September at night, I was under the portico of Dendera on the 5th, whose architecture is as beautiful as its decorative bas-reliefs are bad and repulsive... I wanted to assure myself again, with my eyes and hands, that the cartouches of the lateral inscriptions of the circular zodiac are really empty and were never filled in; this is correct without a doubt and the famous 'Autocrator' is clearly as our friend Jomard likes things best...

The remainder of our voyage until today (11 September) has yielded nothing special. I hope to arrive in Cairo tomorrow night. Nothing will keep me there for more than four or five days; we will leave straightaway for Alexandria and if your cares and the promises of the minister have had their effect, and a solid vessel is ready to receive us, I will disembark immediately in order to get to Toulon. You see there is no longer any question of wintering in Italy. I am counting on being in Paris by then, though deep down this idea horrifies me because of the extreme climactic contrast, and I would need a very warm apartment and am planning on staying in until the first warmth. I shall pretend to be a silk worm.

It was also on the Nile, between Dendera and Haou (Diospolis parva), that we found the two hapless couriers which we dispatched from Thebes to Cairo from the end of June. During all that time we have remained without news from Europe and it was while waiting each day for their arrival that time passed during which we couldn't write to France. Apart from that you must like us be used to lacunae... Thousands of regards to our nestor [M. Dacier]. I hope that he wasn't too annoyed by the fact that his gang — may they perish — placed me below M. Pardessus:¹ it doesn't surprise me. I would have been flattered to have been elevated to the Académie while my discoveries are still disputed, whether sincerely or insincerely that doesn't matter: by electing me its members would then have had a real right to my accolades. I would also have been flattered that they had thought of me while I was crossing the t's on my research and gathering an enormous harvest amidst the ruins of Thebes. I would have regarded my nomination as a kind of national recognition; they have decided on this point to deny this satisfaction to me. Therefore, from now on, I will no longer make gestures in its direction, and, if the Académie elects me, I will be as little impressed with my seat as a connoisseur of wine would be of a bottle of Champaign which was decanted six months earlier. The very water of the Nile inspires revulsion when you are no longer thirsty. May god create peace and happiness.

I haven't had any news from Dubois,² to whom I wrote from Thebes to wherever he may be. M. Mimaut [the new consul replacing Drovetti, who had been called back] sent me a warm letter. According to Cairo gossip, he is a very good man and a bon-vivant. He ran into M. Drovetti at the end of the Pont Neuf, one of them arriving the other leaving. He won't have had the time to absorb any 'good' opinions about people and things: I believe we have lost nothing through this happenstance. I think well of M. Mimaut because he is not into dealing antiquities.

I predicted that the supplementary funds which I petitioned for would arrive when I would no longer be able to make any use of them in Thebes. Nonetheless, it does not matter too much because even if I had received this credit at Karnak I would not have been able to spend a *sous* on searches anyway. I gave up on them a few months earlier as it isn't my forte and the Arab diggers need to be supervised every second lest they do not find anything or make everything they find disappear. Actually, I will nonetheless bring back some interesting objects for the Louvre, though they are of a modest size. As far as large items are concerned, three or four mummies with novel or Greek decorations and with inscriptions, and besides these: the most stunning coloured bas-relief from the royal tomb of Menephtha I (Ousirei) at Biban-el-Molouk. This is a top-quality piece which on its own is worth a collection; it has caused me rather a lot of anxiety and will certainly cost me a lawsuit with the English of Alexandria who pretend they are the legitimate owners of the tomb of Ousirei which was discovered by Belzoni on M. Salt's account. Despite these pretensions, of two things one: either my bas-relief will arrive in Toulon, or it will end up on the bottom of the sea or the Nile rather than fall into the hands of strangers. I have made up my mind about that. [3]

In Cairo I bought from Mahmoud-Bey of Kihaia — still from my savings and own funds — the most beautiful sarcophagus of the present day, past and future. It is made of green basalt and covered on the inside and outside with bas-reliefs, or rather cameos, cut to perfection with unimaginable refinement. It is all that one may image perfection goes in this genre; it would be worthy of being part of a boudoir or salon such is the preciousness and delicacy of its sculpture. The lid shows in half-relief the figure of a woman in a remarkable workmanship. This single piece will discharge my duties towards the royal household, not as far as results are concerned, but from a pecuniary point of view because this sarcophagus is worth at least a hundred thousand compared to the ones that twenty and thirty thousand francs was paid for.

The bas-reliefs and the sarcophagus are the two most beautiful Egyptian objects which have ever been sent to Europe to date. It has a right to come to Paris and follow me like the trophy of my expedition; it will be my present to the Louvre where they will remain in memory of me. Thus, if I find nothing in Cairo with the dealers, who flock to me as if to the messiah after my purchase of the sarcophagus (I paid eight hundred thalaris and would have paid up to twelve hundred), if I do not find with the traders any objects worthy of the Louvre, I said, I will not spend a sous of the credit which has been granted to me, — and if at Marseille, which I will pass by after the Lazaret, I don't find anything either I will have the pleasure of returning to M. La Rochefoucauld an untouched credit letter while also giving him the memorandum on the monuments with which I will be enriching the museum without it costing him a para. Adieu provisionally, I will end this letter in Cairo where I will take it myself.

From the spring of 1828 Viscount de La Rochefoucauld had tirelessly battled against their opponents who wanted to prevent Champollion from undertaking excavations in Egypt. The absence of the Count of Forbin at a meeting on 14 May 1829 made it possible to allocate the money and the official letter announcing victory left on the same day.

Viscount de La Rochefoucauld to Champollion – 14 May 1829, Paris
Royal household, Department of the Arts

It is a great pleasure to announce to you, Monsieur, that as a consequence of the actions which I have undertaken in order to realise your wish expressed in the letter of 1 January of this year, His Majesty has consented that a credit of 10,000 francs should be attached to the budget of 1829 of the Museum in order specifically to effect the acquisition for the Museum Charles X of Egyptian sculptured objects resulting from the excavations about which you informed me. I have no doubt that these new funds, which have been put at your disposal, will present you with the opportunity to add even further to the numerous services which the arts and sciences already owe you, and I congratulate myself on having found myself in a position where I was able to procure for you the funds necessary to facilitate the success of your mission.

I will this very day inform M. the Director of the Museums of the decision regarding the allocation of the 10,000 francs concerned here, and I will invite him to take care without delay of all the arrangements which such a decision may require. I beg you to liaise with him about the details which the nature of this matter may entail.

Kindly, Monsieur, accept my assurance of my very sincere regards

PS – Please trust that I will be delighted to see you after your return after your important work has finished.

Despite this prompt action, the despatch of the new funds was delayed until the 23rd of July.

Champollion to Champollion-Figeac, 15 September 1829, noon,
Cairo [end of the letter of 11 September]

Here I am back in the capital of Egypt where I find no letters, no news from Europe, nor my friend Pariset, who is they tell me in very good health and has left the Syrian countryside with honour. I will go and join him in a few days after having made a visit to Ibrahim-Pacha, whom I would very much like to meet personally. This will be my last letter which I am writing from Egypt, the first one will be dated from the Lazaret of Toulon.... .

Adieu my dear friend, my health is excellent, everything is fine. The Mediterranean is not going to be a shock.

On his arrival in Cairo, Champollion saw, one by one, all the things the dealers in antiquities had set aside for him. Duchesne, who had deserted the expedition towards the end of July, was the reason for this. Having left the expedition at Thebes, he was worried about having abandoned Champollion after only twelve months since the departure from Toulon whereas his contract stated that the members were signing up for twelve to fourteen months.

Duchesne to Champollion – middle of August, Cairo
Monsieur, the sarcophagus is ours. I bought it for 800 talaris and tomorrow I will load it up. I am still overjoyed to be able to announce this unforeseen success to you… I saw another sarcophagus with a man called Antonio Despirro; it is in the shape of a mummy case. The lid is a figure, its arms alongside the body as per usual, a long robe with folds and large cuffs. The hieroglyphs are very well preserved, no cartouches. It is made of grey granite and completely intact… Don't forget to go and see it; I believe it might be a piece which is well worth this trouble. I urge you to do so, I believe we don't have one of that genre. The owner is a commercial grave-digger who needs money; his asking price is 700 pounds. At his place he also has another sarcophagus in the shape of a mummy case; I think it is made of basalt. In the tomb a small figure of calcite and five or six canopic vases were found which I urged him not to separate from the sarcophagus to which they belong. There is also a kind of pyramid in pink granite. A small one…

It is almost certain, it would appear, that M. Rosellini has made no move regarding the sarcophagus. I told M. Mac Ardle, who was helpfulness itself, that, having heard the rumour that Mahmoud-Bey had lowered his expectations and had marked it down to 1000 talaris, you had told me to go by him and see whether this was true and, if so, to buy it and take it with me… The lid and the broken piece of the sarcophagus are still on the riverbank of the Nile, but the most difficult thing has been achieved, the case is on board; there weren't enough precautions I could think of regarding a piece which is so beautiful and costly… All has been accomplished with success; I had the shivers all day, I thought they would never be able to raise it or that it would suffer some mishap; there isn't even a small scratch on it and I am letting you know this with a great sigh of relief; it is quite beautiful! I am extremely proud to be taking it to France.

There is a frigate in Alexandria which is due to be relieved of her duty; if its departure is going to take place immediately I will take all your stuff with me, as you have instructed me. I am writing to you, Monsieur, in greater haste than I would have wanted, I believe nonetheless to have informed you of every important matter. I like Cairo very much, but this is a dreadful country: even the smallest business affair takes forever. What animals! I will leave tomorrow afternoon.

Every dealers in antiquities is waiting for you with apprehension. They think that everything you are not going to buy will be irrevocably tarnished and will never find another buyer. I am going to visit this Antonio again; he very much hopes and wants to sell you his sarcophagus. I have told him that you will doubtless go and see him, but that you are not a man to haggle and that once you had examined it and set a valued you would fix a price, if you felt an inclination to purchase it...'

Champollion to Champollion-Figeac – 30 September 1829, Alexandria
For about ten days, I have been living like a gilded cockerel with our brilliant consul M. Mimaut. He is a charming compatriot whom I cannot praise enough. He is showering me with real affection, which has certainly not happened in the past. My health is excellent, as is those of my young people. Our happiness would be supreme, if we could see pointing on the horizon the sail of the ship which is supposed to pick up, but the sea has remained mute – not even a merchant vessel! So I am to wait here for the contingency as well as emanation of ministerial promises. We are irritated, as you may well imagine. Well, some more patience.

I didn't leave Cairo without visiting Ibrahim-Pacha, who received us in the grandest style. We spoke a lot about the sources of the Nile and I bolstered an idea which he already had, to attach his name to this beautiful geographical conquest, either by sponsoring explorers who would undertake this or by organising himself a small expedition of travellers accompanied with armed men. Perhaps this will be an idea for the future: in any case, the Pasha understands the significance of this enterprise.

I already presented my homage and the expression of my gratitude to Muhammad-Ali. He continues to be well and well-disposed towards the French: enough said.

I am taking the opportunity of this delay to put my papers and immense riches in order. It would take too long to give you any details. The ship charged with this letter and my previous one will sail tomorrow at midday. Goodbye then, my dear friend, goodbye, – to Toulon!

Champollion to Champollion-Figeac – October 1829, Alexandria
Still here, my dear friend, I got quite as far as during the first days of September. The entire Mediterranean continues to lie between us. I left Thebes and Upper Egypt with reluctance, and all that in order to come and waste my time along this depressing riverside. The corvette *Astrolabe* only moored in the harbour two days ago, announcing that it had been charged with returning us to France. One of our Quercy compatriots, M. de Verninac, is in command, a very pleasant young man, well educated, everything I could wish for in the person of a commander. – All this is for the best, but bad luck has it that I won't leave for France until about the 15th of November as the *Astrolabe* first has to transport M. Malivoir, the consul of Aleppo, to Syria. I will thus have to plan on leaving the quarantine of Toulon only during the last days of December. This is a disappointment, a great disappointment.

I am still without any news from all of you since the letters from July. Either the post is very badly organised (frustrating) or you are not writing, – unforgivable. Either hypothesis only depresses me; which I am doing whole-heartedly. Egypt is the most beautiful school in patience that exists in the world, but its lessons don't stick. Adieu. My love to M. Dacier and his family. A greeting to all our friends, a hearty embrace for you.

PS – I won't write any further letters until Toulon. Rosellini and the Tuscans embarked several days ago on a merchant vessel; I will do the same as soon as the corvette arrives. During our forced stay in Alexandria my young people have painted the decorations for the theatre which French amateurs are about to open. And so civilisation progresses! These gentlemen are thrilled with the enthusiasm of our young artists. So I will go to the show while awaiting embarkation.

Champollion to Doctor Pariset – 27 October 1829, Alexandria
Dearest Imouth!
I received your little gallant epistle with delight, – you are triumphant![4] I share your joy with my entire heart; you know well whether or not I ever

doubted your undertaking. Evviva l'allegria!

This letter will be given to you by my three travel companions, who are returning to Cairo in order to sketch its panorama while we are waiting for the 15th of November, the date fixed for our departure. People say that you have a house in which they might find a room to sleep in; if this is the case, let me claim it for them, as I am convinced that I am [only] anticipating your decision.

Will you decide to return to France with me? Now that you have achieved your business, this would be the desire of all your friends. I won't say anymore about it as I feel more and more certain about my conjecture about this matter. While waiting for your news, I embrace you in the same way as my affections, with heart and soul.
Maiamoun

Champollion to Doctor Pariset — 29 October 1829, Alexandria
My dearest Imouth
For the love of the gods of Egypt, return immediately to Alexandria, even if for no more than three days. Your presence is required to an extremely high degree, — and we have so much to tell you![5] I am all yours,

Champollion to Champollion-Figeac — 9 November 1829, Alexandria
As bad weather has prevented the *Astrolabe* to set sail for transporting M. Malivet on the coasts of Syria, my departure won't take place until towards the 20th of this month. So patience!

I would be very pleased I would find upon my arrival at Toulon a letter for the Director of Customs so that I won't have to squabble with these gentlemen: regarding the crates of antique objects which I have addressed to the royal museum; regarding the various curiosities such as woollen mantels, shoes for men and women, veils of embroided muslin, arms and other objects of oriental costumes, which I am importing myself, as are my young people who intend to cloth the dummies in their ateliers when they need to paint Asiatic or African subjects. I beg you therefore to obtain for this purpose and purely artistic interest the free passage of these manufactured goods of the country. It would be good if upon my arrival in Toulon towards the middle of December I would find precise instructions regarding this and officials documents which would raise all problems.

The sarcophagus was stowed on the *Astrolabe* with great ease thanks to our commander, our pleasant Quercy compatriot, M. de Verninac. This is an important thing dealt with. My health is still keeping up; my young people are doing their panorama of Cairo, – and the French theatre whose decorations they painted has made its debut on the feast of the king to the great satisfaction of its French spectators. – Goodbye then, I embrace you as well as all those who are ours. Adieu, all yours with my heart.

Champollion to Champollion-Figeac – 28 November 1829, Alexandria
My dear friend, the great Amon has at last deigned to allow me to say to goodbye to his sacred land. I will leave Egypt heaped with favours from its ancient and modern inhabitants on the 2nd or 3rd of December. The *Astrolabe* is back from Syria and ready to take me on board as well as my trusted aide-de-camp Salvador [Cherubini]. Messrs. L'hôte, Lehoux and Bertin, who have started a chef-d'oeuvre, the panorama of Cairo, want to finish it at all cost and they are right for all the right reasons because it will be a magnificent thing.[6] They will stay for another month in Egypt and I will arrive in Toulon and France before them. Other than that, our health is at its very best and I feel I have enough strength to brave the squalls and blasts of wind which will not be absent from our reception at full sea during the propitious month of our crossing. This will purge us, no more; moreover in order to see France again one would put up with worse than the bad temper of the currents.

This letter will leave tomorrow morning via the brig the *Eclipse*; I am giving it to M. Ouder, aide-de-camp of general Guilleminot. He is a very pleasant young man with whom I struck up a friendship. You will be charmed to make his acquaintance if diplomatic vagaries will allow him to bring it himself to Paris. His arrival in France will precede mine by some ten days because his small ship is must faster than our *Astrolabe*, a corvette made to withstand bombs and the furry of the oceans, which it has braved several times on its voyages around the world.[7] I will probably (because Neptune only allows probabilities) reach the French coast around the 20th to 25th of December and won't be free to go where I want on Christian soil until towards the middle of January.

My quarantine of twenty three days will be in Toulon, if I don't take it at Malta in order to gain a few days. But that depends on the winds which we encounter...

I will arrive with the sarcophagus and eighteen to twenty crates. The important thing is that in quarantine and at customs I shouldn't be asked to unpack all the objects twice in order to expose them to the air and chase away the plague, which hasn't occurred in Egypt for five years. Do me the pleasure of obtaining from a few competent ministers, the one of the Interior for the quarantine and the one for the Treasury regarding customs, all imaginable clemency, particularly as this concerns property belonging to the government...

Goodbye then... The end of the drama is drawing to a close, I hope, as happily as the four first acts. Adieu, yours with heart and soul... Vive la France!

Champollion was not able to realise his project of writing a detailed account of all that had happened to him during his second stay in Cairo and Alexandria. He meant to print such an account as a memoir for distribution to his family and numerous friends rather than for publication in newspapers.[8] His stay in Cairo and Alexandria was tiresome and troubled – but also satisfying. Champollion's first encounter with Ibrahim-Pacha, the son of the Pasha, in the presence of all the members of the expedition had been interesting. But the following day another meeting with the prince in the presence of Linant-Bey alone, was very important in a different way: Ibrahim-Pacha was interested in the proposition of an Egyptian expedition for the sources of the Nile with Linant-Bey as its scientific leader.

Another issue concerned the conservation of the magnificent model hospital and medical school of Abou-Zabel, near Cairo, which had been founded on the directions of Clot-Bey. A friend of Champollion from Grenoble, he had lived in Egypt from 1825 where he had organised a pubic health service and hygienic counsel. Champollion learned before his arrival in Cairo that the Pasha, who up till then had been very proud of the institution, wanted to turn it all of a sudden into a silk factory, which was also to be a model of its kind. The entire city of Cairo was in a state of revolt and Champollion met Clot-Bey, the chief surgeon of the Egyptian army, as quickly as possible in order to find out whether something could be done about this state of affairs. Ibrahim-Pacha promised Champollion that the hospital would be saved.

Relieved about the resolution of these two important matters, and having seen all the ancient sites of the city — there were hardly any worth noticing — he left Cairo, which for him meant leaving Egypt. Having arrived in Alexandria where, it was said, the ship would arrive very shortly, Champollion at last saw Pariset again and two of his colleagues, doctors Laguisquie and Guilhou, who like himself were guests of M. Mimaut, the new consul. During the first days they filed past the Egyptian antiquities which had been gathered for the chiefs of the expedition and which were much more interesting than the ones that had been shown in Cairo. However, a surprise lay in store for Champollion at one of these anti-quarians. Duchesne had left suddenly for Greece instead of going back to Paris with the objects that had been entrusted to him. He had left with this man the sarcophagus mentioned above, as well as the other objects, the most important ones were already missing.

In Alexandria all the members of the expedition presented themselves as early as possible at the Pasha's palace. Arriving from Cairo the day after this official visit, Ibrahim-Pacha went to Mimaut and asked Pariset and Champollion to go with him to Muhammad-Ali, who wanted to talk to them. He was even more excited than normal, which prompted Pariset to bring his medicine chest with him and this was a wise precaution. During dinner Ibrahim-Pacha fell suddenly to the ground, struck by an apoplectic fit. Pariset attended to him very quickly and revived him: in order to complete the cure Pariset had to stay for another week. The Pasha cried and from that intense moment he showered his two guests with favours 'because', he repeated constantly, 'the one resuscitated my son, and the other resuscitated the glory of my country!'

From then on they were allowed to speak frankly before father and son, an opportunity they accepted eagerly. Without any one else being present, they met several times for hours to speak to the two men about the misery in their country which ought to be so prosperous. Champollion pleaded mainly for the cause of the antique monuments to save them from destruction and Pariset for that of modern Egypt and the sanitary improvements which ought to be introduced; but both spoke about measures which would relieve the social situation. Their approaches were very different: Champollion, dubious of the 'enchanter's smile' of the Pasha,[9] constantly forced himself to maintain his reserve while Pariset boldly said things such as: 'Your Highness, give the Arab his soul back!

Wrest the slave from the childishness which holds him back! Restore his human dignity!' Champollion, instead, spoke about the progress of the forty six Egyptian pupils whom Bernardino Drovetti had sent to Paris for their education, to be placed under the direction of Jomard. Knowing them all personally, he was able to give detailed news about them to the Pasha...

Muhammad-Ali often spoke of the architect P.-C. Xavier whose rather abrupt departure in 1827 had offended him. He wanted to know what the reason was exactly for this flight. Pariset who – like Champollion – remembered with what horror Xavier had spoken to them about the misery of the *fellahs*. He bluntly told the Pasha that during the construction of the Mahmoudieh canal[10] Xavier wanted to leave immediately but that only the hope of being able one day to come to aid of the hapless victims had made him stay in Egypt; and that he had left when he lost all hope. Both father and son remained silent. At that moment Champollion showed them a large map[11] of the Delta and the course of the Nile through this area. Ahmed Er-Raschidy, the second *reis* of the *Isis*, had made it and given it to him as a present on 17 September 1828. Fixing his eyes on Muhammad-Ali, Champollion dared to say that the skilful execution of this work by the son of a *fellah*, raised in misery and without any schooling, showed what this race would be capable of if one were willing to educate them. Muhammad smiled and said in a breezy tone, changing the subject: 'Was Ramesses then truly the greatest of the pharaohs?' Champollion, who was about to let his fury rip, had to be restrained by Ibrahim.

Muhammad-Ali loved to talk and to hear people speaking about Napoleon in Egypt. He told Champollion one day about the curious affair of the bishop of Memphis, a Coptic priest sent by the Propaganda office in order to convert Muhammad-Ali. Informed of the arrival of the vessel on which his converter was pacing in full sacerdotal regalia, Muhammad-Ali sent him a message saying: 'My torturer is waiting for you'. The man took his word for it and returned to Naples as quickly as he could and back in Rome he was imprisoned. Ending the anecdote, Muhammad-Ali's smile disappeared and his clenched fist pressed on the head of the lion by his side, which brusquely moved towards Champollion and Pariset. Ibrahim-Pacha stood up but the Pasha calmed the animal down with a movement of his hand. Laughing, he turned to Champollion and said to him in a courteous but sharp tone: 'Of all the doctrines of Europe I would only want for me and my people the doctrine of deciphering the hieroglyphs.' And he asked him to write a summary of the history of ancient Egypt.

Rosellini left on the 7th of October with his three compatriots (Cherubini belonged to the French section) after having received on the previous day 'a superb Persian sabre, richly worked in gold' whose value was estimated at 4,000 francs. Extremely early in the morning of November 4th, the Saint's day of Charles X, Champollion was woken up by a messenger on horseback who arrived in order to present to him in the name of the Pasha a similar honorary saber and to announce an early-morning visit by Ibrahim-Pacha. He personally gave him the official news that the hospital of Cairo would remain a hospital. Lobbied by a large European manufacturer, the Pasha had again changed his mind towards the 29th of October and Champollion had called on Pariset who had told Ibrahim-Pacha that he would, if this happened, guard the entrance and 'rather be chopped in pieces to defend the hospital'.

On the 29th of November Champollion gave the Pasha the summary of Egyptian history he had asked for. In it he wrote 'The first tribes which peopled... the valley of the Nile between the cataract of Assouan [Aswan] and the sea came from Abyssinia or from Sennaar' which explains why Champollion was keen to mount a new scientific expedition passing through the country from which his ancient Egyptians seemed to him to have originated. Knowing that this essay would not be published in France, Champollion places the pyramids at the time of the first dynasties. This he could not yet do in Europe where the first fifteen dynasties were dismissed by the archaeologists of the clergy because of the chronology which had up to that point been adopted as doctrine by Rome. He similarly placed two of the Amenemhets of the twelfth dynasty before the invasion of the Hyksos, a fact which would have compromised him deeply in the eyes of the clergy of that era. The Revolution of July 1830 a few months later would release historians forever from having to take these kinds of precautions. Having taken leave from Muhammad-Ali and his son, Champollion managed to arrange with them the transport of the two obelisks of Luxor – which they gave as a present to France. A M. Besson, Director of the Arsenal of Toulon, was to build a gigantic barge following Champollion's specifications for transport from Luxor to the Louvre.

9.

Back in the Land of the Bells

Champollion to Champollion-Figeac – 25 December 1829, Toulon
Don't worry, everything will be fine!' These are the first words I can address
to you as I am saying hello – you will see that I kept my word, because
here I am on the coastline peaceably undergoing the dispiriting
requirement of my quarantine. My expedition is over now, my dear friend,
and everything has turned out according to your wishes as much as mine.
The anchor of the *Astrolabe* at last caught French soil on the 23rd along
the coast of Hyères,[1] – no doubt in order to celebrate the date of my
birth [23 December 1790] – and for your New Year's gift you will learn
that the wind allowed us to moor along the coast of Toulon today. The
only thing that is thus absent from my pleasure is receiving the letters
which are no doubt waiting for me, either at the post office or at the
office of the maritime prefect. That lies in store for tomorrow.

I have decided to take my quarantine (of only twenty days, I hope) on
board of the *Astrolabe*. I will however take a room at the Lazaret for the
purpose of warming myself up, in order to do a little exercise, and to edit
at my ease the digests of Medinet-Habu, Kourna, of the tombs, of
Karnak, and of Dendera, which will complete the series published in the
newspapers... [2]

I have only brought Salvador, my aide-de-camp with me. Messrs.
L'hôte, Lehoux and Bertin wanted to finish their panorama of Cairo and
to do the portrait of the two Pashas who indicated that they would like
that. – Thousands of greetings to M. Dacier, and to all his family and
ours...

An important matter: the sarcophagus, the great bas-relief and all the crates containing the steles, mummies and other objects destined for the Louvre are on board the *Astrolabe*. It would be risky to disembark and embark these large pieces. Their conservation demands that they are brought to Le Havre by the same vessel. What needs to happen therefore is that M. de La Bouillerie or M. de la Rochefoucauld obtain from the minister of the navy, our good friend,[3] that M. de Verninac, the commander of the *Astrolabe* is charged with keeping them on board in order to take them himself to Le Havre as soon as the season allows this. He could leave as soon as the sea is navigable, i.e. during the first days of February or the first days of March in order to reach Le Havre on the 1st of April. That would be best: do put your irons in the fire. I will write to M. de La Bouillerie and to M. Sosthenes [de La Rochefoucauld].

Attached is a Memo on One of the Temples of Thebes; send me all that has been published of these digests. I will successively pass to you others which are a little voluminous, but tell me what is an economical way to get them to you. Adieu, I await your news.

All yours with my heart and soul.

Champollion to Baron de la Bouillerie, General Intendant of the Royal Household, – 26 December 1829, Lazaret of Toulon

My first desire upon touching the soil of France is to refresh the expression of me utter gratitude to the protective hand which, assisting the lofty views of the King regarding the advancement of historical studies, has furnished me with the means with which to accomplish a series of projects which science showed still needed to be done in the whole of Egypt and on the soil of Nubia. I have striven, through my complete devotion to the important enterprise which you yourself have charged me with accomplishing, not to fail in this noble task and to justify in the best way possible the hopes with which the scholars of Europe have concurred to attach to my voyage.

Egypt was traversed step by step, and I halted wherever time had allowed some remainders of former antique splendour to survive. Each monument became the object of a single study; I had all the bas-reliefs and inscriptions copied which might cast light on the original state of a nation whose ancient name is woven into the most ancient written traditions.

The materials which I gathered have exceeded my expectations. My portfolios are filled with riches and I allow myself to say that the history of Egypt, that of its cults and the arts which it cultivated, won't be well understood and properly appreciated until after the publication of the drawings which are the fruit of my expedition.

I felt a duty to allocate all savings that I was in a position to make regarding excavations in Memphis and Thebes, etc., to enriching the museum Charles X with new monuments. I have been fortunate enough to gather a mass of objects which will complete various series of the Egyptian museum of the Louvre, and I moreover succeeded, after many considerations, to acquire the most beautiful and precious sarcophagus which has ever emerged from the Egyptian catacombs. No museum in Europe possesses such a magnificent Egyptian work of art. I have in addition collected a collection of choice objects of very great importance, among which is a bronze statue of a exquisite workmanship which is entirely encrusted with gold and represents an Egyptian queen from the dynasty of the Bubastites. It is the most beautiful object known of its kind.

I will hasten, as soon as the obligation of quarantine and the state of health will allow, to return to Paris as early as possible in order to have the honour of placing before your eyes, M. Baron, all the results of my voyage. I would count myself lucky if you would want to see in them a sign of my zeal for service to the king, and at the same time evidence of the acute recognition and respectful devotion which I have had the honour to remain yours, Monsieur le Baron, etc.

Champollion to the Viscount Sosthènes de la Rochefoucauld, Director of the Department of Arts of the Royal Household –
26 September 1830, Lazaret of Toulon

I have the honour of announcing to you my arrival in France on the royal vessel the *Astrolabe*, which passed the surf after a crossing of nineteen days and I hasten to bring to your attention at the same time the propitious results of my expedition.

In respect of the scientific research, which was their principal motive, my hopes have been exceeded so to speak: the richness of my portfolios leave little to be desired and the drawings which they enclose clarify a mass of historical points, cast at the same time a piercing light on Egyptian civilisation into its smallest details. Lastly, I gathered incontrovertible ideas regarding history of art, and in particular the one of its development from Egypt to Greece.

It was my duty to attempt to enrich the Egyptian division of the Royal Museum with various kinds of monuments which are missing from it, and of those which might complete the beautiful series which it comprises already. I have not spared anything to reach that goal; everything that I could economise on the funds which the Royal Household and various ministries had agreed to provide for my voyage was employed for the purpose of excavations and for acquisitions of Egyptian monuments of all kinds destined for the Museum Charles X. I had with great difficulty and remove, from the bottom of one of the royal catacombs of Thebes, a very large bas-relief which still preserves almost all of its antique painting. Only this superb piece, coming from the tomb of the father of Sesostris could do full justice the sumptuousness and magnificence of the pharaonic sepulchres. I have in addition acquired a first class monument. This is a sarcophagus of green basalt, covered with sculptures of an admirable refinement of execution and of a most elevated mythological interest; this piece, the most beautiful of this genre which has hitherto been discovered, belonged to Mahmoud-Bey, the Minister of War of His Highness the Viceroy of Egypt.

All the objects intended for the museum were loaded on board the *Astrolabe* and have arrived with me at Toulon. All that remains is their transport to the Royal Museum, and as it is extremely important for the conservation of the sarcophagus, bas-reliefs and several antique paintings, to avoid as much as possible any displacement, it would be very desirable if the corvette the *Astrolabe* on which these precious objects have been stowed were charged to transport them from Toulon to Le Havre as soon as the sea is navigable. By obtaining this decision from the Minister of the Navy you will at the same time both assure the preservation of the monuments and their arrival in Paris towards the 1st of April, the time when it would be essential to receive them in order to at last the arrangement of the lower rooms of the Egyptian Museum.

On the other hand, I will expedite to Paris by haulage eight to ten crates containing several objects of small proportions and which may support with inconvenience transport by soil. The others will arrive by sea with the large objects.

Allow me, Monsieur the Viscount, to beg you to hasten the decision from the Minister of the Navy concerning the dispatch of the corvette the Astrolabe to Le Havre where it will deposit the antiquities belonging to the Royal Museum so that I may, upon leaving quarantine, take all appropriate measures for their safety.

I will end this letter by renewing the expression of all my gratitude for your active benevolence, to which I attribute to a large extent the success of my voyage; please accept at the same time the homage of my respectful and complete devotion with which I have the honour of being yours, M. the Viscount, your etc.

Champollion to Léon Jean Joseph Dubois, –
27 December 1829, Lazaret of Toulon

Fate wanted, my dear friend, that we remained, you and I, deprived for eighteen months of news about each other. At the moment when I was writing to you from Thebes, I learned that you had left for the Peloponnese and that would have to write to me on arrival in order to indicate the point of Greece to which I could address my letter for you. I waited in vain and at my return to Alexandria, a Pole with a Jewish beard, a very excellent man, who had seen you in Elide told me that you had again taken the road for France. The result of all this is that we will have longer to talk to each other while poking our small corner of the fire.

I will nonetheless tell you in advance that all our ideas on Egyptian art (with due respect to the scholar Rochette and the great Quatremère) are from now on for me who has witnessed – what is truly meant by witnessing – them as demonstrable truths. And you will find among my portfolios, which include no less that fifteen hundred drawings of which a large part was coloured on site, things to convince you yourself. My young painters have conscientiously worked and I am not afraid to say that they have observed with a scrupulous fidelity the real and varied style which the Egyptian monuments of various ages display. I have been obliged to redraw almost everything of importance the Commission has published, particularly the historical bas-reliefs of which I have a complete collection and which you will not see without surprise because nothing up till now would have been able to give you even a rough idea of them. I have adopted for these important scenes a large format in order to render even the slightest details and to place more easily on them the numerous explanatory inscriptions which accompany them. One ought to flog publicly the Commission of Egypt, Gau and the English who have dared to publish such shapeless sketches of these large and beautiful compositions.

I have flayed, so to speak, from all the monuments of Egypt and Nubia, from the Pyramids right up to the Second Cataract, their historical views sculpted or written on their walls, and the notebook which I edited of all the bas-reliefs that decorate each monument and of which the main ones were copied with accuracy, give me the certainty that I have left nothing behind which is interesting or important. I have thus gathered work to last a lifetime.

Nor have I forgotten our Egyptian Museum of the Louvre. You know that while allocating the funds which I requested for my expedition expenses the decision was taken to strike from them the sum intended for excavations for the Museum. Despite this, I made unforeseen economies with which to countenance excavations made in Sakkara (Memphis), at Abydos and Thebes. In little time, I was lumbered with mummies and funerary objects; I only kept of all that that which was new – in form or material. I am only bringing back four mummies: two child ones, one beautiful Graeco-Egyptian mummy with long Greek inscriptions, and a beautiful Egyptian mummy with a tight paper covering; – several beautiful alabaster vases and of interesting materials, most of them with legends; – a large braided necklace of Venetian pearls, and the longitudinal inscription, equally braided with pearls of the nurse of king Tharaka, the Ethiopian of the fourteenth dynasty; – several beautiful bronze vases; – a funerary barge with a charming shape, a true jewel with drawers, varnished and painted, in a stunning state of conservation (an extremely remarkable piece); – two pairs of cymbals in striking Egyptian metal; – several bronze utensils; – a throng of small objects of choice of several genres, among them several of those pretty decorated spoons which you like so much; – several ivory objects which are very ancient; – two of the most beautiful vases or scuttles of bronze in existence and in comparison to which the great pail of [Henry] Salt is no more than a insignificant, both of them of very large proportions; – and several steles, small but choice ones as far as the workmanship and inscriptions are concerned.

I dared, in the interest of art, carry a profane saw into the freshest of all the royal tombs of Thebes. I detached from the wall with much luck the famous bas-relief from the tomb of Ousirei showing the king being received by Hathor, who gives him her hand while showing him her necklace. It is this Hathor whose beautiful head you admired on the plaster cast which Belzoni exhibited. This mass of seven to eight feet in height, a choice sample of the great decorative sculpture, is with me on board the *Astrolabe*. I have given it as a companion a sarcophagus of deep green basalt which I bought from my savings of Mahmoud-Bey, minister of war of the Pasha. It is, from the perspective of the number and the extreme refinement of the sculptures, the most pure and most beautiful which you'll find in the catacombs of Egypt – è un pezzo da stordire! It isn't the sarcophagus of a king but certainly the king of sarcophagus.

You must know that people rembered opening credit of 10000 francs for undertaking of excavations in Egypt, and you would be right to suspect that these funds didn't reach me until when I could no longer make use of them. It was in fact upon leaving Thebes and while descending the Nile near Dendera that this announcement arrived. But, as it was evident to me that it was my duty to use the most I could of that sum for the aggrandisement of the Museum, I did not hesitate to take advantage from it in order to purchase choice objects. It is thus that I bring with me to the Louvre the most beautiful bronze that was ever discovered in Egypt. It is a statue of at least two feet high, representing the wife of king Takellotis of the twenty second dynasty, entirely encrusted with gold from head to toe. It is a small masterpiece from an artistic point of view and a miracle from that of the workmanship of its execution. I am certain that you will embrace both cheeks of the princess, despite the oxidation which masks them though only a little and which and which shows through in the shape of a hump between the two shoulders. It is a superb piece;[4] you will be pleased with it. I await impatiently your news. Speak to me about your caravans in anticipation…

Champollion to Constanzo Gazzera, the librarian of Turin University –
18 December 1829, Lazaret of Toulon
I am writing to you a few lines, my very dear friend, in order to announce to you my safe arrival in France where I returned on the royal corvette,

the *Astrolabe*, which left on the 6th of this month from Alexandria where I had been waiting since the 1st of October. Everything went according to plan and my loot is immense. I bring back a mountain of notes, copies, inscriptions and digests which I edited on each monument which is still standing in Nile valley, from the Pyramids to the Second Cataract, more than fifteen hundred drawings, which were executed with all imaginable care and accuracy. I believe that it will only be due to their presence that we will have a correct idea of Egyptian art and the magnificence of the decoration of their temples and pharaonic palaces: a large number of these drawings were coloured in on site, in the presence of the original bas-reliefs, and I made it a rule to finish before the objects themselves what needed to be reproduced. The quick updates of the principal circumstances of my voyage which were published in the French newspapers must have kept you informed about my movements: you will also have obtained an idea of the principal results that were achieved.

I would really like to chat for a few hours with you. Couldn't you make an effort to do so? We are so close! You would be very sweet and I would be so grateful if you would want to make a trip to France to join me in Toulon from 13 to 17 January, or better to Aix from 23 to 24 where I will stay for some eight days in order to study the papyri of the Sallier collection. Do this, my dear friend. I beg Madame the Countess and all of her household (to which I renew my assurances of respect and dedication) to plead my cause with you. I will charge our friend Boucheron to unleash the bolts of his eloquence on my behalf. I enjoin friend Plana to show you mathematically that you must come and join me, and I thus embrace in advance all my advocates as well as my adversary. All yours with my heart.

PS — Address your response to me at the Lazaret of Toulon. Propose this brief to Peyron, while giving him a hug from me. I promise to entertain you for at least four days by showing you pictures.

Champollion to Costanzo Gazzera

I was unable during my stay near Thebes to get to Abydos; at the time when I planned to make the trip the flooding was so far-reaching that it was impossible to reach it. Deep down I regret this setback very little as the notes and research of one of my travel companions [Lenormant] – who visited the ruins during the month of January 1829 – gave me all the information about this place that I could want. The deep burial in sand of the palace does not allow one, except at enormous expenditure, to gather any new information, supposing that one would find any. I know the exact dates of these buildings and their local cults. The wall which carries the royal table is almost destroyed today. I am not wasting any tears about that... I am setting all this out in one of my last letters which will follow those which have already been published. I will collect them all in one volume which will act as a guide to European travellers who visit the antique monuments of Europe. – You will also find among these letters, which I will publish at the earliest convenience, all available information on the papyri of M. Sallier – which actually contains a text relating to the grand expedition of Sesostris against the Scyths and all the peoples of western Asia which were allied and allied to them; and the papyri of M. Sallier is authentic, and must all the more be considered as a contemporary composition of the event, because I found in Thebes in the great palace of Karnak the same text sculpted in large hieroglyphs on the exterior south wall of the palace. You see that it was quite wrong of people to mock M. Sallier when he made my opinion on this precious manuscript public; but these laughers belong to the clique of insincere opinions which you know as well as I do.

This year it will be impossible for me, to make an outing to Leiden; all my time is taken up with editing my Hieroglyphic and Hieratic Grammar, which I want to publish at the end of this year. I am working without respite and you would be pleased, I hope, of this publication which will conclusively quieten all clamours by the envious and idiots.

Champollion to M. Dacier – 1 January 1830, the harbour of Toulon
The great Amon-Ra has wanted to allow me to say goodbye to his sacred soil and the goddess Hathor – your delightful patron – recognising the worship of her which you have always cultivated with such fervour,

deigned out of consideration to you to favour my voyage from Alexandria
to the coasts of the Provence. The quos ego, – uttered by the divine
mouth, – has made my crossing as quick as I could hope for during such
an advanced season.

Having arrived in the land of the bells, as my desert friends say, it has
been necessary to let myself be treated as a plague-carrier and be locked
up in a filthy and depressing Lazaret. Without these accursed sanitary rules,
I would already have the pleasure of embracing you while expressing all
my wishes for the New Year; I am reduced to confiding them to paper but
I will not lose a moment, after I have well and duly been fumigated, to
hasten my return to Paris to repeat them with my own voice. You will hear
with interest, Monsieur, that the results of my voyage across the sea have
surpassed my hopes.

I will arrive with a cargo of beautiful drawings, among them you will
count several which I have been obliged to make because one of your
'proteges', 'The Egyptian par excellence,'⁵ forgot to look carefully at the
originals.

You will be able to contemplate, as you go through my portfolios, the
lifelike portraits of several of your ancient friends, Moeris, the Tuthmosis,
the Amenophes and the Ramesses. I took great care not to forget the
queens, whether Egyptian or Greek; you will find all varieties, white,
brown, black, yellow, even chestnut, some of them pretty, others ugly,
whatever it pleased Amon to grant them in time and place. – As for
battles, they abound in my research and I regret, Monsieur, that you have
lost your great strategist Gail who would have been able to explain to us
all the manoeuvres as well as, at least, Ramesses the Great or Menephtha
his father. I most of all look forward to placing before your eyes a moral
scene of daily life which I had copied with you in mind from one of the
ceilings of the tombs of the kings.

I saw much of Ibrahim-Pacha in Cairo and Alexandria. He is a singular
great man, a most elevated product of Egyptian civilisation. As for his
father, Muhammad-Ali, he is an excellent man, ultimately, having no
other ideas than the one of draining as much money from poor Egypt;
knowing that the ancients represented this area as a cow, he milks and
works it from night till the morning, waiting for it to collapse, which
won't be long. That is the reality of what good and beautiful the noble
advice of Drovetti, the great Jomard and other pastors of people *ejusdem*

farianae is bringing about. Egypt terrifies and evokes pity and I have to say this despite the stunning sabre mounted with gold which the Pasha presented to me as a token of his great pleasure.

I will spend a few days in Aix in order to study the interesting hieratic papyri concerning the campaigns of Sesostris which I found in the collection of M. Sallier. Once this work is done I will immediately go to Paris where I would urgently want to see you to repeat to you, Monsieur, the assurance of my sincere and very respectful attachment...

Champollion to his Champollion-Figeac – 2 January 1830,
Lazaret of Toulon

At last your letters abound. I respond today to those of yours of 26 October, 6 November, 8 December, 23 and finally 25; I need this chain mail in order to acclimatise. – I respond first of all to the matter of lodgings, which I find perfect as long as there are good and thick rugs in my office and my bedroom; it is a crucial item for me. I also need a leather fauteuil, a small desk and a very large table in the middle of the office or the bedroom. As for the bed, I am indifferent. I would still sleep gladly on a sofa: meanwhile, I would be very grateful if this were placed in my small vestibule where it could serve as a bed to give to a friend. Other than that, do everything which you think is good and useful: this will be fine. I thank my nestor for the efforts which he has spent in putting me up. We will be neighbours now and

As for the Rifaud affair, I see from the reports of learned academies that all this is no more than a waste of time. My fifteen hundred drawings of antiquities and hieroglyphic 'subjects' – as these learned men call them – will never suffer from comparison with his. His catalogue is absurd and the flooding prevented me from seeing in Tanis the large pieces which he is proposing for the Museum. They are moreover not worth the transport. I have written to Messrs. de la Bouillerie, de la Rochefoucauld, de Forbin and Cailleux concerning the voyage of the *Astrolabe* to Paris.

My friend Dubois must have received a letter from me: we really must finish our lower Egyptian rooms before his new departure for Olympia. I am spending my quarantine by making progress with my *Notices de monuments*. Here is the sequel of the packet which I sent you. You must press for their insertion. From my end, I will finish this work as early as possible, during the quarantine if time allows it. I aim to leave on the 13th or 14th of this month. I will stay in Toulon for three days, four in Marseille in order to see whether I can spend on purchases for the Museum the remainder of the 10,000 francs that were allocated. From there I will return to Aix in order to study the Sallier papyri.

It won't be until the city of king René [Aix-en-Provence] that I will be able to give you my definitive itinerary for Paris. — I received the document from M. David.[6] — You know that L'hôte is still in Egypt. — Adieu, my dear friend, to your health, and a happy new year! Wish as much from me to all our friends, large and small. I will write to you again from Toulon. Always and entirely yours. Adieu

PS — Answer me by courier-by-courier, poste restante at Toulon, if not in Aix at M. Turcas Sr.[7]

Champollion to Champollion-Figeac — 14 January 1830, along the coast of Toulon

Today, my very dear friend, I counted on regaining my freedom, lose my title of plague-carrier, say goodbye to the Lazaret and hello to the streets of a French city. The health counsel judges otherwise; considering that before taking us from Alexandria the *Astrolabe* had gone to take M. de Malivoir, consul of Aleppo at Latakie, to the coasts of Syria, where a dinghy dropped him off, and that the *Astrolabe* next set sail to return to Egypt, this counsel has increased our quarantine with ten further days, judging us to have a 'rough past.' This absurd decision will prevail because these gentlemen, unfettered by law, do just whatever enters their heads. For five years Egypt has not seen any plague, the bill of health of Latakie was perfect, only the dinghy touched land, forty days and more have gone by since our entrance in the harbour of Toulon after the departure of the *Astrolabe* from Latakie, no illness has manifested itself on board; twenty more days of quarantine in Toulon, expiring on the 13th yesterday, added to the forty preceding ones, amount to two months of evidence of the health of the crew — and yet they require another ten! The most amusing thing, if there is irony in such behaviour, is that the brick the *Eclipse*, with whose passengers and officers we intimately socialised everyday in Alexandria, arrived three days before us in Toulon and was only subjected to twenty days of quarantine. If we did carry the plague, the people of the Eclipse must have got it from us; if they are deemed healthy; that is what we are too.

All this does not make sense, and it would be a good idea if at last limits were placed on the omnipotence of the idiots who form the sanitary counsel and vex the merchant navy and military navy daily with decisions from another world. You must pass these facts on to some devil of the Journal du Commerce who will dress down these good counsellors. The government has no influence over all this, but it is becoming essential that it takes charge a little and drew up some good rules. I won't then leave the cage until the 23 to 24th of January.

I wrote to Messrs. de La Bouillerie, de La Rochefoucauld, Forbin and Cailleux; I already have the answer of the Viscount, but I await above all the official decision of the voyage of the *Astrolabe* to Le Havre. This is the important point in order to leave Toulon with my mind at ease about my cargo.

I await the response from our friend 'the Olympian' [Dubois] and his notes for the purchases to be made in Marseilles where I will go after leaving Toulon and before gluing myself in Aix to the brilliant papyri of M. Sallier who wants at all cost to put me up during my stay of a week or more.

This letter will reach you via M. the Minister of the Navy to whom I have addressed a number of important details regarding the conquest of the obelisk of Luxor. May god want that this beautiful undertaking will happen! This would be glorious for everyone and everything. — I will attach to my letter the *Notice du Palais de Medinet-Habu*, which contains news and which will flatten all the midges baiting me — but only of course if important historical findings have any effect on them.

As for Drovetti, he ought to be deeply ashamed of his behaviour towards me regarding the matter of the excavations and the permissions which he ought to have arranged for. I would not mind perpetuating the impression that I was easily deceived and maintain towards him the appearance of friendship, but I no longer trust him, and I have a very dim view of his tricky character and his behaviour in Egypt — where he only concerned himself with his interests, linked to those with the Pasha, without giving even the slightest care to the national interests he was being paid to protect. All the French in Egypt revile him and I wouldn't dare argue they were wrong. The new consul is adored because he has the heart of a man. — It is in order to shut my mouth that Drovetti is tilting mocha-coffee in yours! I will not refute the eulogies which he received, partly fashioned by you, in my first printed letters, but I will speak of his successor as I must and as I feel. There, that is all I can do.

Nothing else. The Lazaret is the world of uniformity. My health and that of Salvador are excellent,[8] despite the winds, rain and snow and the impossibility of having a fire on board; but I pass part of the day in a bad room in the Lazaret where I warm myself up as much as I can. Write to me quickly. My love to our patron. Remind me to our friends, in particular to M. and Mme de Férussac and that poor Arago,[9] who I feel heartily sorry for. Adieu. Entirely and always yours.

Champollion to the publisher of the Aviso du Journal de la Méditerannée *— 15 January 1830*

Monsieur

You have sought to repeat on trust of several newspapers of the capital that the Pasha of Egypt, to whom I have had the honour of communicating the results of my research regarding the monuments of Egypt and Nubia, has assailed the authority of part of my portfolios. Having received from His Highness nothing but testimonies of the highest protection, or honourable distinctions of the most particular benevolence, it is my wish to counter such an assertion.

I beg you therefore, Monsieur, to make public, by inserting in one of your next numbers, my formal protestation against a supposition which is so little in accordance with the noble character which the Pasha Muhammad-Ali has always deployed in his dealings with Europeans and in particular with the French.

Upon leaving quarantine, Champollion was approached by several senior navy officers whom Drovetti had brought to him so that he could explain to them himself how he thought that the enormous barge for transporting the needle of Luxor should be built. At first, they said to Champollion that it would be impossible to realise his plan. A night of reflection made them change their mind: the next day they sent a letter from Toulon to the Minister of the Navy, in order to recommend to him the construction of the barge and to urge him to talk to king about it at the earliest convenience.

Having been informed about this matter Champollion-Figeac wrote to his brother: '… M. the baron d'Haussez announced to me that he is very seriously occupying himself with the transport of the obelisk from Luxor to Paris; a committee is overseeing the project, but he would like to have your advice and in particular any information *de visu* which would enlighten the committee. I repeated to him what you told me: that it would be necessary to send stone masons and not scholars, and he said that your advice made great sense and that he wouldn't forget it. I want to go through your letters for any information on this which I might find and give to him immediately... Write him what you have to say about the above by starting to thank him for the interest he has shown in your plan. He immediately shared with me his opinion about your arrival... As he is a doer, all you have to do is to give him what you need and he will take care of it. If you write to me at the same time you can put your letter to me in the one for His Excellency, in case he still has his Cularo habits.'

Like, Cularo, the prefect of Isère, baron d'Haussez had opened the letters of the brothers while he was prefect in Grenoble — though outwardly he had concealed that he was their enemy. In this instance he deceived them again because no work was undertaken on the construction of Champollion's barge. Instead a large merchant vessel, the *Dromadaire*, was rigged up for transport of the two obelisks of Alexandria by a baron Taylor, a friend of d'Haussez and Jomard. Taylor set sail during March with the consent of the king who had put 80,000 francs at his disposal in order to undertake 'gigantic excavations'. Thus, at the court there was much less talk of the results which Champollion had achieved than the glorious findings which baron Taylor was going to bring back. None of the obelisks under discussion arrived in Paris while Champollion was alive, but on 25 October 1836 one of the two Luxor ones was finally erected on the Place de la Concorde (where it stands today).

Champollion to Champollion-Figeac — 29 January 1830, Aix-en-Provence
Here I am, my dear friend, installed with the good M. Sallier and hugging the fire in order to distract myself from the stinging cold which still brushes the beautiful climate of the Provence. I shudder at the very idea of going north immediately and bury myself in the fogs of the Seine. Until now the gout has quite spared me from its habitual visit on the first day of the year; a few blunt pricks of pain warned me that it would return at the first touch of humidity which I would encounter.

I left the cursed quarantine on the 23rd of this month, and have only passed two days in Toulon with M. Drovetti, who, having heard that I was in quarantine had come to see me and prolonged his stay until my final departure. We both left at the same moment, on the 26th, he for the east via Nice and I for the west via Marseille, where I arrived on the same day quite early in the morning; I stayed there until the 27th and the night of the 28th. I saw everything worth seeing, that is to say very little in the way of Egyptian antiquities. Just as I was leaving I received the letter from Dubois; also I struck a deal regarding the Egyptian stele of M. Mayer, who has decided to part with it; he will send it directly to the Royal Museum. While disembarking at Toulon, I sent to M. baron de La Bouillerie five large or small crates by ordinary haulage, weighing eight hundred kilograms and containing antiquities, bronzes etcetera, furthermore to your address, seven or eight crates containing my effects and luggage... [10]

I certainly would very much like to see myself in Paris, but the relentless cold which you are experiencing under its blessed sky would give me the shivers; also I have decided to organise my journey in such a way that I will not have to leave the sun of the south until the very last moment in order to deal with the transition. I won't therefore take the Lyon route, which is almost unnavigable because of the snows, particularly between Lyon and Paris. For seven or eight days at least I will have things to do in Aix on the papyri of Sallier; I want to go through them in the finest detail in order not to have to return to them. From there I am planning to go to Avignon to see the Museum Calvet. I will turn to Nimes in order to visit new digs; next to Montpellier, Narbonne, Carcassone, Toulouse et Bordeaux, from there to Montauban and, in order not to lose time, I will visit my sisters either in Villefranche-d'Aveyron, or in Cahors, where I will take the mail coach and will be in Paris in two or three days, that is to say between the 20th to the 24th February...

I found here with M. Sallier several of the documents and pamphlets[11] to which the clique has regaled me during my absence. They are in such bad faith that it makes you want to vomit, and I will never stoop to arguing with that canaille; I will only answer them by continuing what I am doing and by despising these despicable manoeuvres. Envy pokes through everywhere, – such is nature. I spit on it and will press on. Upon my arrival I will resume the editing of my Grammar with an appendix of texts which are word for word translated and annotated. One has to thrust the lance into the visor of these people and treat them with all the scorn they deserve. From now on I will show them my crocodile fangs...

Champollion to Ippolito Rosellini[12] – 29 January 1830, Aix-en-Provence
A letter from Salvador to your amiable wife [Cherubini's sister] must have informed you of our return in the land of the bells after a crossing of nineteen days during which we during which we had chequered good fortune, even experiencing windless planes which lost us five entire days, but in the end there was little to complain about: for a winter-crossing ours was one of the most fortuitous ones. We were submitted to twenty eight days of quarantine and we were free only on the 23rd. After having spent two days in Toulon with M. Drovetti, who agreed to wait for my release in order to chat a little at ease, I reached Marseille where I stayed for a day and a half and where I saw nothing very important in the way of antiquities. I have not been able to spend the funds for purchases which remained. I disposed of part in Alexandria in order to cream off the collection of *khodja*[13] Iani, who showed himself to be polite, obsequious and sweet like a little lamb. I got his beautiful bronze of the queen spouse of Takellothis the Bubastite and some hundred other first-choice objects for a thousand talaris (that is certainly not expensive), furthermore two magnificent bronze vases with images and inscriptions: you saw them perhaps...

I spent some eight days here in order to study and extract the papyri of M. Sallier. You know doubtless that the clique has fiercely mocked this discovery: I will answer them by the publication of a very detailed analysis of this important text.

I went through a number of the pamphlets with which the clique have wanted to regale me during my absence; it is disgusting and one feels that you can only respond to it with scorn and pressing on without worrying about these gnats. My *Grammar* will appear at the end of this year; it is the indispensable preface to our journey. It won't convert, nonetheless, those who are fighting my system and who are deprecating my work because these gentlemen don't want to be converted and they all act in the most iniquitous bad faith. But all this is only natural. I spit on them and go on as before. You know, I falsified the [Chronological] Table of Abydos – because the bad copies by Bankes and Wilkinson do not tally with the drawings by Cailliaud, which are in accordance with the steles, papyri and monuments which separately list each of the kings. What can you say to people who reason with such force? In order to prove that I contradict myself, they cite my changed opinions on certain points, without saying (and hence the bad faith) *when* I said this and when I modified my opinion. But that wouldn't suit them. They quote me as if I made black and white pronouncements on the same day, without taking into account the modifications which the advance of my research has brought to bear on certain points. My entire response is that my voyage has not yielded any modification in the principles of the hieroglyphic system set out in my *Précis*. They are immutable and will remain N-T-T-T [transcription of 'eternal'] because they are the truth which I can only arrive at by more or less felicitous approximations. But let's leave all that aside and make further progress.

Beyond this, all this hurrah of pamphlets hasn't caused a ripple in France: my *Notices of Egypt* crush them and elevate the erudite audience. They are only trying on anything in order to kneed the public to see me being turned away (if they dare) from the gates of the Académie at the next election. They only have a few *apocos* [dullards] to enter: they may succeed. In any case, you know that I will not pull rank. If the Académie wants me, may she nominate me: it is enough for me to have been put forward once, I am not one of those who one refuses several times in a row. I have made up my mind about that and you will no doubt approve of this. Other than that, come what may!

I am here occupying myself with the papyri of M. Sallier. He reckons to make quite some money out of it: I don't know whether he will succeed. The important thing for us is to know extremely well its contents and to have a complete copy, if I can arrange for it; but I believe that that is not part his plans at all. Whatever the case may be, I will draw everything from it I can, lest I cannot do any better. But he will end up having it published in its entirety…

Nothing else to say to you, if only that it is cold and that it is very depressing weather. My urgent compliments to Madame, who will, I hope, not forget the Parisians during the beautiful days in Pisa. Send my regards to your entire family and to all our travel companions. How is the gazelle? All yours with my heart.

In a letter to Sallier, written after his return to Paris, Champollion announced that he would edit another seven or eight letters about his expedition, and that after the last he would give a very detailed analysis of the papyri of Ramesses the Great — by far the most important of the five papyri of Sallier [now in the British Museum]; they would in effect allow him to complete the highly damaged hieroglyphic version of the same text which he had found on one of the walls of the great temple of Karnak. The letters were never written.[14]

Champollion to Champollion-Figeac — 18 February 1830, Toulouse
Here I am, my dear friend, among the troubadours of Toulouse. I sent Salvador away almost as we got in; he will bring along my bulk luggage which contains the drawings and all my notes and descriptions of monuments: these precious documents will act as my front-guard. Then, after having spent several hours among the family here[15] and in Villefranche, I will take the first available mail coach and will proceed to day and night to Paris.

The papyri of M. Sallier detained me longer than I had thought. I had to extend my stay because my excellent host declared having in mind remaining the sole possessor of his book and the wish that I would not make a copy: but I wanted one at any cost and I had to use subterfuge to obtain one. I didn't leave until I had put the most important sections of this curious monument in my portfolio. I studied it more in depth and realised that it contained a dramatised recital of the war of Sesostris against the Scyths (Scheta) allied with the greater part of the western Asian people. The most curious thing is that this text is engraved in large hieroglyphs on the external southern wall of the palace of Karnak in Thebes. It is a highly damaged and almost lost text, — but I am finding it in Aix in its entire integrity: I could not let such a document escape.

Seeking the heat and beautiful sun of the south through the snows which cover the Provence, I went to Nimes where I admired the amphitheatre and most of the all the Maison Carré, which in its present state is certainly the best preserved of all the Roman monuments that exist in Europe. In Montpellier I looked up the excellent M. Fabre who I knew in Italy: he made me see the beautiful museum of sciences in detail as well as the rich library which he has given to has native city. It is a fantastic thing, such an ensemble. Still snow and cold winds upon leaving Montpellier.

What a devilish winter heaven has visited upon us this year. I am suffering very much as a result of it and I fear very much being struck with gout upon arriving in the misty weather of Paris. However it is time that I got back. I sense it, and you shouldn't doubt my longing to do so, but not having gone to Figeac upon my departure it is right that I see our family in passing through. I am awaiting any moment now someone who has hungered to see me again for twelve years and whose attachment I doubt as little as I do yours: it is also a need which my heart has. I yielded and you will forgive me for being a few days late... We will leave immediately for Villefranche where there will be a family reunion for two days at the very most. Our sisters will arrive at the same time. After that I leave and I won't stop except on the courtyard of the great post office of Paris where I left you and where I hope to find you again safe and well, like me, despite several vague pains of gout and the return of the tinnitus in my ear. Have a little bit more patience. You will soon receive my last letter giving you the precise day of my arrival, at least twenty four hours in advance. Adieu then. All yours with my heart.

PS The newspapers put me very much at ease about the king of Naples.[16] He won't be in Paris for a few days after me. Thousands of compliments to our nestor...

Champollion to Champollion-Figeac – 2 March 1830, Bordeaux
Here I am, my dearest friend, having arrived... in the city of 12 March;[17] I will go by the monuments in order to complete my education and my tour because it will tomorrow night, Wednesday 3 March, that I will board the mail coach at ten o'clock at night in order to arrive at last in Paris, Friday, I don't know at what time. You will be able to get exact details and I hope I will find someone to talk to when I get out of the coach. I will say no more. Until Friday then. All yours.

PS Salvador was supposed to drop off my crates with drawings. The other crates have perhaps already arrived? I beg you to let the Louvre know that twelve crates with antiquities are to arrive on the same day addressed to M. de La Bouillerie. That they should therefore be accepted.

On 4 Mach 1830 Champollion arrived in Paris at two o clock at night. An attack of gout meant that he was confined to the apartment at 4, rue Favart, his brother had rented for him. Rosellini and his fellow members, on the other hand, received a rapturous welcome in Florence. At the March elections of the Académie des Inscriptions Champollion was again excluded, though he did become a member at the following election on 7 May 1830. A few months later he heard that he owed the prolongation of the quarantine at the Toulon Lazaret to Minister d'Haussez. Jean-François Champollion died on 4 March 1832, at the same time when he returned from his Egyptian journey two years earlier.

Afterword

There is no doubt that Jean-François Champollion can be regarded as the 'father' of modern Egyptology. His incredible devotion to, and explanation of, ancient Egypt led, as is well known, to his triumphal *Lettre à M. Dacier* in 1822. It 'cracked the code' of Egyptian hieroglyphs that had puzzled scholars for centuries since the last   hieroglyphic inscription had been crudely scratched on the inner wall of the gate of Hadrian on the island of Philae in AD 394. Less than one hundred and fifty years later, in the reign of the Byzantine emperor Justinian (527-565), the temple of Isis was finally closed, as Bishop Theodorus' inscription on the left of the entrance to the sanctuary records.

The basic story of Champollion's achievements is well know, how he schooled himself from an early age to achieve his object, learning several appropriate Near Eastern languages, and not least Coptic, in his quest, and making use of the remarkable basic information and illustrations produced by the French Commission in Egypt in the published engraving of the *Description de l'Égypte*.

While Champollion's work is well known, how much is really known about the man himself? The answer is 'not a lot' in as much as there is no biography of him available in English, although in recent years two have been published in France. It is through his letters written on that momentous journey that he made to Egypt in 1828 to 1829 that we can begin to see the man. Here we share his enthusiasm, both scholarly and almost at times schoolboyish, as he writes to close friends and to elevated people such as the Grand Duke of Tuscany. On his way to Egypt he is very keen to see the Greek temples at Agrigento in Sicily, and then there is the disappointment expressed when they were unable to land because of suspected plague.

When he finally arrives in Egypt, there are the explicit descriptions of the Delta sites, even then ravaged by robbers and sebakh (fertiliser) diggings. As

Professor Gaballa Ali Gaballa, Permanent Secretary to the Supreme Council for Antiquities, has recently pointed out in the Sackler Lecture in the British Museum (18 July 2001), the hundreds of Delta sites, for it is densely packed with them, are now at even more tremendous risk from pressure on land requirement and ever rising water tables.

Champollion writes continuously to his elder brother bemoaning the fact that no letters are reaching him from Europe (they were being deliberately held up), but he nevertheless continues to write in enthusiastic detail with descriptions of what he has seen and of his continuing work. He notes the 'Doric' columns fronting the tombs of the Middle Kingdom nomarchs at Beni Hasan, and is almost lyrical about the Semitic procession depicted on the walls – 'Joseph and his brethren in their coats of many colours' as many Biblically oriented scholars who saw them were convinced. Champollion, however, realised that the 'Doric' columns were indeed far earlier than their Greek counterparts.

At times Champollion is very caustic in his comments about later sculptures and temples, especially those in Nubia, and the temple of Kalabsha in particular. He has no time at all for the later periods and the bastardisation of what he regarded as true Egyptian pharaonic art and architecture. He also has a very poor view of Bernadino Drovetti, the French consul in Egypt (see the recent biography by R.T. Ridley, *Napoleon's Proconsul in Egypt*, London, 2000). Likewise he has a distrust of the British in Egypt in the person of the British consul Henry Salt (see D. Manley and P. Rée, *Henry Salt: Artist, Traveller, Diplomat, Egyptologist*, London, 2001).

Thomas Young, the English physicist, who was also intrigued by and working on deciphering hieroglyphs, has short shrift in some of Champollion's letters. However, one should note that Champollion's teacher in the College de France, Sylvestre de Sacy, wrote to Young in 1815, warning him: 'I think Monsieur, that you are further forward today, and you read a great part at least of the Egyptian text. If I have one word of advice to give you, it would be to not communicate your discoveries too much to M. Champollion. It could happen that he might then claim to have been first'. A later letter says of Champollion that, 'He is prone to playing the role of a jackdaw in borrowed peacock's plumes'. Young was, however generous in exchanging information and, notwithstanding de Sacy's strictures, the final plaudit cannot be taken from Champollion.

Champollion's enquiring mind very soon spotted the anomaly of the female endings in inscriptions alongside an apparently male figure in the temple of Queen Hatshepsut at Deir el-Bahari. Admittedly he read her name incorrectly as Amenenthe, yet despite this he came to an incredible understanding of the complicated Eighteenth Dynasty succession and marriages from Tuthmosis I to Tuthmosis III.

Another recurring theme in Champollion's letters is his wish to remove at least one (he had his eye on both at one time) of the obelisks of Ramesses II before the pylons of the Luxor temple. As it happened, the French did acquire the western one of the pair, which was taken down and re-erected in the Place de la Concorde in Paris in 1836. Much rejoicing attended this feat, and a large variety of contemporary bronze medallions in different sizes commemorate the event.

Champollion is always enquiring about the funds promised to carry out excavation (also held up), and says that, 'with little I will be able to accomplish great things'. This, indeed, he did, but not so much in terms of excavation but more in his recording and publishing, and his work on the *Grammar*.

The publication in English of these enthusiastic letters of description and report not only reveal the man, his weak health that he strove to overcome in his headlong pursuit of his goal, but also the scholar who was prepared to chance all, knowing that he was right, and swim against the tide of resentment that many of his academic colleagues felt. As the Greeks have it, 'Those beloved of the gods die young' – Champollion was only 42 years old when he suffered a stroke in Paris on 4 March 1832, and was laid to rest, appropriately, under an obelisk in Père Lachaise cemetery in Paris, with many of the Napoleonic Commission quite close to him.

Much of the background to the story of the rise of Egyptological studies, the French expedition and subsequent expeditions, will be found in the writer's, *The Rediscovery of Ancient Egypt: Artists and Travellers in the Nineteenth Century* (London, 1982, repr. 1990, and also translated into French, German, Italian and Spanish).

Peter A. Clayton, FSA
Boxmoor, Hertfordshire, July 2001

Endnotes

Introduction

[1] S. Curto, *Archéologia* 52, 1972 p.21.
[2] *Voyageurs et écrivains français en Égypte*, IFAO, p. 152, 1956.
[3] Drioton, Vandier *l'Égypte*, 1972, p. 9.
[4] F. Daumas, *Archéologia* 52, 1972, p. 12.
[5] F. Daumas, *Archéologia* 52, 1972, p. 16.
[6] H. Hartleben, *Champollion* p. 415.
[7] Champollion's friend, the astronomer François Arago (1786-1853), had called Edmé Jomard the 'Egyptian par excellence'. In 1824, variations on this theme rapidly took hold in Paris. Champollion became 'the Egyptian' and Thomas Young 'the Egyptian by juxtaposition'. Others were Goulianoff, 'the Egyptian by imagination, and Gustavus Seyffarth, 'the pseudo-Egyptian'.
[8] H. Hartleben, *ibid*, p. 481.
[9] P. Barguet, *Archéologia* 52, p. 36.

1. Lucky Escape

[1] Jean Letronne, a collaborator of Champollion's who in 1821 had passed a copy of Bankes's Philae obelisk on to Champollion.
[2] Cf. H. Hartleben, 'Introduction' pp. vii-viii, Champollion, J-F *Lettres et journaux écrits pendant le voyage d'égypte* H. Hartleben (ed.), Maspero Edition, 1909, vol 31.
[3] Pap. Sallier I-IV purchased by the British Museum in 1839 (EA 10181-2, 1084-5, and a demotic papyrus, EA 19226). Most of his collection of antiquities is now in the Museum of Aix-en-Provence..
[4] Together with Linant de Bellefonds (Linant-Bey, 1799-1883), an engineer in the service of the Pasha, Léon de Laborde (1807-1869) would travel extensively through Egypt, Abyssinia and, famously, Petra.
[5] 'A few *tois*' ι(approximately 6 feet, *Dictionnaire de L'Académie française* 1835)

2 Treacherous Alexandria

[1] After returning to France, Champollion's physicians would conclude that he had drunk too much unfiltered water and that this had severely harmed his health.
[2] See endnote 5, Ch. 1

3 The fallen obelisk was given to the British government and erected on Victoria Embankment in London in 1878; the (French) upright one was transported to America and re-erected in Central Park, New York, in 1881.
4 Saghir or Caghir is an Arab word meaning 'cadet' 'junior' 'the younger', a nickname Champollion-Figeac had given Champollion when he was sixteen.
5 Dr E. Pariset, a good friend of Champollion and a medical specialist on the plague, thought that the pest was endemic to the Sais and its surroundings. He put forward a plan to investigate how the disease could be combated, but the Egyptian government declined his proposal.
6 Giovanni Battista Belzoni (1778-1823), a former circus strongman and expert on hydraulics from Padua who worked for Sir Henry Salt. The first modern excavator of the Valley of the Kings, he made careful records of his discoveries. Giuseppe Passalacqua (1797-1865), Egyptian curator of the Museum of Berlin. Léon de Laborde, see endnote 4, Ch. 1. Jean-Jacques Rifaud (1786-1852), a sculptor from Marseilles who worked for Drovetti until 1827 and later published his sketches of Egypt.

3. Cairo: Egypt, at Last

1 This 'master piece of stone etching from the dawn of Egyptian art' is the sarcophagus of the Saitic priest Taho (Dja-her). Shipped to Paris by Champollion it is now in the Louvre, Room Henri IV, D9. Its tortuous purchase history is described in several letters below.
2 Linant-Bey was another Egyptologist who was constantly in close touch with William Bankes, but he was also a friend of Champollion and showed him whatever might be of interest.
3 In 1821 William John Bankes brought the Philae obelisk to England from his grand tour, aided by Belzoni and Salt and disputed by Drovetti. Copies of the obelisk's hieroglyphs were circulated widely. Indirectly Champollion received a copy and recognised the name Cleopatra on the obelisk, as had Bankes, though Young had not recognised it.
4 From March 1828 Drovetti urged Forbin, Jomard and others to do their best to prevent Charles X from allocating funds to Champollion for excavations during his expedition. Only in June 1829 did Férussac and Martignac succeed in securing what was needed, by which time it was too late for undertaking excavations (see below).
5 Almeh, girl oracles and prostitutes.

4. Rapture and Decadence: Dendera

1 Achoris (393-380 BC), of the twenty ninth dynasty; his name was one of the first Champollion translated.
2 Youssouf Msarra had been recommended to Champollion by Ibrahim-Pacha; he had served him very well during his repeated voyages to Nubia. Because of this business, however, Msarra thought of some excuse not to join Champollion's expedition.
3 Manetho (4th century BC), a priest with access to temple archives who numbered the pharaonic dynasties in his *Aegyptiaca*. No copy has been found but it is often quoted by the Romans and Greeks. Together with Strabo, a geographer from Augustus's reign, and Herodotus he was the key source of information about ancient Egypt before the decoding of the hieroglyphs.
4 The 'Englishman' was in all probability Caviglia, the Italian from Genoa, who had gone up to Alexandria to meet Champollion, wanting to accompany him for the duration of the expedition. Noticing that most of the young members of the expedition were ridiculing his behaviour, he almost immediately vanished and went into hiding in his little house in Old Cairo: he was no longer involved in excavations at that time. During an encounter with him (without witnesses), Champollion seized the opportunity to scold him for having in 1817 sold to the British one of the four lions that had been grouped underneath the monument until he had shovelled aside the enormous quantities of sand which had covered them.
5 Antoine Bibent, an architect, had been an energetic man when Champollion met him in Italy, but now his health was suffering. He would die within a year after his early return.

6 This remark is glossed in the margin of Champollion's diary and refers to one of the Pepis of the fourth dynasty. He had not yet seen very many manuscripts regarding the early dynasties and he was wary of saying anything about them. He had not been able to do much research on dynasties earlier than the seventeenth but expected to come up with results in Egypt.
7 Actually the 12th dynasty, 20th century BC.
8 A little later Champollion found out that Drovetti was holding back the letters he was waiting for.
9 Sir John Gardner Wilkinson (1797-1875) was the first to make a comprehensive study of the Valley of the Kings – his numbering is still in use. He visited Egypt in 1821, 1824 and 1827-28. Sir William Gell, one of the people Champollion invited to the expedition, had interested Wilkinson in Egyptology. (Gell wrote to Thomas Young: 'I wish you had sent me to Egypt with Champollion who offered to take me, but I had no money.')
10 Paul Lucas, a physician from Rouen, who wrote a well-known Egyptian travel journal in 1704.
11 During this visit Champollion was delighted to see that the drawing of his mentor Vivant Denon, made immediately upon the discovery of the Zodiac, was accurate.
12 According to the bible, Seshonq attacked and took Jerusalem in the fifth year of the reign of Roboam. This victory is depicted on the Karnak bas-relief and depicts the captured city by the bust of a Semitic prisoner as the Semitic people appeared to the Egyptians of the 10th century BC.
13 Champollion's six cartouches produce this order.
14 From Abu Simbel, the architect Jean-Nicholas Huyot had sent Champollion the crucial material with the name of Ramesses in 1822. Here he is blaming Huyot for causing an error.

6. Turning Point: Abu Simbel

1 Louis-Joseph Vicat, a bridge and road engineer, and one of the Champollions' loyal friends.
2 On his earlier visit to Egypt Ricci had measured 52 degrees Reaumur as a result of the extreme density of the air which had been sealed off for centuries.
3 It was the cartouche of Seti I, a mistake Champollion corrected in the Autumn of 1831.
4 Champollion's epithet, given by the ultra-royalists of Grenoble, his adversaries in 1815.
5 On the evening of 31 December it had been agreed that the stele of Ortasen would be given to Champollion. Next morning, while Champollion and Rosellini were occupied with their correspondence, Doctor Ricci nonetheless had the stone stowed on the Tuscan boat, a change of plans which Champollion accepted without a word. (A captain Lyons brought back the lower part of the stele in July 1892.)
6 It had been agreed already in France that Lenormant would only go as far as the Second Cataract.
7 Imouth or Imhotep, the Egyptian equivalent of Aesclepius: a minister of the third dynasty deified as the god of medicine.
8 Two historical lawyers, famous in France: Flaubert would refer to them in *Madame Bovary*.
9 The Tuesday salon of Baron de Férussac.

7. The Mysteries: of Thebes: Farewell

1 For three days consul Acerbi couldn't let go of Champollion and their parting appeared to be very distressing to him; Champollion later heard that William Bankes, Acerbi's protector had written to Acerbi that he must choose between either him, Bankes, or Champollion.
2 Dubois had left Paris for the Peleponnese in February 1829.
3 Temsahh still lived in 1863 and showed Hermine Hartleben a certificate he had received from Champollion: his sons and grandsons had been on the payroll of the Service for Antiquities for a long time, and his family was still one of the richest in Karnak. Champollion gave a similar certificate to Aoueda, his chief excavator on the left bank. Both of them were declared French *protegés*, which protected them and their wives against the normal vexation and tasks required from *fellahs* by their Turkish and Arab

masters.

[4] During Champollion's stay in Egypt, the astronomer François Arago (1786-1853) received a letter at the Académie from Thomas Young, who again reproached him bitterly for making too much of Champollion's discoveries. Jomard, the archaeologist Raoul Rochette and several other members were present and a passionate debate for and against Champollion's hieroglyphic system ensued. Champollion-Figeac arrived afterwards and wrote 'no one could any longer contradict the great defender [i.e. Arago].'

[5] Early on Young, Jomard and Champollion had for a while worked together on improving teaching the poor, based on the system of Joseph Lancaster (the 'monitorial system', grouping pupils by ability and having them teach each other). Jomard saw this system as being French, based on a similar idea by the educationalist Herbault sixty years earlier. Champollion emphasised its Indian origins (he was working on this system when he declined Salt's invitation to join Belzoni at the tomb of Seti I).

[6] Champollion's only child, born in Grenoble on 1 March 1824.

[7] The two sisters of the Champollions lived there.

[8] The mummy of the pharaoh was in fact found (1881) to the south of Deir-el-Bahari, in an entirely different place; today it is in the Egyptian museum of Cairo.

[9] A controversial statement at the time.

[10] A rare mistake by Champollion as this is Queen Hatshepsut and there was enough material available to draw this conclusion.

[11] Pharaoh Sesostris had divided Egypt up in 36 *nome* or regions.

[12] Having heard that Pope Leo XII had died on 10 February 1829, Champollion thought that a planned publication on the Roman obelisks would probably no longer take place and that, for the moment, his presence in Rome was not required. Instead he planned to go to Rome and Turin in the spring of 1830 (a journey which never happened).

[13] An allusion to the equestrian statue of Henri IV which was erected on the Pont Neuf in 1818. Quatremère de Quincy had been instrumental in the government's decision to melt down of Napoleon statue despite loud protests from the Parisians and their repeated offer to provide the necessary bronze for the monument of Henri IV. 'In order to take revenge on this refusal with little respect for the arts, the foundry had inserted in the arm of Henri IV several small bronze reproductions of the destroyed statue of Napoleon in Roman costume.' The new statue was placed on the base of Cherbourg granite on which Napoleon's commemorative obelisk, measuring 180 feet, was to have been placed.

[14] Champollion-Figeac, who was since 1828 one of the curators of the Bibliothèque Royale, lived in one of the annexes of its large building (12 rue Neuve des Petits-Champs). He installed his brother on the second storey of no 4, rue Favart, at a few minutes distance from his own apartment.

[15] Rue de l'Arcade Colbert: where M. Dacier lived. Abbey of St Germain-des-Prés: where Charles Lenormant lived. This refers to Joseph Fourier, Napoleon's administrator of Egypt, who lived near the Pantheon. Upon Champollion's leaving for Egypt Fourier pointed towards the Pantheon and told him: 'Egypt will one day place you in this shrine'. Champollion today rests at Père Lachaise a few steps away from the tomb of Fourier.

[16] Champollion's niece, Mme Falathieu (1815 – 18 March 1903), spoke at length about this power of attraction to Hermine Hartleben, recalling remarkable incidents.

[17] In November 1828 the flooding had likewise thwarted a visit by Champollion to Abydos, which is fourteen kilometres from Baliana and the banks of the Nile. Lenormant, who had passed by in January [18] on his return to France, foresaw what would happen and gathered for Champollion what little new discoveries he could make near these monuments which were at that time already well-catalogued.

8 Plotting the Future

[1] The list of candidates who were balloted during the meeting of 10 April 1828:

	1st	2nd	3rd	4th round
Pardessus	9	13	14	15
Champollion le jeune	6	8	8	9
Thurot	6	7	6	4
Cousin	3			
Guillon de Montléon	1			
Amedée Jaubert	1			

Gail   1
Thierry   1
Champollion-Figeac wrote to his brother: 'this nomination came under extremely fierce attack. *The Journal des Debats*, favourable to the ministry, publicly disowned the schemers, and it is their readers who have dominated the matter for ten years. It was up to the small journals to name them all and for a month there has been an unprecedented turbulence of personal attacks, which hindered the phoneys and forced them to write public letters, and which then serve as the anvil for their opponents. Never before the academic and literary worlds been set ablaze by such a fire... You are the cornerstone and foundation stone of all this, and the names Pardessus and Champollion, who may never meet each other, find themselves associated every morning, being taken aim at together by ten firing mouths...'

2 Though he was the head of the archaeological commission which was sent to Greece, Dubois 'wrote only to his wife' fearing that he would otherwise compromise himself: he refused to grant Champollion-Figeac his wish, who had asked him to send in letters for the *Moniteur*. He returned to Paris on 26 October 1829 and on the day after resumed his place in the Egyptian museum. Champollion had written to him from Thebes to Athens but he received no response in return.

3 Today in the Salle Henri IV of the Louvre. It was already famous in Paris because a very good copy had been included in Belzoni's exhibition of the tomb of Seti I, 1822.

4 This letter informed Champollion that the government of the Pasha had adopted all of the preventative measures against the plague which Pariset had pioneered. The colossal flooding of that year would vindicate his theory that the disease was endemic in Egypt.

5 Champollion and Mimaut.

6 This work was very well paid; nonetheless Champollion gave them 700 francs on top for the voyage from Toulon to Paris, including the cost of quarantine. In addition, Mimaut promised to embark the young artists free of charge when the moment would arrive.

7 The *Astrolabe* had been used in 1828 by Admiral Dumont-Durville for his scientific expedition (under the name of *Coquille*) that lead to the discovery of the shipwreck near Polynesia of the expedition to the Pacific lead by Jean-François de Lapérouse (1785-1788).

8 Aime-Louis Champollion-Figeac (December 1812-20 March 1894) largely provided the information that followed to Hermine Hartleben.

9 Lenormant said of him: 'At the very heart of this gracious smile..., every now and then, you saw him steal leonine glances that felt as if one was only a whisker away from the slayer of the Mamelukes.' Charged by the Ottoman Sultan, Muhammad Ali, an Albanian, had defeated the Mamelukes, something Napoleon had failed to achieve. In the years to come, he would grow more and more autonomous, becoming the founder of a new Egyptian dynasty.

10 Of the 250,000 *fellahs*, whose services could be called up at will, who worked virtually naked and often without bread, almost 21,000 died mainly on the site of the works itself.

11 The map still exists.

9 Back in the Land of the Bells

1 Consul N. Miège, previously vice-consul in Livorno, had invited Champollion to 'spend his quarantine' on Malta, where he would be near him and much more comfortable than at the Lazaret in Toulon.'... After visiting our monuments, you would have only one further leap to make in order to see those of Sicily where you need not fear that they would treat you as a plague-carrier, and from where you could continue your route...' This proposal appealed to Champollion. He rather feared that he would not have any peace of mind, yet Grigenti and the temple of Jupiter beckoned as he would be near them: departing from Alexandria, the decision was made to quarantine at Valetta. At a critical juncture, a fierce northern-eastern wind had swelled and pushed the ship into the sea beyond: they had had to turn to Toulon.

2 These *Notices de Karnac and Dendera* have not survived: either they were not written or they are lost.

3 Baron d'Haussez, minister of the navy; more about him below.

4 Queen Keromama, Egyptian collection, Salle historique, case B, Louvre.

5 See endnote 7, Intr.
6 Senior Customs official. He had sent Champollion a *laisse passer* to give to the commander of the *Astrolabe* for Customs in Le Havre.
7 Champollion wanted to stay with him but a letter from Sallier, arriving in Toulon before his departure, obliged him to accept his invitation.
8 The stove at the Lazaret smoked and the room was exposed to the winds; often the fire had to be extinguished as one risked suffocating if it were left on. Champollion did not tell his brother about these conditions, nor did he inform him about the true state of his health. The exceptional cold which was punishing France was affecting his lungs, which had never bothered him before. Cherubini's delicate health also suffered.
9 Arago's wife had died after a long illness.
10 The list of one hundred and two objects of antiquity brought back by Champollion was found in the archives of the Louvre.
11 On the advice of Sallier Champollion burnt them immediately, which Champollion-Figeac regretted as he would like to have fought back in Champollion's defence.
12 Published in 1884 in Venice, after an original in the possession of the Rosellini family.
13 This is the nominative of the name *khaouagah*, or rather merchant, which the Egyptians and Syrians give to all Europeans; the equivalent of Mr. or Sir.
14 Lenormant published an article which gave an exact picture of the state of Egyptology upon the return of Champollion, March 1830, *Revue française*, t, XIV, p. 159-196.
15 With the older brother of their mother, Doctor Gualieu.
16 The Duke de Blacas had told Champollion-Figeac that the king and queen remembered the 'excellent lessons' which Champollion had given them in Naples and would be delighted to hear news from him about the Museum of the Louvre.
17 1814, the date on which Bordeaux capitulated to Wellington.

Hand-drawn illustrations (except 102): Jean-François Champollion, taken from H. Hartleben, 'Introduction' pp. vii-viii, Champollion, J-F *Lettres et journaux écrits pendant le voyage d'égypte* H. Hartleben (ed.), Maspero Edition, 1909, vol 31

Plates on pp. 8, 45, 39, 63, 99, 101, 135 from *l'Égypte ancienne*, 1839, by Champollion-Figeac

Spine illustration: Jean-François Champollion, by Léon Cogniet, © RMN, Musée du Louvre

Frontispiece: Jean-François Champollion © Rénéaume, collection Rénéaume